Thailand

WORLD BIBLIOGRAPHICAL SERIES

General Editors:
Robert L. Collison (Editor-in-Chief)
Sheila R. Herstein
Louis J. Reith
Hans H. Wellisch

VOLUMES IN THE SERIES

VOLUME 65

Thailand

Michael Watts
Compiler

CLIO PRESS

OXFORD, ENGLAND · SANTA BARBARA, CALIFORNIA
DENVER, COLORADO

218363

016.9593
W 352

British Library Cataloguing in Publication Data

Watts, Michael, 1918-
Thailand. – (World bibliographical series; v. 65)
I. Title   II. Series
016.9593   Z3236

ISBN 1-85109-008-8

Clio Press Ltd.,
55 St. Thomas' Street,
Oxford OX1 1JG, England.

ABC-Clio Information Services,
Riviera Campus, 2040 Alameda Padre Serra,
Santa Barbara, Ca. 93103, USA.

Designed by Bernard Crossland
Typeset by Berkshire Publishing Services
Printed and bound in Great Britain by
Billing and Sons Ltd., Worcester

THE WORLD BIBLIOGRAPHICAL SERIES

This series will eventually cover every country in the world, each in a separate volume comprising annotated entries on works dealing with its history, geography, economy and politics; and with its people, their culture, customs, religion and social organization. Attention will also be paid to current living conditions – housing, education, newspapers, clothing, etc. – that are all too often ignored in standard bibliographies; and to those particular aspects relevant to individual countries. Each volume seeks to achieve, by use of careful selectivity and critical assessment of the literature, an expression of the country and an appreciation of its nature and national aspirations, to guide the reader towards an understanding of its importance. The keynote of the series is to provide, in a uniform format, an interpretation of each country that will express its culture, its place in the world, and the qualities and background that make it unique.

SERIES EDITORS

Robert L. Collison (Editor-in-chief) is Professor Emeritus, Library and Information Studies, University of California, Los Angeles, and is currently the President of the Society of Indexers. Following the war, he served as Reference Librarian for the City of Westminster and later became Librarian to the BBC. During his fifty years as a professional librarian in England and the USA, he has written more than twenty works on bibliography, librarianship, indexing and related subjects.

Sheila R. Herstein is Reference Librarian and Library Instruction Coordinator at the City College of the City University of New York. She has extensive bibliographic experience and described her innovations in the field of bibliographic instruction in 'Team teaching and bibliographic instruction', *The Bookmark*, Autumn 1979. In addition, Doctor Herstein co-authored a basic annotated bibliography in history for Funk & Wagnalls *New encyclopedia*, and for several years reviewed books for *Library Journal*.

Louis J. Reith is librarian with the Franciscan Institute, St. Bonaventure University, New York. He received his PhD from Stanford University, California, and later studied at Eberhard-Karls-Universität, Tübingen. In addition to his activities as a librarian, Dr. Reith is a specialist on 16th-century German history and the Reformation and has published many articles and papers in both German and English. He was also editor of the *American Society for Reformation Research Newsletter*.

Hans H. Wellisch is associate Professor at the College of Library and Information Services, University of Maryland, and a member of the American Society of Indexers and the International Federation for Documentation. He is the author of numerous articles and several books on indexing and abstracting, and has also published *Indexing and abstracting: an international bibliography*. He also contributes frequently to *Journal of the American Society for Information Science, Library Quarterly*, and *The Indexer*.

Contents

Contents

Contents

Introduction

Siam's name was changed to Thailand in 1939, but both names tend to be used as alternatives in historical references. Seventeenth-century material may use 'Siam' either for Ayudhya, which was then the capital, or for the extensive empire which Ayudhya then controlled. Following the transfer of the capital to Bangkok in 1782, Siam became the normal name for the country as a whole until 1939; henceforth it has been known as Thailand.

Thailand is a tropical country within the northern fringe of the influence of the southwest monsoon. Its main climatic variations consist of heavy cloud and rain wind-borne from the Indian Ocean monsoon between May and September, followed by a reversal of wind to the north, producing a pleasant, clear and cooler dry season from October to February, and a spell of stagnant air, with close, humid heat in March and April, leading to the next monsoon.

The principal geographical features are mountain ranges to the west, north and east, containing the basin of the Ping and Chao Phraya rivers, draining southwards into the Gulf of Thailand: this is the central plain or 'rice-bowl', the main populated area and base of the country's economy. The limestone chain in the west separates Thailand from Burma, and trails down the spine of the extended peninsula to the southern border with West Malaysia; to the northeast the basalt Khorat plateau is bounded by the Mekong River, forming the frontier with Laos and breaking to the south to make mountain chains, including the Cardamom Range, which divide Thailand from northern and western Cambodia. In the extreme northeast, at the mountainous tri-border (the 'golden triangle'), Burma and Laos meet, forming a narrow strip separating Thailand from China (Yunnan).

Thailand is slightly smaller than France, with substantially less industrialization, and urbanization, except for the concentration in the

Introduction

capital, Bangkok. The country's overall population density is tending to catch up with that of France; its rate of growth remains a matter of some royal and governmental concern.

Thailand can be likened in shape to an elephant's head seen sideways. The crescent of the inner trunk is peninsular Thailand, containing the long-controversial Muslim provinces converging towards Malaysia. On the front side, bordering the Indian Ocean, is the interesting island of Phuket. The narrow part in between is the Kra Isthmus — an ancient cross-country trade link between India and China, and a principal reason for the location of a Śrivijayan centre some fifteen centuries ago at Chaiya on the Gulf of Thailand. Along the 'nose' is Tenasserim, now part of Burma, a former outlet of Ayudhya to the Indian Ocean trade routes. The forehead and bony top of the head are the tribal mountains bordering Burma, leading to the 'golden triangle'; the back of the head is the part adjoining Laos. The earflap is the northeastern plateau adjoining Cambodia, inhabited by the 'Isan' people, site of earlier subjection to the Khmer empire of Angkor, and marked by its splendid temple at Phimai. The mouth is the estuary of the Chao Phraya River, leading from the Gulf of Thailand to Bangkok and, further up-river, to the former capital, Ayudhya. The cheeks are the great rice-bowl of central Thailand, and the chin the part of the gulf shared with Kampuchea, containing contested oil resources.

The frontiers have been subject to controversy of various kinds. Four provinces in the far south of the peninsula, largely inhabited by Thai-Malays, were the subject of extended negotiations with Britain in the early 19th century. In the northeast, the trans-Mekong area was the subject of controversy with France towards the end of the century; this, too, gave concern to Britain at a time of conflicting colonial interests. The southern border sector of northeast Thailand was the site of extended disputes with Cambodia; and the western borders varied in the 16th and 17th centuries according to whether Burma (Pegu) or Thailand (Ayudhya) had seized control of ports like Mergui, giving access to the trade routes of the Indian Ocean.

The early historians of Thailand, and of Southeast Asia as a whole, tended to exaggerate the influence of India, and to underestimate Chinese, as well as indigenous elements in the social and cultural development of the area. From prehistoric times onwards, indigenous communities, artisans, and artists put a distinctive stamp upon the inflow of exotic influences — Indian and Chinese, Mon and Khmer, and later, European — for which the country provided a nexus: the result was a long period of cultural adaptation and growth towards a strong national homogeneousness of style, land and people, which gave Thai

Introduction

civilization an elegance and 'Thai-ness' essentially its own. The country has become today the hub of a relatively new geographic and political concept — Southeast Asia; as such it is the lynchpin of a new regional, politico-economic group — ASEAN (Association of Southeast Asian Nations).

Its flora and fauna are of exceptional interest and variety. Off its shores swims the largest known mammal, the Blue Whale, while in its mountain caves flies the smallest, the newly-discovered sole representative of an entirely new mammal family, the bumblebee bat. Its jungles abound with the shrieks of elephants, the 'wa-wa' calls of the entertaining gibbon family, and myriads of insects, orchids, birds and butterflies. Its rice is world-renowned, and it is rich in fruits and spices, fish and Crustacea.

The reason for this profusion of flora and fauna is that Thailand is part of a complex transition-zone between two biogeographical sub-regions, the Indian and Sundaic. It occupies a fringe of the Wallacean area of intense speciation resulting from the collision of continental fragments of India and Australia-New Guinea, and has been controversially held to be itself a sub-fragment of the latter. For ethno-botanical reasons many examples of the rich fund of cultivated plants, fruits and spices of this active area, which centred originally on Celebes and neighbouring islands, were gradually introduced into the southern Asian belt of land which includes Thailand; and for all this variety of species, the country offered the ideal moist, warm and stable climate for survival and propagation.

The Thai nation has gone through two main formative stages. The first consisted of its gradual separation from the Tai tribal family. This probably began in Annam, northern Indochina — a region credited with being an original centre of wet-rice cultivation, an art which the Thais brought eventually down the Ping and Chao Phraya river valleys into what is now Thailand. The second formative stage consisted of the gradual coalescence of early settlements within Thailand with petty kingdoms under Khmer tutelage, which formed a central Thai state.

Its people were, and have remained, substantially Thai, though incorporating significant residues from indigenous as well as immigrant tribal communities, Mon-Khmer predecessors, Indian Brahmin court advisers, and traders.

Recent archaeological results tend to minimize the importance of mass migrations in the social and cultural evolution of Southeast Asia. Oceanic inundations, followed by partial recessions, between the seventh and third millennia BC left most of the Southeast Asian lowlands under water, at the same time providing better access by water to the remain-

Introduction

ing islands and mountain ranges, and emphasizing catchment areas like
the Mekong, Tonle Sap and Chao Phraya river basins as zones of seden-
tary cultivation. In Thailand coastal swamps, which are now well inland,
supported settlements which were open to exotic trade contacts. They
used, but probably did not yet domesticate, wet rice; excavation of
some of these, and of other settlements further inland, has shown
that they had advanced by the end of the first millennium BC to
domestication of animals, sophisticated fishing technology, bronze and
iron metallurgical skills, arts of decorated pottery and jewellery, and
highly stratified social organization. The suggestion is that sometimes
rapid (as in the case of iron) idea-diffusion, and selective development
of exotic cultural systems by ruling élites, played roles comparable in
importance to that of the early tribal immigrations.

The principal non-Thai element within Thai society today consists
of the Chinese. Thailand acquired, over several centuries of immigration
from China's southern provinces, a substantial Chinese minority. The
Chinese now form an unobtrusive, and, on the whole, a well-assimilated
sector of perhaps 10 per cent of the population. To a great extent they
arrived, and have remained engaged in trade at all levels.

Why were the Thai by far the most successful of the tribal groups,
able to evolve a great and always independent modern kingdom? Again,
two principal reasons come in for consideration. First, they were a lowland people, occupying river valley sites with access to water, and they
had the secret of wet-rice cultivation to make the best use of the fertile
soils which these offered. Second, they became the heirs to a whole
complex of great cultural traditions, nurtured for millennia by the
neighbouring civilizations of India and China, and transformed and
handed on by their Mon and Khmer predecessors.

In a sense, these two reasons converge. For the Hindu civilization
which the Thai inherited was intensely concerned with water, the
surrounding element of Mount Meru, the cosmological centre of religion
and kingship, and of a human social order which sought to imitate the
order of the gods and thus to acquire harmony with nature and the
universe. When the Khmer established a new kingdom based in Angkor,
it was at a river confluence near the great Tonle Sap Lake. Their Meru
temple could then replicate the Hindu heaven by being surrounded
with water; and the first thing they did was to use this water to cultivate
rice. This provided both the basis for an expanding labour force —
always in short supply in Southeast Asian kingdoms — and the necessity
for a strong, centralized administration to control the irrigation systems.

Similar considerations applied to the process of kingdom-formation
in Thailand, itself initially under Khmer suzerainty. Ayudhya was con-

xiv

structed (in the 14th century, after the decline of Angkor) at the confluence of three rivers, virtually occupying an island. It was thus
prosperous in rice, fish, fruit, timber and other natural produce, and
also, being accessible from the sea, could attract foreign trade contacts
stretching from Europe to China, Japan and the Spice Islands.

In the meantime Thailand had acquired the legacy of Mon culture,
first in the Indic civilization of Dvaravati, and later from Theravada
Buddhist Pagan. The first all-Thai kingdom of Sukhothai (13th-15th
century) synthesized all these trends into an unprecedented efflorescence of Buddhist art, culture and learning. In particular, Sukhothai
brought the Buddha image to perhaps its finest forms anywhere,
typified by superb beak-nosed, lime-chinned seated Buddhas in gold,
glowing with seemingly incandescent inner power, and by walking
Buddhas showing an effortless fluency of line and movement. Each
image symbolizes a part of the life or teaching of Buddha in posture or
hand positions (*mudras*), the most frequent of which in Thailand's
Theravadist canon being the *bhumisparsa mudra*, with fingertips touching the ground to symbolize Buddha's appeal to the Earth Goddess to
witness his purity on the eve of his enlightenment. (The walking posture
symbolizes Buddha's return from preaching to his mother in Indra's
Himalayan 33-god heaven.)

At the same time temple murals began to acquire a characteristic
fineness of line, which was to develop ultimately into the gold-leaf-on-
black-lacquer artwork of late Ayudhya, and the murals which are the
artistic highlight of the Thonburi-Bangkok period from the last quarter
of the 18th century through the first half of the 19th century and up to
1868.

The subject matter of this art is almost entirely restricted to
traditionally selected episodes from the life of Buddha, from *jatakas*
(selected stories of previous lives of the Buddha), and from the
Ramakien (the Thai version of the Indian epic, the *Ramayana*). This
concentration on religious themes left considerable scope for individual
detail, in the handling of which the distinctive character of Thai art is
well exhibited in a way which gives many insights into the country's
own social history — for instance, in scenes showing the popular
shadow-plays in action, or showing the national sport, Thai boxing.
Even the Indian religious figures represented in these art forms acquired
recognizably Thai personalities, often of impish or voluptuous minor
gods and goddesses, seen disporting in the mythical Himalayan uplands
of Hindu legend.

Of the two artistic influences — Mon and Khmer — which immediately preceded the early Thai kingdoms, the first could be said to

Introduction

resemble Greek influence in Europe, bringing delicate, refined architecture and sculpture, while the second in more than one respect resembles Europe's experience of Rome. The solid, decorated lintels and corbelled arches and terraces of the temple site at Phimai typify the heavier Khmer architectural style; other parallels with Rome can be drawn from the harsh and rigid administration practised by the kings of Angkor upon their own subjects and upon vassals or mercenaries like the Thai, and from the Khmer habit of building military roads to connect Angkor with outer provincial centres like Phimai and Lopburi.

The contrast is also evident as between the blunt *prangs* (Khmer towers) of Angkor, which were copied in temples built during the early Ayudhya period, and numerous, more typically Thai, slender, tapering structures, like the copies of several early periods grouped together at the Grand Palace in Bangkok. Immediately opposite the palace, on the other side of the river, can be seen the earlier Temple of the Dawn (Wat Arun), a fine example of the Khmer-style *prang* spire.

It might be said of Sukhothai that it represented the Mon element more than the Khmer in these respects, while Ayudhya reverted to a more Khmer style, exemplified in temple-building and later in a rigidity of government, which persisted into the early stages of the Bangkok period. Many of the early Thai kings had a propensity to prefer Buddhist piety to statecraft, as evidenced by periods of decline in Lan Na (Chiang Mai), Sukhothai, and early Ayudhya, which intermittently fell victim to Burmese raiders, the last assault in 1767 leading to its destruction and abandonment as the capital.

Under King Narai (1656-88) Ayudhya had become a glittering cosmopolitan capital, a centre of world trade, the most important city in Southeast Asia, in touch (among other potentates) with Louis XIV, and with a Frenchman, ex-Greek buccaneer Phaulkon, as first minister to the king. French, English and Dutch traders' accounts of the city at this time are of particular interest.

The destruction of Ayudhya – a cultural disaster of world proportions – led to a period of transition and strife, from which it was rescued by Taksin, a half-Chinese general from the northern province of Tak. Taksin founded a new capital down-river at Thonburi, immediately opposite the Chinese trading village of Bangkok. There he reconstituted the religious heritage of Theravada Buddhism in beautiful temples, murals and scriptures, but, being accused by his rivals of religious excess amounting to madness, was executed in 1782. He was thus the sole representative of the new dynasty which he founded.

Introduction

Generals who had aided Taksin in pacifying the north and eliminating the Burmese then founded the Chakri dynasty, and proceeded to create a new palace-capital on the other side of the river, near the village of Bangkok, partly because it seemed safer from Burmese attack, and partly because it presented less marshy building ground. The new Grand Palace was surrounded by water, in the traditional style, by the introduction of a system of canals (*klongs*), which were developed from the Chao Phraya River as 'streets', making the city a 'Venice of the East' — a reputation from which it has retreated in recent years with the filling in of many of the *klongs* to make way for road-building, with a corresponding increase of seasonal flooding.

The Grand Palace compound, augmented by successive kings and dominated by shimmering golden spires, remains the central wonder of the city. It houses in the magnificent Royal Chapel the Emerald Buddha, talisman of the dynasty, brought from Vientiane by the founding generals and giving the régime its period name of Rattanakosin ('precious jewel of Indra').

The first three kings of the Chakri dynasty (later given the name of Rama by the sixth king) concentrated on restoring the religious, legal and administrative structure of Ayudhya without intentional change. It was Mongkut (Rama IV) who, emerging from a senior monastic position to assume the throne in 1851, saw the need to modernize the country in the face of growing European pressures. Mongkut's treaty with Britain, negotiated on an equal footing in 1855 with Sir John Bowring, set a landmark in modern Asian history. Mongkut's son, Chulalongkorn (Rama V 1868-1910) completed the process of social reform begun by his father. Both these reformist monarchs were greatly assisted by leading members of the monkhood and the oligarchic élite families like Prince-Patriarch Vajiranana (1860-1921) and the great educationalist Prince Damrong (1862-1925).

Thai society remains traditionally compartmented. At the lower level both town and village life is guided by the monkhood, though the people have never abandoned ancient animist beliefs and practices, which they continue to observe alongside Theravada Buddhism. At the top, kingship remains essentially a Hindu cultural tradition, imported and operated from the earliest times by Indian Brahmins. Ceremonies conducted by the king are vital to the rhythm of society and its agricultural life. Around the kings, administrative functions have grown steadily, in a pattern largely discharged by lesser members of the royal family, or by descendants of oligarchic families ennobled by the kings.

This system has created widening circles of an educated middle class, supported for over a century by a modernized monastic and state educational framework; but the sense of deference and obligation within a rigid social stratification has persisted, tending to obviate the natural development of an independent middle class capable of sustaining a viable Parliamentary democracy. In these circumstances attempts at post-war elections have soon wilted. Despite the incessant introduction of new constitutions since the constitutional period began in 1932, governmental change has been largely by military coup, albeit usually after seeking the king's permission. Bloodshed has been restricted to a few rare cases, notably the student rising in 1973 against an exceptionally oppressive military-police governing triumvirate. But by 1985, still with a military government, and with some signs that the middle, 'Young Turk', officers resent the role allotted to the army by politicians, it is evident that pressures within the system are intensifying.

Yet the country is economically stable and reasonably prosperous. It still has problems; among them, how to achieve a more equitable distribution of the national income so as to improve the situation in some depressed agricultural and inner-city areas, and how to stimulate diversification of a still mainly rice-based economy. Steps to prepare the way towards steady economic growth have already been taken by developing the country's infrastructure.

Strategically, Thailand has inherited problems, especially of refugees, from the conflicts on its eastern borders during the years since the Second World War. Economically, it has had to accommodate to the withdrawal of American involvement in those conflicts. In the mid-1980s, retaining military alliances with the West and working politically within ASEAN, it continues to show itself a reliable bulwark against the spread of subversive forces into Southeast Asia from the communist-inspired war zones of Indochina.

Religion and kingship

Thailand is a Buddhist country. Its monasteries practise and profess the type of Buddhism known as Theravada, which it received from Sri Lanka at the outset of the formation of the first independent Thai kingdoms in the 13th century. Most Thais, including the king, expect to shave the head (the tonsure ceremony, equivalent to 'coming-out'), don the yellow robe, and spend some time in a monastery as neophyte monks.

But Thailand has never excluded other religious or philosophical traditions; King Mongkut encouraged Western Protestant missions, as part of his modernization policy after his accession in 1851, although he was himself until then the abbot of an important Buddhist monastery. This attitude is founded in the essentially syncretic character of the

Introduction

religious traditions which reached Thailand from India by several quite different routes from the 5th-13th centuries AD.

Hinduism and Buddhism had common origins, rooted in Vedic hymns and rites – especially those codified in the *Rgveda* (ca. – 1.2m) – and in the Sanskrit commentaries (*upanisads* etc.) which grew out of these from the first millennium BC. Three types of religion emerged: first, Brahmanic sects preferring one or another of the Hindu gods, Śiva, Viṣnu or Brahma; then came the two forms of Buddhism – Mahayana and Hinayana – the latter couched in the Theravada scriptures in Pali.

The syncretist element in the religion of Thailand arose from the merging of these various teachings and beliefs at many stages (most notably in Cambodia) on their way to the country. Thus, Buddha is depicted in Thai temple murals attended by the Hindu gods Indra, Viṣnu (the preserver), and Brahma (the universal – depicted with four faces).

The king may enter a monastery, but is not crowned by the Buddhist Patriarch; and kingship, introduced by Brahmins from India, retains many of its original Hindu traditions. Versions of Viṣnu's name can be found in personal and place names (for instance, Narai, the 17th-century king of Ayudhya, and Phitsanulok, the provincial town); and important royal occasions, such as the funeral and cremation ceremonies, which are attended by Buddhist monks, celebrate the power of the Hindu god Śiva, creator and destroyer.

The tribes

The tribes form a highly complex 'interdigital' pattern of often migratory village settlements in all Thailand's border areas. Many of these are common to neighbour countries, and even spill back and forth across the borders. They amount to several dozen distinct peoples, some of common origin but separated by culture and dispersal, others of totally different stock. They can be classified according to language – the various Tai tribes (White Tai, Black Tai, etc.), and Shan, Lao or Yuan being of the Tai language family, while the T'in (the third most numerous group in Thailand), in north Thailand and Laos, are among a number of tribes of Mon-Khmer linguistic origin. The second most numerous, the Hmong or Meo, spreading right across northern Thailand and northern Indochina, and the Yao of northern Thailand and the southern provinces of China, speak languages with Chinese affinity and mix their shamanist beliefs with Taoism. The Negritos of peninsular Thailand and Malaya are aboriginal inhabitants of wide areas of Malesia, and seem to have migrated northwards, against the normal stream. Thailand's most numerous group, the Karen, are settled in villages

Introduction

spread from north to south along the Thai-Burma border, and were probably original inhabitants of that region. They inhabit upland and lowland river terraces, build longhouses of bamboo for up to thirty families and for rice granaries, and speak their own Karenni tongue.

The level at which the tribes live and migrate, and often the related factor of whether they build their houses of bamboo on stilts or of wood on the ground, provide further evidence of tribal distinctness. The Meo are hilltribes, while the Shan, like the Thai themselves, have always moved along lowland river valleys with wet-rice cultivation.

The crop habits of the tribes vary from primitive upland slash-and-burn culture, with opium poppy growing, to wet-rice, and different types of domesticated animals. Hill hunter-gatherers, like the Pear people of the Cardamom mountains along the Thai-Cambodian border, who rely on trading cardamom and other finds such as deer-horn velvet for cloth, salt and iron, have tended to lose their identities through acculturation and intermingling with lowland villages.

Meo opium cultivation in the so-called 'golden triangle', encouraged by the remnant KMT (Kuomintang) army, presents a trading-contact problem; the Thai government and the King personally have been seeking to wean these tribespeople away from their traditional opium cash crop by training them in alternative crops, and by improved general education.

On the whole, the tribal composition of this great tract across northern mainland Southeast Asia is changing as contacts with modern neighbours are increasing; and it is partly this factor which has made the tribes such an interesting and urgent study, to which much expert research has been given in the decades since the Second World War.

Language and literature

The Thai language belongs to a distinct family of languages, the Tai group. Its nearest neighbours are Sinitic and Tibeto-Burman. Like the other principal tonal languages of Asia — Chinese, Vietnamese and Burmese — but unlike Japanese, Malay, Mon-Khmer and Sanskrit, it is tonal and non-agglutinative (i.e. distinguishes apparent homonyms by using variant tones, and adds words instead of modifying them to make plurals, tenses, etc.).

Its lexicon is basically monosyllabic, with a few dissyllables. It has a relatively minor loanstock from southern Chinese (e.g. the primary numbers parallel Cantonese), and an important loanstock of mainly literary, religious, royal and administrative terms from Sanskrit or Pali: these are mostly complex polysyllables, to which Thai has added tones.

Introduction

The Thai script consists of a 'transitional alphabet' — i.e. an alphabetic system in which some vowels are inherent, or unwritten; for instance, the dissyllable *thanon* (street) is written 'thnn'. It was devised, from Khmer, one of the early scripts derived from Sanskrit, by King Ramkhamhaeng of Sukhothai: its first extant example is a royal inscription composed by him in 1292 and incised on a stele at Sukhothai.

The script, written left to right, uses no spaces between words within a phrase, and has no internal punctuation. Following the Sanskrit system, the forty-four consonants dominate; the thirty-six written vowels distinguish short from long sounds, and each of these may comprise one or up to three or more symbols, written above, below, left or right of the consonants. Tones are indicated by the selection of consonants, which are classified into high, middle and low for the purpose, sometimes with the addition of diacritics. The script has remained virtually unchanged since the 13th century. The following line is a modern example:

อุทยานประวัติศาสตร์สุโขทัย

meaning: The Sukhothai (Archaeological) Historical Park.

Different forms of speech are used for addressing superiors or inferiors, and a totally different lexicon for formal address to royalty. The first person pronoun is different for men and women, as are the frequently used polite interjections *kha* (by women) and *khrab* (by men); when used alone, these interjections constitute simple affirmatives. These variants lend a distinctive charm to colloquial spoken Thai.

Thai has two sets of numerals, one classical and convoluted, derived fairly closely from Sanskrit, the other modern, identical with European Arabic. Both sets, being alike of ultimately Indic origin, include O (for zero), which is missing from Roman, though current usage of classical Thai numerals as an alternative to Arabic is otherwise in some ways parallel to that of Roman in Europe.

The Tai group, probably having had a common ancestor (unknown), includes many of the tribal languages of Thailand and adjacent areas. These are of decreasing mutual intelligibility with time and distance of migration from a probably Annamese parentland: thus, the differences tend to be cultural rather than ethno-linguistic. Among the closest to Thai today are Lao and Shan.

Most of the tribal languages are pre-literate; a few (e.g. Yao, and others with close affinities to southern China) make some use of Chinese characters. Thai, however (like Ahom, the member of the Tai group which migrated to Assam) developed a complete Indic script by the 13th century, in which valuable chronicles were set down, on beaten and sized bark (Ahom) or corypha palm leaves (Thai).

A main and continuing element in Thai literature was developed in the form of Theravada religious scriptures, either in the Pali language (in Thai script since it had none of its own), or in Thai. Pali, the religious language of Hinayana Buddhism, is still the basic language of religious learning and offices in Thai monasteries, paralleling Latin in the Roman Church. The *Tripitaka*, a compilation of Hinayana scriptures and precepts, is available in Thai libraries in some forty-five volumes. The *Traibhum*, a shorter Thai compilation of Theravada texts dating from the 14th century, has gone through many recensions. Some, accompanied by splendid didactic miniature paintings on folded sheets of brown paper up to 50 metres in length, are among the treasures of Thai literature.

Another important para-religious work from an Indian source is the *Ramakien*, a Thai epic derived in several recensions, ultimately from the *Ramayana*, the northeast Indian story of Prince Rama, his consort Sita, and Hanuman, the white-monkey general who rescues her from the demon Totsakan — the Thai personation of Ravana, the evil king of Langka (Sri Lanka). The *Ramayana*, in 24,000 verses derived from earlier oral traditions, and based on characters stemming from as far back as the *Rgveda*, is attributed to the hermit poet Valmiki (ca. —4c). The long evolution of episodes in this drama has conferred important moral and religious overtones upon it, for instance making Rama an incarnation of Visnu. In the form of a magical fairy-tale, it is to be found in serial murals in many temples of Thailand, especially Wat Phra Jetupon (Wat Po) in Bangkok. It has been the most influential single literary, dance and musical inspiration of the country, and indeed of all Indianized Southeast Asia.

The didactic monastic literature of Thailand takes a similar epic form, consisting of episodes from the life of Buddha, and from his previous incarnations, especially the last, or Great Ten, of the 550 *jatakas*, showing his progress towards buddhahood. The main and last of these, the long *Vessantara Jataka*, exemplifying the virtue of giving away possessions, is recited in procession with painted banners by the monks at the end of the Buddhist Lent, conferring merit on all those who stay to listen.

Without detracting from the central importance of these religious canons or epics, a secular literature grew by Ayudhyan times in both epic and poetic form. Pseudo-*jatakas*, like the northern story of Prince

Introduction

Sang Thong, gained popularity, and the *nirat* love poetry of King Narai's court, exemplified by the young poet Si Prat, and by works of the early Bangkok period by Sunthon Phu, set a fine tradition of lyric, sometimes sensitively erotic, poetry comparable in style and content to Elizabethan lyric verse. Among moralist epics perpetuated from oral tradition, an important place was occupied by versions of the traditional classic *Khun Chang, Khun Phaen.*

Until the social reforms of the mid-19th century the kings, commanding both court and monastic patronages, remained the chief patrons, just as they were often also among the exponents, of all expressions of art; and most of it, including literature, was inseparable from their religious inheritance from Hinduism and Buddhism.

With the arrival of the first printing presses after 1824 (products of the English East India Company and of American Protestant missions) modern literature with an ever widening diversity of publishers and authors began to take off. One of its best examples of today is M. R. Kukrit Pramoj's 'Four reigns', a popular historical novel in Galsworthian style.

The bibliography

A bibliography of this type is like a snapshot of a running, flashing stream. The compiler hopes to capture sufficient samples of both the deep water, and the surface scintillations, to convey a lasting impression of what must be an ever self-renewing flow.

The bibliography assumes no prior knowledge of the subjects it treats. Its presentation is not designed for specialist students or scholars — except in so far as their interest in their own fields may draw them into other, tangential or related, fresh fields. Specialists will have their own, much fuller and more detailed bibliographic sources. Some avenues leading into these are indicated at various levels.

Source materials concerning Thailand are worldwide. Relevant monographs, articles and serials available in London alone probably exceed 100,000. They represent materials originated not only there, but also in Paris, Tokyo, Kyoto, Bangkok and Singapore, and at universities in the United States, Germany, Australia, and so on. A bewildering array of specialisms in many languages.

Entries in this bibliography are of materials mainly in English, with some in French or German, and one in Dutch. Some are translations from, or contain references to, primary or secondary sources in Thai, Shan, Burmese, Khmer, Chinese, Malay, Arabic, Japanese and other languages.

Introduction

Among material excluded is, for instance, the considerable, mostly untranslated, fund of Russian scholarship — though the 'thick journals' (*tolstiye zhurnaly*) like *Voprosy Istorii* (Problems of History) continue to treat Far Eastern religious, historical and similar topics. Some of this material, and also some examples of the copious political propaganda from Moscow to or about Southeast Asia, can be found in the 'Summary of World Broadcasts', part I (q.v.). Some examples of Thai and Western radical and communist writing on Thailand will be found in the bibliography.

The overall selection consists of 818 entries, or about 1,000 with subsumed references. Bibliographic references cited indicate over 30,000 further material sources.

In making this selection I have been guided by four main considerations: Is the book or other item 'a good read' in its own right? Is it likely to stand up into the '90s? Does it convey fairly a type of general interest or specialism at one particular level? Finally, has it a good bibliography for further or extended reading on its subject area? If an item seems to satisfy at least one, or perhaps more than one, of these desiderata I have given it preference.

The wide spectrum of Thailand's cultural and political connections, both past and present, makes it difficult to draw a line at which a neighbouring country's interests, or a subject of general regional interest, becomes of too little relevance to warrant inclusion. I have tried to provide sufficient material from the country's religious inheritance from ancient India, and of its cultural and tribal origins in China and Indochina, to provide an adequate picture of its initial background, and enough on its neighbours Burma, Cambodia, Malaysia, and its general Southeast Asian context (especially the relatively new one of ASEAN) to convey a good account of its degree of contact and common heritage with these. This applies particularly, for example, to Ayudhya's European and world trade context in the 16th and 17th centuries, concerning which a number of contemporary European as well as modern accounts have been included.

Archaeology in Thailand has made important contributions towards an understanding of early Southeast Asia; among aspects covered here are the controversial discoveries at Ban Chiang near the Mekong River, which caused a world sensation in the early 1960s by seeming to antedate Middle Eastern and Chinese metalworking and rice cultivation, and the interesting questions surrounding the social and ritual use of bronze drums.

Thailand's peculiar experience of the Second World War, as at the same time a nominal enemy and yet an actual collaborator of the Allied

Introduction

side, with its own resistance movement, and the unique, and in many ways interesting, fate of Allied prisoners-of-war, are fully reflected.

The entries include a representative taste of the mass of material on Thailand's flora and fauna, and also of the extensive literature explaining the ethnobotanic and biogeographic reasons for its exceptional diversity. Indications are also provided as to potential sources of extended reading and continuing research in these fields which, though of considerable interest, are too voluminous for further coverage in a bibliography of the present scope.

The bibliography necessarily contains many entries which cover more than one subject. Their arrangement in chapters is therefore not always conclusive; for fuller coverage of particular topics, recourse should be had to the general index. On some administrative matters, and defence organization, handbooks and yearbooks may be found to be the most useful and up-to-date reference sources.

Two final points in this general look at the bibliography: the glossary has been drawn up to provide some further background information, in addition to its function as a quick-reference guide on apparently obscure elements in some of the titles listed. Cf., for example, no. 258, glossary entries under 'tamnan', 'Kengtung', and 'Chiang'. Similarly, the chronology is designed to augment some of the general observations on political and art history in the introduction.

Transliteration

Many attempts have been made at a roman transliteration of Thai. A Thai word is meaningless, or given an incorrect meaning, without its proper tone. There are five alternative tones for each syllable (some authorities stipulate a sixth). Western names or loanwords tend to be spoken in level tone throughout. The ordinary Thai word romanized as *chang*, to take an example at random, can mean elephant or smith, according to how the reader supplies the tone. The context will of course tend to dictate the answer; most Thai speakers will automatically supply the correct tones for isolated words, phrases or proper names romanized without tonemarks, and it is only for total accuracy (for instance, in some modern computer transliterations of book or article titles), or for lengthy passages or linguistic material, that some system of tonemarking is indispensable.

There are two other hurdles for the Western transliterator. Indic voiced and unvoiced, and aspirated and unaspirated, consonants have to be distinguished, though to the untutored Western ear the difference is hard to detect. The distinction is best made in roman by adding 'h' (tat, that; pra, phra). In a few Sanskrit loanwords 'd' and 't' are used

Introduction

interchangeably for the sound 't' (Thani, or Dhani). The addition of 'h' to show aspirated consonants does not imply a different basic sound, as it would in English in 'than', or 'phase'; 'v' and 'w' are used interchangeably to represent the consonant ว , which is pronounced between English 'v' and 'w'; the same Thai letter is also used for the vowel romanized as 'ua'.

The second problem concerns final consonants. Spoken Thai has fewer of these than written Thai. Thus written final 'r', 'l', and 's' are pronounced as 'n', 'n', and 't' respectively. They are sometimes romanized one way and sometimes the other; thus Phibul follows the Thai spelling, and Phibun reproduces the same name phonetically. The name of the present king, Bhumibol Adulyadej, is pronounced Phumipon Adunyadet. Initial 'j' (from Sanskrit) can come out as 'ch' or 'dzh' in sound, while as a final letter 'j' comes out as 't'. Long or short vowels are sometimes indicated in material requiring technical accuracy (including, again, linguistic material).

Finally, there is the problem of loanwords, especially personal names, derived from Sanskrit or Pali. These may be transliterated into Thai either in full or in shortened form, as they are spoken, and therefore into roman with the same alternative forms. Thus common final syllables ending in 'a' (which is not sounded in Thai) like -tiara may become -tian (as spoken). Such unspoken, or 'arabesque' letters are marked with superscript [s] (there is an example in the specimen line of Thai script above). The same symbol is used when Western names are transliterated into Thai, e.g. above final 's', which remains unspoken when preceded by another consonant, e.g. in the English name Watts.

The Thai Royal Institute transliteration is given in the *Journal of the Siam Society*, vol. 33, part 1 (Jan. 1941), p. 49-65. A very thorough system for linguistic purposes using phonetic and diacritic tonal and other symbols is given by Mary Haas in *Thai-English student's dictionary* (q.v.). A simplified adaptation, following Thai spelling but without added phonetic symbols, diacritics, or doubled vowels (for length), and with 'ae' for the vowel sounded as 'a' in Anne, is used in the text of this bibliography. Transliterations in titles are as published:

Chinese Wade-Giles is used, and not the newer, official Pinyin system.

Sanskrit 'ś' (palatal) and 'ṣ' (retroflex); both pronounced as 'sh' in English shade; semi-vowel 'ṛ', pronounced as 'ri' in English rig or

Introduction

'Sanskrit'; this also occurs in a few Thai words: e.g. *angkrit*: England, English.

Thai names, ranks and name-indexing

Thai personal names usually comprise first-name and second, or family name, in that order. Second names were not used until the 20th century, and Thai names are still often indexed according to first names. Royal styles and titles may run to extensive groups of Sanskrit words. Some essential elements of these are: Chao Fa, for princes born as first generation offspring of a king and queen, and Phra Ong Chao, for royal offspring by lesser consorts or subsequent generations if both parents are not of equally high rank. Royalty or commoners may have ranks conferred by the king, indicating administrative responsibilities such as minister, e.g. Mom Chao, Chao Phraya (regent — also the name given to the Bangkok river), Krom and Kromamun. These are normally also referred to as Prince. The female title in Thai adds Ying, e.g. Phra Ong Chao Ying.

The normal practice in English is to use Prince or Princess with first name only for all the above. Thus, Prince Damrong, for Prince Damrong Rajanubharb, is used in this bibliography for entries and indexing.

The next generations of royalty, unless they come from spouses of equal rank, are Mom Rachawong (M. R.), Mom Luang (M. L.), and thereafter the normal civil form of address, Khun, equivalent to the polite forms Mr., Mrs. or Miss. This is used for both men and women on all polite occasions, and is also normal usage within the family circle. The parallel is with the polite form of address to a British knight using first-name only, e.g. Sir Richard.

Either the first or the second names are commonly used for indexing Thai authors, and when in doubt it is recommended to search under both alternatively. In this bibliography the normal Western practice has been followed, i.e. indexing by second name except for royalty.

Acknowledgements

A number of people have been most kind and helpful in preparing the way for this undertaking; without them it would not have come about. First, I would like to express my gratitude to Professor E. H. Stuart Simmonds, the late Dr. Peter J. Bee, and Dr. Manas Chitakasem, of the Department of the Languages and Cultures of Southeast Asia and the Islands, and to the late Professor Charles A. Fisher, and Dr. Philip A.

Introduction

Stott, of the Department of Geography, of the School of Oriental and African Studies, University of London, for their encouragement, advice and instruction over a number of years.

In Bangkok, I would like to express my respects and gratitude to HRH Princess Chumbhot na Nagara Svarga and her museum assistants at the Lettuce Garden Palace (Wang Suan Pakkad) for their enlightenment and guidance, and to thank other Thai friends too numerous to mention individually, in both London and Bangkok, and Judy Stowe and other members of the BBC Far Eastern Service, for their help on political points.

In London, my thanks are due to Mr. J. E. Hill and Mr. P. D. Hillyard of the Zoology Department, British Museum (Natural History), for expert guidance on the bumblebee bat and spiders, respectively, to the late Dr. W. S. Bristowe, on spiders, and at the Royal Botanic Gardens, Kew, to Dr. John Dransfield, on palms, and, in Bournemouth, to Mr. Peter Collins, on philately. I would also like to express my appreciation and gratitude to the library staffs of the School of Oriental and African Studies, of the British Museum (National History), of the Royal Botanic Gardens, Kew, and of the British Library, for their unfailing professional assistance; and to Talat Stonehouse at Clio for her work on the manuscript.

Last, and indispensable, my thanks are due to Ben and Alec Knox, without whose timely guidance of my first steps into the mysteries of computerland I would have found the problems of production a great deal less tractable than they were. None of the aforementioned people was in any way directly responsible for the selection or annotation of any of the material in this bibliography, errors and omissions in which must be laid entirely at my own door.

Michael Watts
Blackheath
January 1986

Glossary

Sanskrit − skr.; Pali − p.; Thai − th.; Lao − l.; Khmer − kh.;
Malay − m.; Shan − s.

BE	Buddha Era; subtract 543 for AD.
ban	th. (long 'a' as in English barn): village; house.
bang	th. (long 'a'): riverside village or locality; reach.
Bangkok-Thonburi	full Western name of the combined capital (cf. Budapest); th.: *Krungthep* (city of angels ...). The pre-capital Chinese fishing village, Bang Kok, remains a city district.
bodhisattva	p.: buddha (enlightened person, freed from further reincarnations) in waiting, remaining at the human level to practise works of merit and virtue; a previous incarnation of the Buddha.
bot	*see ubosoth.*
Chakri	*see* wheel of the law.
chao	th.: part of royal titles, chief; in northern area: tribal chief; s.: *saohpa, sawbwa.*
chao phraya	th.: senior minister; regent; Menam Chao Phraya, the Chao Phraya River (often wrongly called 'Menam').
chedi	th. from p. *cetiya*, skr. *caitya*: tapered, flame-shaped reliquary shrine, containing Buddha relic or funerary ashes of kings; stupa.

Glossary

Chiang
th. from Tai-yuan (northern dialect); s. *Jeng, Keng*: city; Chiang Mai ('new city') capital of Lan Na, founded by Mangrai 1292: Chiang Saen, north of Chiang Mai, gave its name to an earlier, disputed art period.

corypha
species of fan-palm (*corypha lecontei*), cultivated in temple sites; used in monks' screen-fans; leaves used for chronicle books. Another species (*borassus flabellifer*), referred to as talipot (skr. *tala* [palm], *pat* [leaf]), gives *talipoin* (monk, in Burma – via Portuguese). In Assam, in the absence of the fan-palms, the Ahom chronicles were inscribed on sized aloes-wood bark.

dharma
skr.: th., p. *thamma*: the law or doctrine of Buddha; law; *Thammasat*: the Law University, Bangkok.

Dvaravati
skr.: name given to the first kingdom, of Indian origin, known in Thailand – based at Nakhon Pathom, and prominent at Lopburi; also to the Theravada Mon art period associated with it (6-11c). Its last outcrop (13c) was at Haripunchai (Haripunjaya) near Lamphun.

farang
th.: Westerner, European.

flora
(as a book): botanic checklist with descriptions of the plant population of the stated country or area, in one or a continuing series of volumes.

garuda
skr.: mythical eagle with human arms and torso; Thai state emblem; th.: *khrud*.

hikayat
m.: historical account, chronicle.

Hinayana
skr.: 'lesser vehicle': school of Buddhism giving rise to Theravada in Ceylon.

ikat
m. (th. *madmi*): 'knotted': hand-woven style of batik cloth, noted for original, traditional designs.

Indra
skr.: king of the Hindu 33-god heaven at the summit of Mount Meru; represented in Hindu kingship by the reigning monarch.

Glossary

Isan	th.: northeastern dialect, close to Lao; the Khorat plateau (q.v.) district of Thailand, bordering Laos; also its Lao-related people.
jataka	skr.: didactic recitation or story of a previous incarnation of the Buddha.
Junkceylon	(also Thalang): former name for Phuket Island.
Kengtung	ancient Shan royal and monastic city, now part of Burma, northeast of Chiang Mai and Chiang Saen; chronicles are in Khün script, close to Tai-yuan (northern Thai): they include some Pali. See also Chiang. The Padaeng ('red forest') monastery in Kengtung was founded ca. 1350 AD.
Khmer	(Mon-Khmer family): language of Angkor and the Khmer empire, also used in Thailand in pre-Thai inscriptions.
Khorat	plateau of central northeast Thailand; also colloquial name for its provincial capital, Nakhon Ratchasima — captured by a Lao vassal, Anu, in 1827, the eventual defeat of whose rebellion led to the sack of Vientiane and to large precautionary shipments of Lao people across the Mekong River into Khorat Province, creating later Isan (q.v.) separatist unrest.
khun	th.; formerly, a rank (lord); in modern times, a polite first-name prefix, equivalent to Mr., Mrs. (sometimes *nang*), or Miss.
klong	th.: canal, especially in Bangkok; rice-carrying trunk canals were also made.
Kwai	name (incorrectly) given by prisoners-of-war to the river Khwae Noi.
Lan Na	th.: name ('million ricefields') given to the area in northern Thailand of several 11-13c Tai kingdoms, especially that established by Mangrai at Chiang Mai. Its neighbours were the disputatious buffer state of Nan-chao (in Yunnan) to the north, and Lan Chang ('million elephants'), the Theravadist kingdom based at Luang Prabang (Laos) to the east.

Glossary

Ligor former name for Nakhon Si Thammarat.

Lopburi provincial town in the northeast; Khmer vassaldom of Lavo or Louvo; site of King Narai's alternate (summer) palace.

Mahayana skr.: 'greater vehicle': school of Buddhism of wider canon; brought from India and practised by early, pre-Thai kingdoms.

Malesia biogeographical name given to Peninsular and archipelagic Southeast Asia, when the terms Malaysia and Indonesia became political expressions.

Mekong (or Mekhong) the river: *Mae* (*Nam*) *Khong* (th., l., kh.), from 'river' (literally *mae*, 'mother' + *nam*, 'of waters' and *Khong*, transliterated from skr. *Ganga*, i.e. Ganges, the Hindu sacred river. 'Mekhong' is also a popular brand of Thai rice whisky.

Menam name formerly (incorrectly) given to the Chao Phraya River (q.v.).

Meru skr.: central mountain of the Hindu cosmos, surrounded by water and continents, and having Indra's 33-god heaven at its summit; in temple architecture, the Meru (*chedi, stupa, prang* [kh. from skr.]) is the spire, and the remainder of the temple is a replica of the cosmos; *Men* (th.); also phallic symbol of Śiva.

Mon (Mon-Khmer family): language of Mon people who brought the Buddhist Dvaravati civilization to Thailand (+6c).

muang th.: traditional territorial concept: nation, country, district, locality or its people, town, now mainly colloquial. (The vowel, though conventionally romanized like 'ua', is in this case the more complex diphthong sounded as German ü, or French u + a). s.: *mong, möng*.

naga skr.: mythical half-human snake, protector of Buddha; used in Thai temple finials, and over some Buddha images, which are also seated on its coils.

Glossary

nagara   skr.: city, town (sometimes state); *nakhon* (th.); *angkor* (kh.), giving Angkor Wat ('temple city').

nakhon   th. (from skr. *nagara*): town, city; sometimes transliterated 'nakorn' (phon.).

Nan-chao   *see* Lan Na.

nang   th. (long 'a'): lady, Mrs.; (short 'a'): shadow-play (see *wayang*).

nirat   th. (*niras*, from skr. *nirasa*: 'deprivation'): genre of love poem expressing pangs of separation.

Pali   (Indo-European family, Middle Indo-Aryan branch): religious language of Theravada, (Hinayana) Buddhist scriptures, developed in Ceylon; parallel with Prakrit, the simplified, popular offshoot from Sanskrit; Pali having no separate script, countries receiving the Pali canon used their own for its inscription.

phra   th. (from p.): Buddha image; monk; honorific prefix for monks, or for kings.

Phra Malai   p.: monk in Ceylon, who visited the underworld to seek instruction from Maitreya, the Buddha of the future; a favourite Thai legend, associated with funeral rites.

phraya   th.: next highest conferred rank, after *chao phraya* (q.v.).

phya   th.; a shortened form of *phraya* (q.v.).

Rama   hero prince of the *Ramayana*, giving the Bangkok Rama (Chakri) dynasty its name.

Ramakien   th. (skr. *Ramakirti*): version of the Indian *Ramayana* epic, adapted in Thailand as dance drama, and theme for temple murals. (Transliteration conventional, for *Ramakian.*)

Rattanakosin   th. (from skr.): 'precious jewel of Indra'; name given to the Chakri dynastic period, denoting the Emerald Buddha.

Glossary

Ṛgveda

skr. (sometimes 'Rigveda', phon.): collection of Vedic hymns and rites (ca −1.2m), resulting from the Aryan invasion of northern India (ca −1.5m); a foundation of the religious philosophy of Hinduism and Buddhism, also of the *Ramayana*; skr. *ṛg*: 'stanza, verse'; *veda*: 'knowledge, canon'. Vedic is the equivalent of Greek, and Sanskrit or Pali of Latin, for Thai language and literature.

sangha

skr.; p.: order of monks or nuns, monkhood. One of the 'three jewels' (*triratana*) of Hinayana Buddhism, the others being the Buddha, and the law, or doctrine (*dharma*).

Sanskrit

(Indo-European family, Old Indo-Aryan branch): the religious and philosophical language of Brahmanism in northeast India, and of Hindu scripture and literature following Vedic (ca −1.5m); skr. *sanskrit*: 'polished, refined'; its Brahmi script (−3c) was the prototype for modern Indian scripts and, in its elegant Pallava 'leaf-bud tip' style, for Mon, Khmer, Thai, and others of Indianized Southeast Asia, including the 'tamarind-pod' (l., th.: *fak kham*) Lao script, derived from Mon, which preceded Thai.

śastra

skr.: canon, used in combination-words.

sepha

th. (from skr. *sebha*): genre of epic recital, derived from ancient India, using voice changes for dramatic effect.

siamang

m.: long-armed black gibbon.

Singora

former name for Songkhla.

Śrivijaya

skr.; Mahayanist maritime empire of Indian origin, influential (ca +8c) in Indonesia and Thailand, with bases at Palembang (Sumatra) and Chaiya (Kra Isthmus).

Sukhodaya

skr. form of Sukhothai, capital of the first independent Thai kingdom (13c).

suphasit

th. (from skr. *subhasita*: aphorism, parable): morality poem; story incorporating a precept.

stupa

skr.: solid, bell-shaped commemorative Buddhist shrine, sometimes called a pagoda.

Glossary

swidden   Old Anglo-Saxon term for primitive agriculture; somewhat misapplied by some writers to the 'slash-and-burn' techniques adopted by Southeast Asian hilltribes.

tamnan   th.: chronicle; history of state or religious foundation; legend.

thamma   *see* dharma.

Theravada   p.: 'teaching of the elders'; Hinayana doctrine of a monastic sect in Ceylon, imported into Burma (Pagan) and Thailand.

traibhum   th. (from p.; also *traibhumi* + *katha*, 'sermon'; skr. *trailoka, tiloka*): 'three worlds': collation of Buddhist scriptures, 14-19c.; source of illuminated captioned miniatures for murals; also transliterated traiphum.

ubosoth   (also *bot*) th. (from skr.): main assembly building of a monastery, housing its principal Buddha image.

vinaya   skr., p.: the Buddhist monastic disciplinary code; one of the three divisions of the canon, or *tripitaka* (p. *tipitaka*).

wat   th.: an entire temple complex; may include *ubosoth* (q.v.), one or more *viharns* (chapels − skr.: *vihara*), many *chedis*, a library or scriptorium, and *sala* (monks' hall).

wayang   m.: theatrical performance; *wayang kulit*: leather-puppet shadow-play of Javanese origin, practised in the Malay-Thai peninsular region; th.: *lakhon* ('play') + *nang* (short a: 'buffalo-hide'; 'puppet'; by extension, modern cinema film).

wheel of the law   sculptural symbol of Buddha's doctrine; *chakra*, skr. ('wheel'): symbol of levels of the cosmos, represented by nine rings on temple-spires; discus (spiked missile): attribute, symbolizing authority, of gods, or of kings. *Chakravartin*, skr.: (Buddha as) Universal Emperor. *Chakri*, th. ('discus-bearer'): high official, general, or king; title initially assumed by the Bangkok dynasty.

Chronology

−2000	Ban Chiang culture (NE Thailand)
−1000	Dongson culture (Indochina-mainland SE Asia) Hoabinh culture (?) Proto-Tai in Yangtse area (?) or South China
−200	Early Tai in North Indochina
+200	Tribal Tai dispersals (−+1000)
+500	Chinese-influenced empires of Champa, Funan Indian-influenced empires of Dvaravati (6-11c), Śrivijaya (7-12c), and Khmer (8-13c) begin to spread Buddhism and Śivaism in SE Asia
+750	Nan-chao empire (8-13c); threat to T'ang
+900	Nan-chao, T'ang in decline
+1000	Tai tribes occupying SE Asian river valleys (via Nan-chao?) Pagan (11-13c) centre of SE Asian Theravada Buddhism Lopburi under Khmer rule
+1100	Khmer Hindu-Mahayana temple built at Phimai; road from Angkor Angkor Wat built; frieze shows Thai as mercenaries
+1200	Kublai Khan drives south; accelerates Shan, Thai migrations Angkor in decline Haripunjaya (last Dvaravati outpost) falls to Mangrai (1281)

Chronology

1250-1438	first Thai Kingdom of Sukhothai
1259-1564	northern (Tai-yuan) Kingdom of Lan Na Mangrai moves capital from Chiang Saen to Chiang Mai (1292)
1351-1767	Kingdom of Ayudhya (taking in Lopburi)
1767	Ayudhya sacked by Burmese; Taksin moves capital to Thonburi (−1782)
1782	Rama (Chakri) dynasty established at Bangkok Coup introducing constitutional monarchy (1932)

Kings of Thailand

1279-98	Ramkhamhaeng (Sukhothai)
1346-70	Lü Thai (Sukhothai)
1355-85	Ku Na (Chiang Mai)
1441-87	Tiloka (Chiang Mai)
1656-88	Narai (Ayudhya)
1767-82	Taksin (Thonburi)
1782-1808	Phutthayotfa (Bangkok — Rama I)
1809-24	Phra Puttaloetla (Rama II)
1824-51	Phra Nangklao (Rama III)
1851-68	Mongkut (Rama IV)
1868-1910	Chulalongkorn* (Rama V)
1910-25	Vajiravudh (Rama VI)
1925-35	Prajadhipok (Rama VII)
1935-46	Ananda Mahidol* (Rama VIII)
1946-	Bhumibol Adulyadej (Rama IX)

*acceded as a minor

Abbreviations

ASEAN   Association of Southeast Asian Nations (members: Thailand, the Philippines, Singapore, Malaysia, Indonesia)

BEFEO   Bulletin de l'Ecole Française d'Extrême Orient

BIOSIS   Biological Sciences Information Service

BMA   Bangkok Metropolitan Administration

BSOAS   Bulletin of the School of Oriental and African Studies, University of London

EFEO   Ecole Française d'Extrême Orient (volume numbers refer to Publications of the EFEO)

ISEAS   Institute of Southeast Asian Studies (Singapore)

JMBRAS   Journal of the Malaysian Branch of the Royal Asiatic Society (others are, or have been, Straits Branch, Chinese Branch, etc.)

JRAS   Journal of the Royal Asiatic Society

JSS   Journal of the Siam Society

PMBC   Phuket Marine Biological Centre

RTG   Royal Thai Government

SOAS   School of Oriental and African Studies, University of London

SWB   Summary of World Broadcasts, published by the BBC

USOM   United States Operations Mission (Thailand)

Note: Information and xerox copies of published theses can be obtained from: University Microfilms International, 300 North Zeeb Road, Ann Arbor, Michigan 48106 USA; and White Swan House, Godstone, Surrey RH9 8LW, UK.

The Country and Its People

1 **Thailand: land of temples.**
John Audric. London: Hale, 1962. 190p.
This is a concise general guide to Thai life and institutions, culled mainly from official sources, by a former government adviser.

2 **Bangkok: a Thai diary.**
Ruth Thompson Bendel. Singapore: Asia Pacific Press, 1972. 124p. illus.
This account of the daily life of a Thai family is pleasingly presented in large format with wide-spaced, simple text aided by drawings. This book could be of use to Western families about to take up a short- or a long-term residence in Bangkok.

3 **Thailand: its people, its society, its culture.**
Edited by Wendell Blanchard. New Haven, Connecticut: Human Relations Area Files Press, 1958. 528p. bibliog.
Though dated, this fully comprehensive handbook remains a useful reference source.

4 **People of the sun.**
John Blofeld. London: Hutchinson, 1960. 192p.
The author provides some profoundly observed character sketches of a representative selection of types encountered during a journey through Thailand in search of its soul: a prince, a hill tribesman, a monk and a scholar.

The Country and Its People

5 **The kingdom and people of Siam.**
Sir John Bowring, introduction by David K. Wyatt. Kuala Lumpur: Oxford University Press, 1969. 2 vols. (Oxford in Asia Facsimile Reprint).

Sir John Bowring visited Siam in 1855 to conclude the trade treaty with King Mongkut, which became a prototype for similar arrangements by other European powers. Bowring's model description of the land and people, published in 1857, contains astute observations and a great deal of information. It is still of considerable interest today. The two volumes, with contemporary plates, deal with diplomatic relations (Burney, Crawfurd and others) and with Siam's customs, products, legal system, and the country in general as Bowring saw it, and as he could learn of it from extant sources (especially Bishop Pallegoix's then recently published *Description du royaume Thai* [q.v.]). David K. Wyatt's introduction outlines Bowring's remarkable and many-sided career as reformer, administrator, and linguist.

6 **Thailand: a country study.**
Edited by Frederica M. Bunge. Washington, DC: Army Department HQ, 1981. 352p. bibliog. (American University Foreign Area Studies).

This is a concise total handbook of Thailand, updated from an occasional sequence (last publication 1971). Main subdivisions are: history (Robert Rinehart); society and environment (Irving Kaplan); the economy (Donald P. Whitaker); government and politics (Rinn S. Shinn); national security (Harold D. Nelson).

7 **Contributions: in memoriam Phya Anuman Rajadhon, late president of the Siam Society.**
Edited by Tej Bunnag, Michael Smithies. Bangkok: Siam Society, 1970. 397p.

This compilation covers a subject range which includes history, language, literature, art, and historical cartography.

8 **Culture shock Thailand and how to survive it.**
Roben Cooper, Nantatha Cooper. Singapore: Times Books International, 1953. 237p.

The authors have compiled a handbook of procedure and custom to enable the tyro visitor to get by in matters ranging from politeness and posture to bribery without offending Thai susceptibilities.

9 **Thailand: the modern kingdom.**
Frank C. Darling, Ann Darling. Singapore: Donald Moore for Asia Pacific Press, 1971. 122p. map. bibliog.

This is a concise, well-presented general profile of Thailand as it is today.

10 **Directory for Bangkok and Siam.**
Bangkok: Bangkok Times Press, 1888-1937. ca.450p.

This directory was the predecessor of the *Siam Directory* (1947-). The issue of 1932 (held in the library of the School of Oriental and African Studies, University of London), makes a complete research instrument in itself, containing an encyclopaedic profile of the country on the eve of the institution of constitutional monarchy. Among the material set forth is: a description of the temples of Bangkok; a diplomatic directory; a registry of foreigners residing and working in the capital; a list of their clubs and businesses; national defence establishments and personnel; and outlines of history, festivals and civil and educational networks of the country.

11 **Thaïlande. (Thailand.)**
Jacques Dumas. [Paris?] : Renée Moser, 1980. 127p.

This excellent, large-format collection of colour photographs is arranged according to selected districts or topics. It will be of particular interest for its section on the River Kwai and bridge area. Other sections cover the 'Golden triangle', elephants, dance drama, and cremation ceremonies.

12 **La transmission de l'imprimerie en Thaïlande: du catéchisme de 1796 aux impressions bouddhiques sur feuilles de latanier.** (The transmission of printing in Thailand: from the catechism of 1796 to Buddhist impressions on palm leaves.)
Gerald Duverdier. *Bulletin de l'Ecole Française d'Extrême-Orient,* vol. 68 (1980), p. 209-59. 2 plates.

Written records in Thailand were in manuscripts on palm leaves, or sometimes on brown paper, until 1835. The first internal press was introduced in 1868, at the end of King Mongkut's reign, though it was not this reformist abbot-turned-monarch, but his younger brother, the Chao Fa Noi, and the *Dhammayutiana* (Young Siam movement), who were responsible for the innovation. This article gives an illustrated account of tradition and change in this field in the Bangkok period.

13 **Siamese tapestry.**
F. K. Exell. London: Hale, 1963. 192p.

The author was a teacher on government contract; the book consists of his impressions of the idyllic conditions of the *farangs* (Westerners) and teak-wallahs living in Thailand before the war.

14 **Felicitation volumes of Southeast Asian studies presented to H. H. Dhanivat Kromamun Bidyalabh Bridhyakorn on the occasion of his 80th birthday.**
Bangkok: Siam Society, 1965. 2 vols.

The two volumes marking the 80th birthday of a distinguished president of the Siam Society consist of collected essays and articles on historical and other Thai subjects. They make a useful source of easy access to a variety of selected materials by leading contributors to the society's journal.

15 **My village in Thailand.**
Sonia Gidal, Tim Gidal. New York: Pantheon, 1970. 60p. illus.
(My Village Series, no. 21).

The 'My Village' team pause for a while among the dwellers in teak and bamboo
houses clustered alongside the Bangkok *klongs* (canals), and also visit the elephant-
training site at Surin, seeing ordinary events through simple villagers' eyes. This
liberally illustrated book would make a good family introduction to these aspects
of Thai life.

16 **Siam: a handbook of practical, commercial and political information.**
Walter A. Graham. London: Alexander Noring, 1924. 2nd ed.
2 vols. map. bibliog. illus.

The original publication of this handbook on Thailand was by the Royal Asiatic
Society (of which the author was a member) in 1912. It covers all aspects of the
country, including geography; religion; trade; industry and agriculture; flora,
fauna and minerals. The work remains an excellent general introduction. It can
also be used as a basis for assessing the extent of changes brought about by
modernization.

17 **H. M. King Bhumibol Adulyadej.**
Bangkok: Public Relations Department [n.d.] . 15p. plates.

This is a short, official profile of the reigning king, who acceded on 9 June 1946.

18 **Studies of contemporary Thailand.**
Edited by Robert Ho, E. C. Chapman. Canberra: Australian
National University Press, 1973. 416p. (Research School of
Pacific Studies, Department of Human Geography, no. 8).

This is a useful compilation of background papers on industry and development;
the environmental limits imposed on agriculture; the hydraulic society and central
plain irrigation; rice in northeast Thailand; the opium problem; and Thai Muslims
in the border provinces.

19 **Mai pen rai means never mind.**
Carol Hollinger. Boston, Massachusetts: Houghton Mifflin, 1965.
237p.

This is a lively and attractive account of daily contacts by an American foreign
service wife in Bangkok. The *mai pen rai* (phonetic) of the title literally means
'it is nothing'. An expression, very frequently heard, which expresses something
of the Thai charm and relaxed attitude to life.

20 **Bangkok.**
Martin Hürlimann, translated from the German by A. Ross
Williamson. London: Thames & Hudson, 1963. 99p. illus.

An intelligent, well-observed photographic and descriptive essay. Bangkok is
captured in pictures by a distinguished Swiss photographer.

21 **Thai titles and ranks, including a translation of traditions of
royal lineage in Siam by King Chulalongkorn.**
Robert B. Jones. Ithaca, New York: Cornell University Press,
1971. 147p. bibliog. (Southeast Asia Program Data Paper no. 81).

The paper outlines the history of a complex area of Thai nomenclature, and
includes a translation of writing by King Chulalongkorn on the subject. Thai
royal titles and ranks have evolved from tribal élites and equivalents in Sanskrit
through a succession of dynasties. Princely styles and titles (*chao fa, phra ong
chao,* etc.) acquire accretions, such as *krom, kromamun,* to mark administrative
responsibilities undertaken by members of the ruling family. When duties of this
kind become devolved to members of élite commoner families, rather similar titles
(*phraya, chao phraya,* etc.) are conferred on them. For a further exposition cf.
also a review article by M. Vickery in the *Journal of the Siam Society,* vol. 62,
part 1 (1974), p. 158-73.

22 **Phya Anuman Rajadhon: a reminiscence.**
Charles Fenton Keyes, W. J. Klausner, Sulak Sivaraksa. Bangkok:
Satirakases-Nagapradita Foundation, 1973. 73p. bibliog.

The subject of this memoir was one of Thailand's most prolific writers on many
aspects of the country's traditional life and customs. This work was published to
celebrate his 80th birthday and it provides a four-page bibliography of his work.

23 **Tales from Siam.**
Germaine Krull, Dorothea Melchen. London: Robert Hale, 1966.
192p. photos.

This is a chatty account of a stay in several places in northern Thailand, showing
a picture of ordinary family life which could be useful for families about to visit
or stay in the country.

24 **Bangkok editor.**
Alexander MacDonald. New York: Macmillan, 1969. 229p.

The founder of the main English-language daily newspaper in Bangkok gives his
impressions of the post-war setting.

The Country and Its People

25 **Siam: nature and industry.**
Ministry of Commerce & Communications. Bangkok: The
Ministry, 1930. 315p. 5 maps.

Though dated, this general compendium of official information, like its counterpart *Siam: general and medical* (q.v.), is still of value for its material of archival
interest relating to the end of the period of absolute monarchy.

26 **Thailand: its people, its society, its culture.**
Frank J. Moore, political chapters by Clark D. Neher. New Haven,
Connecticut: Human Relations Area Files, 1974. 607p. map.
bibliog.

This is an exhaustive general handbook on all aspects of Thailand. Its twenty-nine
chapters cover social structure, politics and political organization, administration,
finance, education, religion, agriculture, trade, and other useful information and
statistics of the country. It subsumes earlier handbooks of similar type, such as
the 'American Area Handbooks'.

27 **Everyday life in Thailand: an interpretation.**
J. A. Niels Mulder. Bangkok: Duang Kamol, 1978. 223p.

This general impression of everyday life in Thailand is written from a sociological
and ethnological standpoint. Cf. also the author's *The cultural context of development planning in Southeast Asia* (Bielefeld University Working Paper, 1974. 17
leaves), and *Individual and society in contemporary Thailand and Java as seen by
serious Thai and Javanese authors* (Bielefeld University, 1981. 40 leaves).

28 **Thailand in the 1980s.**
National Identity Office. Bangkok: Office of the Prime Minister,
1984. 304p. maps. illus.

This is a revised edition of *Thailand into the 1980s*, and gives an all round impression of the state and prospects of the country.

29 **Life and ritual in old Siam: three studies of Thai life and customs.**
Phya Anuman Rajadhon, translated from the Thai by W. J. Gedney.
New Haven, Connecticut: Greenwood Press, 1979. 191p.

The author exemplifies his theme of life in old Siam by means of three studies
taken from farming, family religious practice, and childbirth. The treatment is
sensitive, though somewhat idealized.

30 **Guide to Bangkok, with notes on Siam.**
Erik Seidenfaden. Kuala Lumpur: Oxford University Press, 1984.
reprint of 1920 ed. 364p. 250 illus.

A classic introduction to Bangkok and its social and economic condition of the
early decades of the 20th century.

31 **The Thai peoples; the origins and habitats of the Thai peoples with a sketch of their material and spiritual culture.**
Erik Seidenfaden. Bangkok: Siam Society, 1958. 177p. 19 plates. Book one.

Though dated, this remains an interesting collection from the Siam Society of information and illustrative material on the history and anthropology of the peoples of Thailand.

32 **Selected articles from the *Siam Society Journal.***
Bangkok: Siam Society, 1954-59. 10 vols.

Published to celebrate the Siam Society's 50th anniversary, these volumes collect together selected articles on a wide variety of Thai-related topics from the society's journal (q.v.).

33 **Thailand: land of colour.**
Hubert Sieben. Wellington, Sydney: Sevenseas, 1967. ca.100p. illus.

This large-format volume consists of about a hundred fine, full-page colour photographs without any text. It is introduced briefly in English, French, German and Japanese.

34 **The star sapphires.**
Gerald Sparrow. London: Jarrolds, 1958. 192p.

Bangkok, in 1945, was recovering from the extraordinary circumstances of the Japanese occupation. Westerners of several nationalities who (like the author, a British legal representative) had been interned in the city, emerged to find themselves involved in some strange adventures. The intrigues of the time are engagingly told in this story.

35 **Portrait of Bangkok.**
Larry Sternstein. Bangkok: Bangkok Metropolitan Administration, 1982. 152p.

The bicentenary of the Chakri dynasty was the occasion for both celebrations and publications in Bangkok, of which this portrait of the city was one. Issued under official auspices, it presents an illustrated series of essays, derived largely from the author's previous writings. His long experience of Bangkok makes the book a useful and interesting addition to the descriptive literature of the capital.

The Country and Its People

36 **Tattooing in Thailand's history.**
Barend Jan Terwiel. *Journal of the Royal Asiatic Society*, no. 2 (1979), p. 156-66. bibliog.

This article gathers together recorded foreign observations of the now dying practice of tattooing in Thailand, from that of the 19th-century, French, some-time-vicar of Bangkok, Bishop Pallegoix. The author demonstrates that the purposes served by tattoing varied, being sometimes of animist origin (for instance, to secure invulnerability to weapons of attack by an enemy), or in more sophisticated social-administrative situations, it served to register class obligations or domicile.

37 **Thailand Culture Series.**
Bangkok: Fine Arts Department, 1953-54.

This series consists of seventeen pamphlets by Thai authorities on various fields of art and culture, including: (Phya Anuman Rajadhon) – 6. animist spirits, 7. chedis, 13. marriage, 17. history of the Thai alphabet; (Silpa Birasri) – 4. architecture and painting, 10. sculpture; (Chen Duriyanga) – 8. music; (Prince Thani and Dhanit Yupho) – 11. & 12. masked and shadow theatres; (Boribal Buriband) – 9. Buddha image.

38 **Thailand-Studien.** (Studies on Thailand.)
Frankfurt-am-Main, GFR: Alfred Metzner, 1962. 84p. (Hamburg University, Asian Institute Papers, no. 15).

This remarkable little book was issued to mark the centenary of German-Thai relations. It covers succinctly topics ranging from anthropology, poetry and philology to the French ultimatum of 1893 and Thai-German collaborative medicine; even non-fluent readers of German, interested in Thai script and poetry, should find in Klaus Wenk's exposition (a clear Thai textual illustration of the life and work of the 17th-century poet, Si Prat), a model of the genre. The book contains a short, good bibliography of modern books in German (some of these have also been published in English) on Thai anthropological and other subjects. Cf. also another compilation of concise contributions on Thai topics in the same series, 'Hamburg University, Asian Institute Papers, no. 8' (1960).

39 **Lotus land.**
P. A. Thompson. London: T. Werner, 1906. 312p. pullout map.

These are the anecdotes and observations of a surveyor in Thailand just after the turn of the century on places (includes Lopburi), temples, monks, art, food and similar everyday matters.

40 **Bangkok.**
William Warren, photographs by Marc Riboud. Boston, Massachusetts: Houghton Mifflin, 1970. 275p. illus.

Provides a good pictorial review of Bangkok, with many colour plates. The text, fitted in among the photographs, relates the historical background in an interesting and informed manner, dealing, for instance, in some detail with the religious and social antecedents of that noticeable landmark, the giant swing.

41 **The legendary American: the remarkable career and strange disappearance of Jim Thompson.**
William Warren. Boston, Massachusetts: Houghton Mifflin, 1970. 275p. photos.

Written three years after Jim Thompson's strange disappearance at a central Malayan highland resort, this volume deals with such evidence as there is of that event, and with the legend which grew up subsequently about that remarkable American businessman, founder of a still flourishing silk trade. Jim Thompson built a traditional Thai house made of teak alongside one of the *klongs* (canals) in Bangkok and stocked it with Thai and Indian *objets-d'art*. Now a museum, the house is of interest in itself, and also displays a number of his major art acquisitions and antiquities; some, unfortunately, have been stolen. This fascinating mystery story conveys the distinctive flavour of cosmopolitan Bangkok.

42 **Consul in paradise: 69 years in Siam.**
W. A. R. Wood. London: Souvenir Press, 1965. 175p.

This charming book consists of vignettes reflecting the delight which its author, the first modern Western historian of Thailand, found and continued to enjoy into his nineties in Chiang Mai. Wood was permanent consul at the palatial and distinctively Victorian British consulate, and he chose to establish his home and family life here.

43 **Twentieth-century impressions of Siam.**
Edited by Arnold Wright, Oliver Breakspear. London: Lloyd's Greater Britain Publishing Company, 1908. 302p. map.

This is one of a series of publications on foreign countries at the turn of the 20th century edited by the editor of the *Yorkshire Post*. In large-format photogravure resembling the *Illustrated London News* style, it gives an excellent all-round account of the country at the time and is valuable especially for its contemporary photographs. The sections are by various authors; those on manners and customs and the teak industry are of interest.

Geography and Geology

General

44 **The Southeast Asian world: an introductory essay.**
Keith Buchanan. London: G. Bell & Sons, 1967. 176p. 28 maps.
This is a useful introductory survey by a geographer, emphasizing the prospects for social development.

45 **Siam: das Land der Tai.** (Siam: the country of the Thai.)
Wilhelm Credner. Suttgart, GFR: J. Englebhorns, 1936. 422p.
12 maps. bibliog.
A very comprehensive survey of Thailand's geology, rainfall and climate, land and water resources continues to be cited as a basic reference work.

46 **The five faces of Thailand: an economic geography.**
Wolf Donner. London: C. Hurst, for the Institute of Asian Affairs, Hamburg, 1978. 930p. maps. bibliog.
This is a complete handbook of the location and development of the economic products of Thailand. The country is considered in general and then in respect of the five regions: central and southeast; south; northeast; north; and Bangkok.

47 **Thailand: a geographical analysis.**
Ashok K. Dutt. In: *Southeast Asia: realm of contrasts.* Edited by Ashok K. Dutt. Boulder, Colorado; London: Westview Press, 1985.
3rd rev. ed. 268p.
The section on Thailand in this large-format, popular geography of Southeast Asia forms part of a compendium describing the physical geographical perspectives of the region as a whole, and of each of its component countries in detail. The treatment is light and stresses economic development prospects. For beginners or for educational purposes, the book is calculated to stimulate interest without stifling it.

48 **Southeast Asia: a social, economic and political geography.**
Charles A. Fisher. London: Methuen, 1966. 831p. 110 maps.
bibliog.

This is the best and most comprehensive general and applied geography of Southeast Asia. The author begins by treating Southeast Asia as an emergent geographical personality in its own right. Part two describes the region's political geography before and after the Western impact on it. Part three deals with the tropical mainland countries ('Thailand' p. 484-528).

49 **The geology of the tin belt in peninsular Thailand around Phukhet, Phangnga and Takua Pa.**
M. S. Garson, A. H. G. Mitchell, B. Young, B. A. R. Tait. London:
HM Stationery Office, 1975. 112p. maps. plates. large-format ed.
(Overseas Memoir, no. 1).

This paper, from the Institute of Geological Sciences, London, describes the stratigraphy and mineral-bearing economic geology of the important tin zone of southern Thailand. There are marginal resources of gold, diamonds and some other deposits, in addition to tin. Cf. also C. K. Burton, *The geological environment of tin mineralization in the Malay-Thai peninsula* (International Tin Council, 1969. 17p.).

50 **Geography and the environment in Southeast Asia: proceedings of the Jubilee Symposium of the Department of Geography and Geology, University of Hong Kong, 21-25 June 1976.**
Edited by R. D. Hill, Jennifer M. Bray. Hong Kong: Hong Kong
University Press, 1978. 485p. maps. bibliogs.

The aim of the symposium from which these papers were taken was to draw together academics, government officials and consultants to look at environmental problems in a constructive manner. Contributions of particular relevance to Thailand included are: 4. 'Exorcising the bedevilled city of angels', by Larry Sternstein; 8. 'The impact of urbanization on the environment: a study of Bangkok', by Shao-er Ong, 'Urbanization and rural change: Tambon Om Noi', by Koichi Mizuno, 'A study of land use and socio-economic and demographic change in the suburban areas of Bangkok', by Aurapin Bunnag, 'Upland development and prospects for the rural poor: experience in northern Thailand', by E. C. Chapman; and 15. 'The environmental impact of some dams in Southeast Asia' (with map of the Lower Mekong p. 219), by Prachoom Chomchai. Useful bibliographic references are included in each paper.

51 **Mineral investigation in northeast Thailand.**
Herbert S. Jacobson. UN Development Project of the Mekong
Committee, Royal Thai Department of Mineral Resources, 1969.
96p. maps. (Geological Survey Professional Paper, no. 618).

This is a useful basic research paper on the mineral resources of northeast Thailand.

52 **Phanerozoic plate boundaries in mainland Southeast Asia, the Himalayas and Tibet.**

A. H. G. Mitchell. *Journal of the Geological Society of London*, vol. 138 (1981), p. 109-22.

The author of this article identifies south Tibet and Burma-Thailand as missing fragments of the Australia-New Guinea component which was a result of the break-up of the Antarctic supercontinent of Gondwanaland. The considerations, though inconclusive, in favour of locating the missing fragment of the northwest continental margin of Australia in this region are adduced in T. C. Whitmore, 'Wallace's line and plate tectonics' (q.v., p. 22). Whitmore stresses the biogeographic importance to the Malay peninsula of the middle Eocene collision east of Iran between India and Eurasia. Cf. also M. S. Garson and A. H. G. Mitchell, 'Transform faulting in the Thai peninsula', *Nature* (London), vol. 228 (1978, p. 45-47).

53 **Thailand: aspects of land and life.**

Robert L. Pendleton. New York: Duell, Sloan & Pearce, 1963. 321p. 16 plates. (An American Geographical Society Handbook).

Though dated, this handbook contains useful basic geographical and other information, and continues to be much cited as a background reference work.

54 **Tin-bearing granite and tin-barren granite in Thailand.**

Kaset Pitakpaivan. Bangkok: Thailand Department of Mineral Research, 1969. 100p. roneoed. maps. tables.

This paper, prepared for the International Tin Council's Second International Technical Conference on Tin, consists of a detailed tabular statistical report of granite testing during a field observation.

55 **Thailand: the environment of modernisation.**

Larry Sternstein, maps by Peter Daniell. Sydney, London: McGraw-Hill, 1976. 200p. bibliog. illus.

This is an excellent, large-format, economic geography of Thailand, liberally provided with charts and general illustrations (including an interesting map of Bangkok as it was in 1870), and with admirable, full-page thematic colour maps. The author covers an exhaustive range of subjects, from historical, ethnic and soil-geological to modern agriculture, forestry, minerals, planning and foreign trade. The book has a good subject bibliography.

56 **Proceedings, Regional Conference on the Geology of Southeast Asia. Collection of papers.**
Edited by B. K. Tan. Kuala Lumpur: The Conference, 1973. 324p.

A collection of geological papers on Southeast Asia includes a study of the formation of the Shan-Tenasserim massif, in a preliminary synthesis of the geological evolution of Burma by Maung Thein (p. 87-116). There is a useful bibliography of Thai as well as Burmese interest, and a study of the early stages of the Burmese-Malayan geosyncline by Teiichi Koboyashi (p. 119-28). Also included is a useful bibliography referring to Thai aspects of the subject. Cf. also T. Koboyashi, 'Notes on the geological history of Thailand', *Japanese Journal of Geology and Geography*, vol. 31 (1960), p. 128-48), and C. S. Hutchinson, 'Dating tectonism in the Indosinian-Thai-Malayan orogen', *Geological Society of America Bulletin*, vol. 79 (1968, p. 375-86).

57 **Geology of Laos, Cambodia, southern Viet Nam and the eastern part of Thailand: a review.**
D. R. Workman. Bangkok: Economic Commission for Asia and the Far East, 1972. 148p. maps. (Geological Sciences Institute Report, no. 19).

This UN report gives a full description of the regional geology and mineral resources.

Maps and atlases

58 **Administrative division boundaries of Thailand.**
Army Map Service (Technical Services Division), Geographical Names Branch. Washington, DC: The Branch, 1959. 9 leaves. 8 col. maps.

This atlas shows *changwat* (province) and *amphoe* (district) boundaries as at February 1959.

59 **Atlas of living resources of the seas.**
Food and Agriculture Organization of the United Nations, Fisheries Department, 1981. 4th ed. 23p. 69 plates of col. maps.

Contains useful reference material on the important sea regions of interest to Thailand for fisheries and maritime research.

13

60 **Thaïlande & Laos: guide pratique de voyage.** (Thailand & Laos: a practical travel guide.)
Marcel Barang, Francis Meyer. Paris: Assinter, 1977. 132p. map.

This guide, in French, adds little touristic information to more extensive publications in English; but the large, pull-out map is full and particularly useful for place-names associated with the war and insurgency zones across the Mekong River.

61 **Atlas of the physical, economic and social resources of the lower Mekong basin.**
Engineer Agency for Resources Inventories. Washington, DC: Department of the Army & Tennessee Valley Authority, 1968. 257p.

These are well-produced maps with narrative information on the natural and human resources of the Thai and other riparian lands skirting the lower Mekong.

62 **Gazetteer of the maps of Thailand.**
Washington, DC: Office of Geography, Department of the Interior, 1966. 675p. map. (Official Standard Names Gazetteer, no. 97).

This is an exhaustive gazetteer of geographical names in Thailand, including towns, villages, rivers, and administrative divisions. Since most Thai place-names have meanings, it also gives a coded indicator of these in addition to the location, both by latitude and longitude and by reference to six sets of maps of various scales, which are named in the introduction. A glossary is also provided for geographical terms in Thai or Malay. The gazetteer gives romanized transliterations, but does not print Thai equivalents. Cf. also *Geographic map of Thailand* (scale 1:1,200,000, Bangkok: Survey Department, 1962).

63 **Guides Madrolle: cartes et plans.** (Madrolle guides: maps and plans.)
Paris: Hachette, 1906. vol. 9 (Indes du sud. Siam: p. 103-29).

This set of guidebooks provides travel information for itineraries by ship to various places in the Orient (carrying advertisements for P & O). Volume 9 goes via Djibouti, Bombay and Ceylon to Siam, and describes excursions to Bangkok, Ayudhya and Lopburi. Volume 5, *Vers Angkor*, has an interesting pullout map of French Indochina at the turn of the century, with adjacent areas of Thailand, and disputed provinces in the area of Battambang. Volume 11 describes Yunnan Fu in South China and includes a map.

64 **Hildebrand's travel map.**
Frankfurt-am-Main, GFR: Karto-Grafik, 1984. scale 1:2,800,000.

A good, very large folding map showing Thailand, Burma, Malaysia and Singapore with city plans and tourist information added.

65 **Notes of a journey across the Isthmus of Kra made with the French government survey expedition in 1883.**
Commander A. J. Loftus. Singapore: [RGS?], 1883. 55p. maps.

This diary-booklet is of value both for its large-scale foldout maps, and for the notes of the author on conditions in and around the isthmus, such as 4 ft tides.

66 **The Hamlyn historical atlas.**
General editor R. I. Moore. London: Hamlyn, 1981. 176p.
88 col. maps.

This atlas is divided into four main sections, dealing with the ancient world, its heirs, the age of European supremacy, and the emergence of the modern world. Siam, or Thailand, appears on six of the maps, demonstrating its pivotal position in the relationships described in the text interleaved with the maps. The cultural heritage of Gupta India, one of whose extensions occurred in the Dvaravati empire in Thailand is discussed by J. G. de Casperis, University of Leiden; the Far East in the 17th century is described by Gordon Daniels of the University of Sheffield. The book includes a tabular survey of the maps by date and region.

67 **Reference map: Vietnam, Cambodia, Laos, Thailand.**
Washington, DC: National Geographic Magazine, 1967.
ref. no. 02242.

A good map of Thailand and its immediate neighbours. Its dimensions are 31.5 x 39 inches. scale 1 inch represents 30 miles.

68 **Routes in Upper Burma, including the Chin hills and Shan states.**
Delhi: Cultural, 1983. 2 vols.

This collation of 1,236p. in two volumes draws upon the earliest available maps, travellers' records and notes. For any tour or expedition into the sparsely mapped north and northwestern border areas of Thailand and Burma it should provide both useful and interesting background material.

69 **Thailand national resources atlas.**
Royal Thai Survey Department, Supreme Command Headquarters.
Bangkok: The Department, 1969. 55 leaves. scale 1:2,500,000.

This is a larger resources atlas (78 cm as against 52 cm) than the Army Mapping Department portfolio (q.v.); it was published earlier (1969 as against 1976-). The atlas covers physical, human, social and economic resources, and the legends are in English and Thai.

70 **Natural resources atlas of Thailand.**
Thailand Army Mapping Department. Bangkok: The Department,
1976- . 44 leaves, loose-leaf portfolio.

This portfolio of maps, mainly coloured, shows the natural, human and economic resources of Thailand. Legends are in English and Thai. It is published in loose-leaf form for updating and additions.

Travel, Tourism and Guidebooks

Travellers' accounts

71 **English intercourse with Siam in the 17th century.**
John Anderson. London: Kegan-Paul, French & Trübner, 1890.
503p. foldout map. bibliographic notes (*passim*).

This is an absorbing and historically valuable account. The occasion of the volume was a mission in the 1880s on behalf of the Calcutta Museum. The author was able to collect, in addition to the specimens of marine fauna which were the professional object of the expedition, a variety of extant reports of Siam's relations, via the ocean ports which it possessed at the time, with English, French, Dutch, Japanese and other foreign traders. The book cites material from Mergui, Ligor, Singora, Patani and Penang, dealing in part with piracy, then often a secondary function of trade, and among other merchant adventurers of the day, with the noted English swashbuckler, Will Adams.

72 **The mask of Siam.**
David Barnett. London: Hale, 1959. 189p.

The author, an initially disillusioned traveller, gives an astringent, intense analysis of a journey in search of a deeper meaning behind the smiling faces he met, first in Bangkok, and later among the hunter-tribes in the teak forests of northern Thailand.

73 **Voiage de Siam.** (Voyage to Siam.)
Pierre Bouvet, with an introduction and biography by J. C. Gatty.
Leiden, The Netherlands: Brill, 1963. 157p. foldout map.

The close relationship of trade and politics with the French 17th-century religious expeditions to Siam is among the points brought out in this interesting contemporary account of a mission by Pierre Bouvet. The book includes a modern introduction in French and four pages of facsimile reproductions of the original.

74 **The voyage of Jan Huyghen van Linschoten to the East Indies.**
Edited by A. C. Burnell, P. A. Tiele. (From the old English translation of the Dutch publication of 1598). London: Hakluyt Society, 1881-85. 2 vols. (nos. 70 & 71).

Linschoten's voyage is of exceptional interest. Volume one gives an account of Arakan, Pegu, Ayudhya and Malacca (all trade-port areas of concern to 16th- and 17th-century Siam); and volume two describes flora, fauna and products of the region, including the Martaban jars, famous for their use over a long period, by Indiamen, for carrying produce in bulk.

75 **Siam in the 20th century.**
J. G. D. Campbell. London: Arnold, 1902. 322p. map.

A good, first-hand account conveying the atmosphere of the later stages of King Chulalongkorn's reign.

76 **The kingdom of Siam.**
Arthur Cecil Carter. New York: Putnam, 1904. 280p.

This is a good contemporary account of Siam in King Chulalongkorn's reign, which was prepared to commemorate the 1904 Louisiana Purchase Exposition in St. Louis.

77 **Voyage to Siam by six Jesuits in 1685.**
Abbé François T. de Choisy, translated from the French. London: Robinson & Churchil, 1688. 298p. maps. drawings.

This is the best of several contemporary publications concerning the embassy of the Chevalier de Chaumont to the courts of King Narai at Ayudhya and Louvo (Lopburi) in 1685-86 at the behest of Louis XIV ostensibly to bring about a trade treaty, but with it, also the conversion of the king to Christianity. The book contains descriptions of royal barge processions, palaces and ambassadorial dwellings at Ayudhya, the summer palace at Bang Pa-in, the city of Lopburi, and evidence of Phaulkon's favourable attitude to the Jesuit mission and to Chaumont's embassy. The six Jesuit mathematicians and astronomers whose mission is the subject of the book were sent abroad to conduct observations for the Academy of Science then recently founded by Louis in Paris.

78 **Cross-cultural trade in world history.**
Philip D. Curtin. Cambridge, England: Cambridge University Press, 1984. 293p. maps. bibliog.

The subject-matter of this interpretation of world history is the effect of long-haul trade contacts between (rather than within) major cultural regions. Topics covered *passim* include Siam's historical trade interests via the China seas and Indian Ocean routes, Siamese trade enclaves in Java, Malacca, and the Riau Islands (in association with those great Malay seafarers from Celebes, the Bugis). The author refers to the role of the early Rama kings in promoting foreign trade.

79 **Mango summer.**

Cynthia Ellis. London: Hodder & Stoughton, 1960. 254p.

This is a perceptive and enthusiastic account by a British Foreign Office shorthand-typist of people she had met and places she had visited in several different areas of Thailand. Among the travels recounted is a journey down the Mekong River from the ancient northern capital, Chiang Saen, to Luang Prabang, the royal capital of Laos.

80 **Avenue to the door of the dead.**

Harold Elvin. London: Anthony Blond, 1961. 320p.

This book consists of scenes from the author's travels by bicycle in the company of an engaging young Indian (known as 'Tiger') through much of Thailand and as far as Angkor (the 'City of the Dead'). The pair, often penniless, taste the seamy side of life, and are befriended by an assortment of local types from bandits to prostitutes.

81 **Some yeares of travels into divers parts of Asia and Africa.**

Sir Thomas Herbert. London: Jacob Blome, 1638. 399p,

Sir Thomas Herbert's account of his travels, which began in 1626, via Persia and the trade ports of the Indian Ocean to Ayudhya and the Spice Islands, constitutes one of the classic stories of the 17th century. His description of Ayudhya itself includes references to the trade goods such as spices and aloes, and silver from Japan, and evidence of the accreditation of rich trade missions paying tribute. Other editions are an imprint by Stansby (1634), which is held in the library of King's College, Cambridge, England; a facsimile reprint (Amsterdam, 1971); and an edition in French (Paris, 1663).

82 **Foreign records of the Bangkok period up to A.D. 1932.**

M. L. Manich Jumsai, Committee for the Publication of Historical Documents. Bangkok: Office of the Prime Minister, 1982. 268p. bibliog.

This compilation by an *ad hoc* committee of Thai and European historians was published as a souvenir volume to mark the bicentenary of the Chakri dynasty in Bangkok in 1982. In addition to some old illustrations of Bangkok, the book contains an interesting collection of quotations from lesser-known records and reports from English, French and other sources. These records reflect contemporary impressions of life in the capital under successive reigns of the Rama kings up to that of Prajadhipok, the last absolute monarch.

83   **The English governess at the Siamese court; being recollections of
     six years at the royal palace in Bangkok.**
     Anna Harriette Leonowens (*née* Crawford).   Boston, Massa-
     chusetts: Fields Owens, 1870. 321p. Reprinted, Bangkok:
     Chalermnit, 1979; New York: Roy, 1964. 267p.

This is the original, largely fictitious publication on which the film, 'The King and
I' was based. Mrs. Leonowens' name was adapted from that of her Indian Army
husband Leon Owens; the name persists in trading concerns founded in the north
of Thailand by her son Louis cf. W. S. Bristowe's *Louis and the King of Siam*
(q.v.). Anna also published several articles in Boston magazines, purporting to
sensationalize 'harem life' in Bangkok; these later formed the subject of another
book by her called *The romance of Siamese harem life* (q.v.).

84   **The romance of Siamese harem life.**
     Anna H. Leonowens.   London: Trübner, 1873. 277p. Reprinted,
     London: Arthur Baker, 1952, with an introduction by Freya Stark.

The reprint, which includes an uncritical introduction by Freya Stark, excludes
prints which were included in the original publication. This volume is of interest
because of the light it sheds on what a contemporary publicist considered likely
to attract a Victorian readership.

85   **A new historical relation of the kingdom of Siam.**
     Simon de la Loubère.   Kuala Lumpur: Oxford University Press,
     1969. 2 vols. (Oxford in Asia Historical Reprints).

This account, by a leader of an imposing Jesuit mission which was sent to Ayudhya
in 1687 by Louis XIV with the purpose of converting King Narai to Christianity,
went into several editions (including an English translation), before the end of the
century. It remains one of the best available contemporary impressions of that
fraught occasion and of the remarkable life and times of Narai's kingdom.

86   **Peter Floris: his voyage to the East Indies in the Globe 1611-1615.**
     Contemporary translation from the Dutch, edited by W. H. More-
     land.   London: Hakluyt Society, 1934. 164p. 3 maps.

An account of the 17th-century voyage of the Dutch mariner, Peter Floris,
contains an interesting contemporary description of Ayudhya.

87   **Eye of the day.**
     Tarquin Olivier.   London: Heinemann, 1964. 179p.

This is a discriminating collection of impressions by an Old Etonian, travelling in
hippie mode, on a journey from Northern Thailand to the Shan states and into
Indonesia.

88 **Description du royaume Thai ou Siam, comprenant la topographie, histoire naturelle et coutumes.** (Description of the kingdom of the Thai or Siam, comprising topography, natural history, and customs.) Jean-Baptiste Pallegoix. Paris: 1854. 2 vols. Facsimile reprint. Farnborough, England: Gregg International, 1969.

The impressions of this early French visitor were acutely observed and have been used widely as source material by subsequent writers, not least by Sir John Bowring in *The kingdom and people of Siam* (q.v.). An English translation by R. F. Martins was published in Shanghai in 1877, but may be difficult to obtain.

89 **Suma oriental.**
Tomé Pires, translated from the Portuguese and edited by Armando Cortesao. London: Hakluyt Society, 1944. 2 vols.

Tomé Pires was an important observer of the trade world of the Far East, as it was being opened up by Portuguese mariners in the 16th century. His account, written in Malacca (conquered by Albuquerque in 1511), in 1512-15, includes descriptions of 'Siam' (Ayudhya), Mergui, Kedah and Malacca itself; all areas of interest to Ayudhya and its foreign trade partners from both East and West at the time.

90 **The Hakluyt handbook.**
Edited by D. B. Quinn. London: Hakluyt Society, 1974. 2 vols. maps. illus.

This handbook provides a guide and introductions by various authors to the most extensive contemporary publications of accounts of the 16th-century voyages of discovery. Three major collections were published by Richard Hakluyt between 1582 and 1600; further material, collected by Hakluyt up to 1625, was published by his self-appointed executor, Samuel Purchas. The introductory and explanatory materials in these volumes refer also to the sources which Hakluyt used, and also to the few he did not (chiefly the compilation of his Italian rival, Ramusio). This record is therefore a complete one for the period. See, especially, Donald F. Lach, *The Far East*, vol. 1, p. 214-22. Numerous plates show contemporary maps and title pages. The society, formed to commemorate Hakluyt, is itself responsible for the modern publication of numerous volumes on subsequent voyages and related topics, of which the handbook is one example.

91 **A description of the government, might, religion, customes, traffick, and other remarkable affairs in the kingdom of Siam.**
Joost Schouten. In: *A true description of the mighty kingdoms of Siam and Japan,* François Caron, Joost Schouten, translated from the Dutch by Roger Manley, revised, abridged and edited with appendixes by Charles R. Boxer. London: Argonaut Press, 1935. 197p. maps. bibliog.

Schouten's description of Siam, first published at The Hague in 1638, and from 1645 bound with Caron's observations of Japan, is one of the most important 17th-century Dutch accounts. The translation by Manley appeared in London in several editions in the 1660s. This Argonaut edition of 1935 (on vellum, limited to 475 copies) reproduces the edition of 1663 in Manley's translation from the original Dutch (Schouten, p. 95-111), with facsimiles of parts of the text and maps (one pullout). The entire volume is of interest for the extensive introduction and notes by Charles R. Boxer, and for Caron's account of his voyage to Japan, and of Batavia, the headquarters of the Dutch East India Company (VOC), as well as for Schouten's description of Ayudhya. Professor Boxer's edition brings out the versatility of VOC directors like Caron and Schouten – equally at home with pen, sword, or builder's protractor. Cf. also Charles R. Boxer, *The Dutch seaborne empire 1600-1800* (London: Hutchinson, 1965), and *The Dutch in 17th century Thailand,* by George Vinal Smith (q.v.).

92 **A physician at the court of Siam.**
Malcolm Smith. Kuala Lumpur: Oxford University Press, 1982. 164p. bibliog. (Oxford in Asia Reprint).

This entertaining book, first published in 1947, relates vignettes of life at court, as seen by the author who was a physician employed at the royal palace in pre-war Bangkok.

93 **Five years in Siam.**
H. W. Smyth. London: John Murray, 1898. 337p.

The sojourn described in this account is of interest because of the author's observations of nature and animals seen in the country at the end of the 19th century.

94 **A study of the Arabic texts concerning navigation in Southeast Asia.**
G. R. Tibbetts. Leiden, The Netherlands: Brill, 1975. 294p. maps in pocket. (Royal Asiatic Society, Oriental Translations Fund, no. 44).

This is a valuable series of translated extracts from Arabic texts, mainly of the latter part of the 1st millennium AD, concerning oriental voyages, many of them to or near Siam.

Travel, Tourism and Guidebooks. Travellers' accounts

95 **Histoire civile et naturelle du royaume de Siam.** (The political and natural history of the kingdom of Siam.)
François Renée Turpin. Paris: Costard, 1771. 2 vols.

French Jesuit missionary sources provide the basis for this much cited contemporary account of life and customs at Ayudhya. The first volume deals with the natural history of Siam. The second recounts the rise and fall of French influence against a background of court procedure and monastic trial-by-ordeal in what the author describes as the prelude to the revolution of 1688; Phaulkon and Taksin are mentioned. For an English version cf. *Voyages and travels*, vol. 9, translated by John Pinkerton (London: Longman, Hurst, Rees, Orme & Brown, 1811, p. 573-655). An English translation by A. O. Cartwright, *A history of the kingdom of Siam to 1770* (Bangkok, 1908) is not wholly reliable.

96 **The short history of the kings of Siam.**
Jeremias van Vliet, translated from the Dutch by Leonard Andaya from a transcription by Miriam J. Verhijl-van den Berg, edited by David K. Wyatt. Bangkok: Siam Society, 1975. 97p.

Jeremias van Vliet was probably the most prolific of all the Dutch East India Company's residents to leave his impressions of 17th-century Ayudhya. This edition has the added value of further editorial work by David K. Wyatt.

97 **Siam and Cambodia in pen and pastel.**
Rachel Wheatcroft. London: Constable, 1928. 296p.

This is an attractive travel account with the artist and author's illustrations and comments on the passing scene of the day, including games and kite-flying. She also describes excursions to China and Burma.

98 **The kingdom of the yellow robe.**
Ernest Young. Kuala Lumpur: Oxford University Press, 1982. 399p. (Oxford in Asia Facsimile Reprint).

This is a facsimile of a classic descriptive work on Thailand. The original publication of 1898 is reproduced, with sketches by E. A. Norbury and photographs by the author, showing scenes of domestic and religious life in Siam in the last decade of the 19th century. The author deplores the traditional laundry methods, and is aghast at the practice of betel-nut chewing.

Guidebooks

99 **Berlitz tourist guide.**
London: Berlitz; Bangkok: Asia Books, 1984. 128p.
A good pocket guide, with useful tourist information and phrases.

100 **Thailand: a travel survival kit.**
Joe Cummings. Victoria, Australia: Lonely Planet, 1982. 131p.
This is a well-organized, practical, travel guide, providing hints for tourists who may encounter unsuspected problems.

101 **Thailand a complete guide.**
William Duncan, sketches by Ikuko Duncan. Rutland, Vermont: Tuttle, 1976. 384p. maps.
A good all round guide, with sketches to aid impressions of places worth visiting.

102 **Guide to the Sukhothai historical park.**
Bangkok: Public Relations Department, Fine Arts Department, 1978. folded sheet. plan. illus.
This guide to the 20-square-kilometre archaeological park containing the ruins of the ancient city of Sukhothai consists of a folded sheet, with plan and photographs. It includes a brief historical background and an account of current development plans for the site. The guide, available in English or Thai, can be obtained at the excellent museum on the site. (The title of the guide in Thai script is reproduced in the 'Introduction' [q.v.]).

103 **Ayutthaya: the former Thai capital.**
Edited by Nidda Hongvivat. Bangkok: Muang Boran, 1980. 63p. maps. illus.
Published by the archaeological publishing house in Bangkok, this is a beautifully illustrated guidebook with captions and background history.

104 **Chiang Mai: the cultural center of the north.**
Edited by Nidda Hongvivat. Bangkok: Muang Boran, 1980. 64p. illus.
The publisher of this well-informed, descriptive guide with colour plates also publishes an archaeological journal produced in Bangkok.

105   **Hildebrand's field guide: Thailand, Burma.**
Dieter Rumpf.   Frankfurt-am-Main, GFR: Karto-Grafik, 1985.
189p.

Accompanied by a good, folding map, this pocket guide is packed with historical and cultural information on places to visit, and includes notes on local festivals. Illustrative plates are placed in a separate section. This guide could be useful as a weight-saver for tourists planning to visit Burma as well as Thailand.

106   **Bangkok by night.**
John Sinclair, photographs by John Everingham.   Hong Kong: CFW Guidebooks, 1981. 63p.

Some people fear that tales of Bangkok's night-life are exaggerated, the author remarks, adding that such fears are groundless. This attractively illustrated guide to the night-life provides useful information on everything from Thai boxing and classical dancing to nightclubs, bars and shows on Patpong Road.

107   **Thailand travel talk.**
London: Tourist Organisation of Thailand, 1970- . bi-monthly.

This is a brief collection of items of tourist interest, available from the London office of TOT.

108   **Panorama of Thailand: a guide to the wonderful highlights of Thailand.**
Thong-in Soonsawad.   Wichita, Kansas: Kansas State College, 1966. 135p. 3rd rev. ed. photos.

The religious backgrounds of *wats* (temples) in Bangkok, Lopburi (an important early capital in the northeast under Khmer influence) and other sites are outlined in this handy, illustrated guidebook.

109   **Bangkok: portrait of a city.**
Philip Ward.   Cambridge, England: Oleander, 1974. 136p. illus.

This is a good, compact guide to the places of cultural interest in Bangkok, including the Thompson House Museum.

Flora, Ethnobotany and Fauna

Flora

110   **A dictionary of the economic products of the Malay peninsula.**
Henry Burkill.   Kuala Lumpur: Governments of Malaysia and
Singapore. 1965. 2nd ed. (amended 1935 ed.) 2 vols. bibliog.
notes.

The author of this dictionary was curator of the Singapore Botanic Gardens.
The work consists of a compilation of material on the history, and the medical,
culinary, industrial and other uses of plant and animal products in Malaya, with
extensive gleanings from relevant literature going back to the earliest times. It
remains the standard reference work in its field for the Malay and neighbouring
regions, including Thailand, and is a principal source for botanical entries in
McFarland's dictionary. McFarland's dictionary makes a useful companion to
Burkill's dictionary for students of Thai; it includes a section of addenda (39p.)
listing birds, fishes, and flora of Thailand under scientific and Thai names –
referring back to the relevant entries. Cf. George Bradley McFarland, *Thai-English
dictionary* (Stanford: Stanford University Press; London: Oxford University
Press, 1944. 2nd ed.).

111   **Florae siamensis enumeratio: list of the plants known from
Siam with records of their occurrence.**
W. L. Craib.   Bangkok: Siam Society, 1931. 2 vols.

This is a classic and much-cited flora. The author was professor of botany at
Aberdeen.

Flora, Ethnobotany and Fauna. Flora

112 **Contributions to the flora of Siam.**
William Grant Craig. Aberdeen, England: University of
Aberdeen, 1912. 2 vols.

The author's material includes extracted monographs from the *Kew Bulletin* (1913-40).

113 **Vegetables in Southeast Asia.**
G. A. C. Herklots. London: Allen & Unwin, 1972. 525p. bibliog.

This is an admirable collection of descriptions of the common vegetables and spices used in Chinese and other cuisines of Southeast Asia, with good coverage of those rarely encountered elsewhere, e.g. the delicious ginger variant *Boesenbergia pandurata*. Vernacular names, including Chinese ones, are given and the book contains numerous well-defined drawings of the plants.

114 **Beautiful Thai orchid species.**
Haruyuki Kamemoto, Rapee Sagarik. Bangkok: Orchid Society
of Thailand, 1975. 186p. bibliog. illus.

Orchids constitute one of Thailand's most beautiful products, both wild and commercially farmed. This fine volume gives a detailed account of their botany and cultivation, with numerous colour plates.

115 **Aromatic plants of India.**
Edited by S. Krishna, L. Badhwar. *Journal of Scientific and Industrial Research,* parts 1-16, in vols 6 (Dehra Dun, 1947) & 12 (Delhi, 1953).

This collection of papers on aromatic plants of India may prove to be a useful reference source on the botany of the numerous species and sub- or variant species of spices and other aromatics, which Thailand shares with India.

116 **Vegetables of the Dutch East Indies.**
Jacob Jonas Ochse. Amsterdam: J. Asher, 1931. 1,005p.
Reprinted 1975, with amended scientific plant names. illus.

This is a classic work by the distinguished Dutch author (1892-1970) on the tubers, bulbs, rhizomes, herbs and spices, and other edible vegetables of Southeast Asia. Most of the plants covered, including special varieties familiar in Thai markets and used in Thai cooking, will be found in Thailand. The volume includes a survey by Bakhuizen van der Brink of indigenous and foreign pot-herbs and side-dishes. Entries include the botany, usage and sketches of the plants.

117 **A preliminary survey of the vegetation of Thailand.**
Husato Ogawa, Tatuo Kira. *Nature and Life in Southeast Asia,*
vol. 1 (1961), p. 21-157. bibliog. 13 plates.

An extensive survey which is the result of a field expedition from Osaka University in 1957-58. Types of forest vegetation are analysed and illustrated.

118 Medicinal plants of East and Southeast Asia: attributed properties and usages.

Compiled by Lily M. Perry, Judith Metzger. Cambridge, Massachusetts: MIT Press, 1980. 620p.

This substantial compilation is essentially an updating, and setting out of new information on medicinal plants of the region and their therapeutic uses; it omits material already extensively documented (e.g. the citrus family). The book is arranged and indexed according to diseases treated, as well as by scientific names of plants, and accommodates to the regional medicinal concepts, for instance, 'hernia' in references to Chinese medicine is taken as inclusive of abdominal pain in general.

119 Spices.

W. J. Purseglove, E. G. B. Brown, C. L. Green, S. R. J. Robbins. London: Longman, 1981. 2 vols. bibliogs. glossaries.

This work provides a specific extension of *Tropical crops* (q.v.), dealing with the modern spice industry and the background history of the trade conflicts in Southeast Asia and elsewhere which gave rise to it. Volume one contains a brief history of spices; volume two covers the 'classical' spices (pepper, cinnamon, nutmeg, mace, cloves, ginger and others). The authors describe the botany, chemical ingredients and industrial production of each plant. The two volumes form a useful background to the early trade wars affecting Thailand, and describe the actual or potential industrial uses of some of the country's indigenous plants.

120 Tropical crops: dicotyledons, and Tropical crops: monocotyledons.

W. J. Purseglove. London: Longman, 1968 (vol. 1) & 1972 (vol. 2). 2 vols. bibliogs. glossary.

Research students and general readers requiring fuller information on tropical crops, their origins, cultivation and dispersal, should find all they need in these two authoritative handbooks containing all the angiosperms that are grown as crops throughout the tropics. The two volumes cover plants of both the East Indies (with all the main varieties of Thailand) and the West Indies. Many of them are common to both tropical regions as a result of transport in either direction by early traders. The author offers new data which tend to modify Vavilov's theory on centres of origin of key food plants.

121 Flora of the Malay peninsula.

H. N. Ridley. London: Reeve, 1922-25. 5 vols.

This is the classic flora based on the Singapore Botanic Gardens and covering collections from the part of mainland Southeast Asia adjoining Thailand. These volumes should be consulted as a reserve reference work for plants found in this country.

Flora, Ethnobotany and Fauna. Flora

122 Dioptericarpaceae of northern Siam.
E. D. Ryan, A. F. G. Kerr. *Journal of the Siam Society*,
vol. 8, part 1 (Jan. 1911), p. 1-24. 5 plates.

This description of forestry will be of interest, particularly for the photographs, dating from 1910. In addition to northern taxa, the article also lists dipterocarps found in the south.

123 The orchids of Thailand: a preliminary list.
Gunnar Seidenfaden, Tem Smitinand. Bangkok: Siam Society,
1959. 4 parts. drawings.

The four parts of this descriptive listing provide a very comprehensive account of Thailand's orchids.

124 The botany of mangrove forests in Thailand.
Tem Smitinand. Phuket, Thailand: The Seminar Workshop on
Mangrove Ecology, 1975. 37p.

This paper was presented at the Seminar Workshop on Mangrove Ecology in 1975. Mangrove forests are an interesting and economically significant type of coastal terrain in Thailand, as in other coastal regions of the tropics. Mangrove swamp and coastal strips tend to subspeciate flora and fauna; this paper indicates the range of Thai mangrove flora.

125 Flora of Thailand.
Edited by Tem Smitinand, Kai Larsen. Bangkok: Applied
Scientific Research Corporation of Thailand, 1970-75. 2 vols.
3 parts.

This (in English only) is in many ways the best flora of Thailand, consisting of report papers by botanists working in Thailand who also contribute similar material on specific plants or genera to the *Kew Bulletin* (e.g. intermittent reports from Thailand by Kai Larsen). The well-produced drawings may be more useful in exhibiting details than the more attractive colour plates of other popular floras.

126 Plants of Khao Yai National Park.
Tem Smitinand. Bangkok: Friends of Khao Yai National Park
Association, 1977. 74p. col. illus.

This attractively illustrated flora, published to support the park's amenities, includes food usage and English translations of Thai folk- or common names. No visitor to this large and exciting wildlife reservation should be without it.

127 Thai plant names: botanical name — vernacular name.
Tem Smitinand. Bangkok: Royal Forest Department, 1980.
379p. map.

An inventory, in Thai and English, of botanical and common vernacular plant names, indexed and easy to use for students interested in the botany, ethno-botany and Thai lexicon of the flora of the country.

28

128 **Wild flowers of Thailand.**
Tem Smitinand. Bangkok: T. Smitinand, 1975. 228p. photos.
This flora, which is in Thai and in English, gives brief, botanical descriptions of a wide collection of wild flowers encountered in Thailand. It includes numerous colour plates.

129 **Recent trends in the classification and mapping of the dry deciduous dipterocarp forests of Thailand.**
Philip A. Stott. London: P. A. Stott, 1975. 30p. map. bibliog.
This paper was presented to the Malesian ecology Symposium at Aberdeen in 1975. The author describes the dry dipterocarp forest dispersals, which constitute nearly half of Thailand's forestlands. The tables and good location map will be found useful.

130 **Flora of Thailand.**
Chote Suvatti. Bangkok: Royal Institute of Thailand, 1978. 2 vols.
A comprehensive flora, giving concise botanic descriptions in Thai and English.

131 **Flora malesiana: being an illustrated systematic account of the flora of Malaysia.**
General editor C. G. G. J. van Steenis. Jakarta: Nordhoff-Kolff, 1948- . (Series 1, Spermatophyta, vols. 1-10, Pteridophyta, vol. 1-).
This is the major current flora of the region of the Malaysian archipelago. Its outstanding general editor is the most distinguished senior representative of a long line of Dutch botanists specializing in the flora of the Indonesian world, covering flora common to mainland Southeast Asia including Thailand.

Ethnobotany

132 **Malayan fruits: an introduction to the cultivated species (with Thai and Tamil names).**
Betty Molesworth Allen. Singapore: Donald Moore, 1967. 245p.
The fruits of Thailand form an important element in the country's culture, cultivation and marketing. Some cultivated fruits (e.g. *lamyai* in the north) are a distinctive local product, others (e.g. *rambutan*) are common products of Thailand and the Malay peninsula. The author's comparison of Thai and Tamil common names makes an interesting ethnobotanic study.

29

133 **Evolution des paysages végétaux en Thaïlande du nord-est.**
(Evolution of vegetation in Thailand's northeast landscape.)
Jean Boulbet. Paris: Ecole Française d'Extrême-Orient, 1982.
36p. vol. 136.

This large-format study in French with numerous tabular annexes traces the
species development of the vegetation of the northeastern Korat plateau of
Thailand. It describes the effects of its settlement by man from the earliest times
and includes the Khmer temple complex at Phimai, where there was resettlement
of a neolithic site. The study follows the distribution of dipterocarps, Zingiberaceae, and other plants important to man.

134 **Science and civilization in China, vol. 6: biology and biological
technology, pt. II: agriculture.**
Franceska Bray. Cambridge, England: Cambridge University
Press, 1984. 724p. maps. bibliogs.

See especially p. 42-45, and note (a) on p. 42 for the arguments which have been
advanced by various authorities for and against a Hoabinhian culture in the
Bronze Age and in earlier Southeast Asia. The author discusses the possibility of
an independent regional origin of cultivated plants (foraging supported by plant
tending) in northern Indochina, and the domestication of animals, including the
water buffalo – the typical draft animal of wet-rice cultivation – and still an
important factor in the village economy of Thailand. This volume has an extensive
bibliography in Western languages.

135 **Nan-fang ts'ao-mu chuang: a fourth-century flora of Southeast
Asia: introduction, translation, commentaries.**
Hui-lin Li. Hong Kong: Chinese University Press, 1979. 168p.
bibliog. illus.

The author of this attractive slim volume, a professor of botany at the University
of Pennsylvania, provides the first English translation and commentary of Chi
Han's *Flora of Southeast Asia*, written in 304 AD; Chi Han's book is much quoted
in Chinese flora from Sung times onwards, as well as by later Western writers
(Hirth, Bretschneider, *et al.*). The book contains added illustrations consisting of
drawings from a late Sung materia medica (1279 AD), and also carries a late Sung
version of Chi Han's text. Chi Han's work records the first Chinese references to
the use of spices and other plants in China and the region south and southwest
of China. The author's introduction contains some ethnobotanic notes on Yüeh
culture in the region concerned, including dragon-worship, magical use of bronze
drums, rice cultivation and agriculture by vegetative propagation. The work sheds
light on cross-country trade from Funan and Champa into southern China in the
early centuries of the 1st millennium AD. The bibliography provides a useful
summary of material on the history of cultivated plants. For further inferences
from bronze drums found near Tali, Nan-chao, Yunnan, cf. Michele Pirazolli-
T'serstevens, *The bronze drums of Shihzhai shan* (q.v.).

136 **Tung-nan-Ya tsai-p'ei chih-wu chih ch'i-yüan.** (The origin of
cultivated plants in Southeast Asia.)
Hui-lin Li. Hong Kong: Chinese University Press, 1966. 29p.
bibliog. In Chinese, with a summary in English.

In this inaugural address the author examines the findings of DeCandolle in
Origin of cultivated plants (London, 1884), Vavilov in 'The origin, variation,
immunity and breeding of cultivated plants' (*Chronica Botanica* vol.
13, 1951),
and Ames in *Economic annuals and human culture* (Cambridge, 1939) with
reference to the regions of origin for cultivated plants in Europe, Asia and
America. The author proposes a more precise division of the regions relating to
southern and eastern Asia, consisting of four lateral belts comprising the legumi-
nous loess zone of northern China, southern and subtropical China, southern
mainland Asia, and archipelago Southeast Asia. He discusses the origins and
dispersal, on phytogeographical and ethnobotanical grounds, of important plants
of subtropical China and Southeast Asia, including rice, coconuts, spices and
bananas — one species of the latter having been extensively used in this region to
make banana-fibre cloth. For an interesting account of the close relation between
the evolution of tribal culture and the plant environment in the Cardamom mountain area of Cambodia adjoining northeast Thailand, cf. Marie A. Martin, *Introduction à l'ethnobotanique du Cambodge* (Paris: CNRF, 1971, 257p. [Ethno-
linguistic Atlas Series, no. 61]).

137 **Rice and religion: a study of old Mon-Khmer religion and culture.**
Gordon H. Luce. *Journal of the Siam Society*, vol. 53, no. 2
(July 1965), p. 142-52. 9 pull-out plates.

This paper read to the Siam Society outlines the author's proposal that irrigated
rice cultivation — one of the great economic discoveries of humanity — originated
in the Mon-Khmer-speaking regions of Tongking. Rice cultivation caused a population explosion which spread this method, under pressure of the incoming
Vietnamese, northwards into Yunnan (Nan-chao) and thence westwards to Shan
and Upper Indian areas, leading eventually to the major regions of settled wet-rice
cultivation along the valleys and deltas of the Red, Menam (Chao Phraya) and
Irrawaddy rivers. The argument is supported by pull-out charts showing the
diffusion of Austro-Asiatic and Mon-Khmer language borrowings among the
Malayan peninsular Semang, the Munda-speaking Indians, and some other peoples
of the areas considered.

138 **Nature and man in Southeast Asia.**
Edited by Philip A. Stott. London: School of Oriental and African Studies, University of London, 1978. 182p. maps. bibliogs. illus.

The papers in this collection are from a series of open lectures delivered at the School of Oriental and African Studies (University of London), in 1975. Their general import was concerned with the correspondence between the region's plant ecology and human cultural evolution, evidenced partly in linguistics. A number of the contributions deal specifically with Thailand and with the ethnobotanic evolution of the region. See, especially, 'Man and land in southeast Thailand', by Ronald Ng (p. 34-48); 'Observations on folk taxonomy in Thailand', by E. H. S. Simmonds (p. 128-41). 'Restricted faunas and ethnozoological inventories in Wallacea', by Roy F. Ellen (p. 142-64, with map); and 'The red forest of Thailand: a study in vernacular forest nomenclature', by Philip A. Stott (p. 165-76). The bibliographies attached to each paper will be of particular value. Cf. also Philip A. Stott, *Historical plant geography: an introduction* (Allen & Unwin, 1981. 151p. maps. bibliog.).

139 **Noms vernaculaires des plantes (Lao, Meo, Kha).** (Vernacular plant names [Lao, Meo, Kha].)
Jules Vidal. *Bulletin de l'Ecole Française d'Extrême-Orient*, vol. 49, no. 2 (1959), p. 435-608. 12 b/w plates. map. bibliog.

This article consists of an exhaustive compilation of trans-Mekong tribal plant nomenclatures, with references to scientific names and equivalent vernacular names with Lao script. It also provides a selection of plant photographs. The entries are coded to indicate special usages, e.g. masticatory and medicinal. For Thai equivalents cf. *Siamese plant names* (Bangkok: Siamese Forest Department, 1948), names the author refers to; for a Shan plant nomenclature cf. Dewan Mohinder Nath, *Botanical survey of the southern Shan states* (Rangoon: Burma Research Society, 1960. 418p.).

140 **The Malay archipelago.**
Alfred Russel Wallace. London: Macmillan, 1869. 2 vols. illus.

Wallace proposed his line of division of the flora and fauna of the Indonesian archipelago in a letter in 1858; later he published this detailed account of a journey confirming his opinion from relevant Indo-Malayan and Austro-Malayan taxonomic discoveries, and providing further references to volcanic and deep-sea aspects of the proposed line, then drawn to the west of Celebes. He afterwards changed it to run east of the island; modern research has broadened it into a zone (Wallacea), comprising the entire island.

141 **Wallace's line and plate tectonics.**
Edited by T. C. Whitmore. London: Oxford University Press,
1981. 91p. maps. bibliog. illus. figs.

Peninsular Thailand occupies a fringe of the Malayan archipelago, while central
and northern Thailand participate in the biophysical zone stretching from
northern India via Burma and Indochina into southern China. This unique situation
is responsible for the remarkable richness and variety of the country's flora and
fauna. The material in this well-aggregated collection of specialist contributions
on the causes and biological effects of the tectonic upheaval, first noticed by
Wallace in 1858, within the Malay archipelago is essential towards an understanding of Thailand's natural evolution in its broadest phytogeographical
context. The material deals especially with important advances between 1960-80
in our knowledge of ocean-floor and continental movements contributing to the
dispersal of flora and fauna, and also with outstanding enigmas concerning the
bihemispheric distribution of some angiosperms which overlap in the Malay
archipelago which is one of the sharpest zoogeographical divisions in the world.
Cf. also M. G. Garson and W. G. Mitchell, 'Transform faulting in the Thai peninsula', *Nature* (London), vol. 228 (1978), p. 45-47; and T. C. Whitmore, *Tropical
rainforests of the Far East* (Oxford University Press, 1975).

142 **The Graminaceae of monsoonal and equatorial Asia. I: Southeast
Asia.**
Robert Orr Whyte. *Asian Perspectives*, vol. 15 (1977), p. 127-51.

The grasses were chosen for this analysis of the dispersal and domestication of
cereals through wide bands of tropical Asia, including Thailand and Malesia.
The article and its successor 'II: West Asia', *Asian Perspectives* vol. 21, no. 2
(1978), p. 183-206, carry extensive bibliographies on the dispersal and domestication of cultivated plants.

143 **Cultural, ecological perspectives of Southeast Asia: a symposium.**
Edited and introduced by William Wood. Athens, Ohio: Ohio
University Press, 1977. 192p. bibliog. (Center for International
Studies, Southeast Asia Series, no. 41).

The themes of this compilation range over the palaeology, prehistory and emergent
agriculture of Southeast Asia, exhibiting aspects of the interaction of man and
nature in the dispersal of plants and the development of human cultural patterns.
The broad bibliography is a useful contribution, cf. especially, C. Sauer, *Dispersal
of plants* (1952), and also Henry N. Ridley, *The dispersal of plants throughout
the world* (n.d.).

Fauna

144 **Oribatiden Thailands.** (Thailand's Oribatidae.)
   Ju-nichi Aoki. *Nature and Life in Southeast Asia*, vol. 4 (1965),
   p. 129-93. bibliog. 104 drawings.

This article (in German) deals with ground-mites (acarina) of Thailand. The Oribatidae, to which they belong, constitute one of the world's least-known fauna. The extensive bibliography on the general subject, covering Africa, South America and Southeast Asia, is mainly in Spanish, German and other Western languages, with a few English references.

145 **List of the odonata from Thailand.**
   Syoziro Asahina. *Kontyu*, 1982-83. 3 parts. bibliogs
   (parts 1 & 2). illus.

A three-part article by a Japanese specialist which describes over forty species of dragonflies found in Thailand during several recent research expeditions. Part 1 (Agronidae), vol. 50, no. 3 (Sept. 1982), p. 454-66; part 2 (Protonucidae), vol. 51, no. 1 (March 1983), p. 90-99; part 3 (Plastictidae), vol. 52, no. 4 (Dec. 1983), p. 583-95. Each part is well illustrated with drawings; parts one and two contain full bibliographies.

146 **The alpheid shrimp of the Gulf of Thailand and adjacent waters.**
   Albert H. Banner, Dora M. Banner. Bangkok: Siam Society,
   1966. 168p. map. bibliog. 62 plates. drawings. (Monograph no. 3).

This report on shrimps is based on a collecting expedition, in 1960-61, in offshore waters from Trad to Songkhla. Specimens were also made available by the Malaysian National Museum in Singapore. Evaluations were conducted at the Hawaii National Maritime Laboratory. The record was considered definitive enough for publication as a monograph. It contains descriptions and locations of 63 species and subspecies, 40 per cent common to Indo-Pacific waters, and the remainder showing a bias towards Pacific taxa.

147 **The natural history of West Malaysian mangrove faunas.**
   A. J. Berry. *Malayan Nature Journal*, vol. 25, no. 2 (1972),
   p. 125-62. plates.

This article describes the fauna of the mangrove areas typical of the coasts of Malaysia and Thailand, with special reference to the interesting and economically significant varieties of Crustacea.

148 **Production ecology of ants and termites.**
Edited by M. V. Brian. Cambridge, England: Cambridge
University Press, 1978. 409p. bibliog. (International Biological
Programme Study, no. 13).

This exhaustive study deals with the interaction of ants and termites with their
environments. The work contains material which could be of value to students
interested in relevant insect-pest problems in Thailand.

149 **Insects and other invertebrates for human consumption in Siam.**
William S. Bristowe. *Transactions of the Entomological Society
of London*, vol. 80 (Dec. 1932), p. 387-454.

Based on studies conducted in Thailand and Laos, the author, a specialist in
spiders, discusses the types of nutrition or delicacy enjoyed there, which might be
regarded as abnormal fare in a cold climate: such as water-snakes and cobras
(considered aphrodisiacs); large brown-bodied scorpions; and soft-bodied spiders,
both prized for the crispness of the outer shell and softness of the interior when
toasted. The author mentions Shan and Karen use of beetle larvae, crickets and
moths as food, and the medicinal use of the balled web of the giant-orb spider,
capable of trapping small birds as fare for itself. Among the author's many papers
on island spiders, cf. especially, 'Preliminary note on the spiders of Krakatau'
(*Proceedings of the Zoological Society of London*, 1931, p. 1389-1400), in which
he discusses the dispersal of spider and other flora and fauna of the Indonesian
region in the light of the re-inhabitation of Krakatau after 1883.

150 **Spider superstitions and folklore.**
William S. Bristowe. *Transactions of the Connecticut Academy
of Arts and Sciences*, no. 36 (1945), p. 53-85.

Spiders are very much a worldwide phenomenon and it is interesting to see how
far the superstitions and folklore that have grown up around them is also common
to many different regions. The author of this article considers facets, such as
respect offered to spiders as recipients of transmigrated souls, the pouncing of
spiders on their prey as the source of dances ('caper' derived from old French, to
seize), and their purtenance in medicinal charms.

151   Checklist of the ants (Hymenoptera: Formicidae) of Asia.
      J. W. Chapman, S. R. Capco.   Manila: Manila Bureau of Printing,
      1951. 327p. (Monograph no. 1).

Ants are an interesting and ubiquitous feature of the wilder regions of Thailand,
where a felled teak-tree will often disperse treetop colonies of leaf-cutter or red-
and-black ants of unexpectedly large size. This volume describes species to be seen
in the region. Jungle areas of Thailand are also the habitat of the 'white ant',
whose destructive presence can become spectacularly apparent when the monsoon
breaks and they erupt like masses of boiling honeycomb from flooded underground
galleries and mud-covered tree-trunk runways which they build as protection
from direct sunlight. Though popularly classed as ants, the white ants are from
a different order of insects, Isoptera. For a checklist of those found in Thailand
cf. Muzasser Ahmad, *Termites of Thailand (Isoptera)*, a monograph article in the
Bulletin of the American Museum of Natural History, vol. 131 (1965) p. 1-113,
with figures and a bibliography for further reading.

152   Butterflies of the oriental regions.
      Bernard D'Abreca.   Victoria, Australia: Hill House, 1982 (part 1);
      Melbourne, Australia: Hill House, 1985. (part 2). 2 vols. bibliog.
      col. plates.

These splendid, extra-large-format volumes cover the entire butterfly population
of the region east, west and southeast of Thailand, which forms an area of conver-
gence for species from all three regions i.e. South China and Indochina, Upper
India and Burma, and the Indonesian Archipelago including the Philippines. Some
of the species of butterflies illustrated and described by the author are of quite
restricted habitat; some, common to all, or to major sectors of the region, including Thailand. Most, if not all, of Thailand's 800 or more species are included:
part 1 — Papilionidae, Pieridae, Danaidae and part 2 — Nymphalidae, Satyridae,
Amathusiidae. The second part has a dedication to Hans Frühstorfer (1863-1962)
and includes a photograph of him. Frühstorfer pioneered the expansion of collection and identification of butterfly species of the region at the end of the 19th
century.

153   English vernacular names of the birds of Thailand.
      E. C. Dickinson, J. A. Tubb.   *Natural History Bulletin of the
      Siam Society*, vol. 21 (1966), p. 293-319. bibliog.

This article lists 790 bird species found in Thailand, giving scientific and English
vernacular names. Cf. also H. G. Deignan, 'Checklist of the birds of Thailand',
US National Museum Bulletin, vol. 226, p. 1-263.

154 **A field guide to the reef-building corals of the Indo-Pacific.**
Hans Ditlev. Rotterdam: W. Backhuys, 1980. 291p. bibliog.
illus.

This handy field guide is intended to help the non-expert to find and identify the
reef-building corals of the oceanic region which includes the Gulf of Thailand
and the west coast of peninsula Thailand, including Phuket. The author provides
hints on where to look, and a complete picture guide to all the species. Cf. also
the author's 'Stony corals (Coelenterata, Scleractina) from the west coast of
Thailand', *Phuket Marine Biological Centre Research Bulletin*, no. 13 (1976),
14p. map.

155 **Elephants and their diseases: a treatise on elephants.**
Lieutenant-Colonel George Henry Evans. Rangoon: Government
Printer, 1910. 343p. bibliog. photos.

Part one of this comprehensive handbook on elephants in Burma deals with the
handling of working elephants, their gear, dragging, river crossing, feeding and if
humanely necessary − shooting. The origin of Burma's working elephants in
Assam and Siam, between the head waters of the Salween and Ping rivers, is
noted, and the tribes which herd them are mentioned. The second part deals with
elephant hygiene, anatomy, diseases and veterinary care.

156 **On the mammalia of Siam and the Malay peninsula.**
S. S. Flower. *Proceedings of the Zoological Society of London*
(1900), p. 305-79.

This descriptive listing of mammals of the central and peninsular regions of
Thailand illustrates the state of knowledge at the turn of the century and provides
a comparative basis for assessing population changes in the intervening period.

157 **The whales, porpoises and dolphins known in Malayan waters.**
C. A. Gibson-Hill. *Malayan Nature Journal*, vol. 4, no. 2 (1949),
p. 44-61. bibliog. photos.

This article describes the Cetacea, who have appeared relatively rarely on the
Malayan coastlines. The author identifies resident species, especially the Blue
Whale (the largest mammal known), and distinguishes them from occasional
visitors. Cf. also A. J. Berry, D. R. Wells, C. K. Ng, 'Bryde's Whale in Malaysian
seas', *Malayan Nature Journal*, vol. 26 (1973), p. 19-25, bibliog. photos. which is
about whales stranded from Thai waters during the northwest monsoon.

158 **Birds collected by the Swedish zoological expedition to Siam 1911-12.**
Count Nils Gyldenstolpe. Uppsala, Sweden: Almqvist & Wicksells, 1913. 76p. illus. (K. Svenska Vetenskapsakademiens Handlingas, vol. 50, no. 8).

This large-format report contains some superb colour plates of birds found during the expedition to northeast Thailand. A second expedition, in 1913-14, produced further zoological results, published in 1916 in the same series (vol. 56, no. 2; vol. 53 no. 3; vol. 55 no. 4), dealing respectively with birds (II), snakes, lizards and batrachians. Cf. also Kitti Thonglongya, 'Note on type locality of some birds and mammals collected by Count Nils Gyldenstolpe in Thailand', *Natural History Bulletin of the Siam Society*, vol. 22, no. 1 (1967), p. 185-87, retracing part of the expedition and confirming some taxonomic locations.

159 **Freshwater molluscan fauna of Thailand.**
Tadashige Habe. *Nature and Life in Southeast Asia*, vol. 3 (1964), p. 45-66. plate.

Describes many varieties of snails, including the popular edible snails of Chiang Mai.

160 **The myzomyia species of anopheles (*cellia*) in Thailand with emphasis on intra-interspecific variations: (Diptera Culicidae).**
Bruce A. Harrison. *Contributions of the American Entomological Institute*, vol. 17, no. 4 (1980), p. 1-195. bibliog. (Medical Entomology Studies, 13).

This study deals with anopheles mosquitoes in relation to their role in human malaria. The author describes eleven species found in Thailand, of which two (a. *aconitus* and b. *minimus*) are known vectors of the disease. He discusses material on the suspected implication of *minimus* in promoting malaria in POW camps near Kanchanaburi during the Second World War.

161 **Bats from Thailand and Cambodia.**
John Edwards Hill, Kitti Thonglongya. *Bulletin of the British Museum (Natural History) Zoology*, vol. 22, no. 6 (1972), p. 173-96. bibliog.

This is a descriptive list of bats collected by Dr. J. T. Marshall of SEATO's (South-East Asia Treaty Organization) US army medical component. The collections are in Bangkok and Paris (Cambodian species, mainly common to Thailand as well).

162   **A new family, genus and species of bat mammalia: (Chiroptera) from Thailand.**
John Edwards Hill. *Bulletin of the British Museum (Natural History) Zoology*, vol. 27, no. 7 (1974), p. 303-36. bibliog. 8 figs.

Thailand has a rich bat fauna. This paper announces and describes a new species which also marks the discovery of an entirely new genus and family of mammalia (an exceedingly rare occurrence in this century), of which this bat is the sole representative: *Craseonycteris thonglongyai*, the hog-nosed or 'bumblebee' bat. It was found near Kanchanaburi in 1973, and is the smallest known mammal (the size of a bumblebee), weighing less than two grammes. It was discovered in a small cave complex, its only known habitat partly screened by a waterfall not far from the celebrated bridge over the River Kwai, by Kitti Thonglongya, a Thai naturalist. Thonglongya's death in the following year left it to his collaborator, the author of the present paper, to complete the study, the taxonomic allocation, and the announcement of man's most diminutive mammalian cousin. The 'bumblebee' bat is listed as an endangered species. For a description with photographs, cf. *Mammals of Thailand*, by Boonsong Lekagul and Jeffrey A. McNeely (1977, q.v.).

163   **Phytoplankton from Lake Borapeth in the Central Plain of Thailand.**
Minoru Hirano. *Contributions from the Biological Laboratory, Kyoto University,* vol. 24, no. 4 (1975), p. 187-203. 13 plates of drawings.

This illustrated paper on organisms found in the water taken from Lake Borapeth by a Japanese research team, is one of several papers discussing the evidence of organic and other types of pollution found in water. For a further indication of coverage of Thai biological topics in this journal (q.v.) cf. Matsufumi Matsui, 'A small collection of amphibians from Thailand', vol. 25, no. 4 (1975), p. 295-302.

164   **A pilot study of the social life of the white-banded gibbons in northwest Thailand.**
Syunzo Kawamura. *Nature and Life in Southeast Asia*, vol. 1 (1961), p. 159-69. bibliog.

This study of the gibbons of northwest Thailand commends C. R. Carpenter's *Field study of the behaviour of Thai gibbons* (1940).

165   **A field guide to the birds of Southeast Asia.**
Ben F. King, Edward C. Dickinson, illustrated by Martin W. Woodcock. London: Collins, 1975. 480p. endpaper maps. 64p. of plates (mostly col.).

A recommended, well-illustrated and standard field guide to the bird populations of Thailand and its mainland neighbour countries.

Flora, Ethnobotany and Fauna. Fauna

166 **Bird guide of Thailand.**
Boonsong Lekagui, E. W. Cronin. Bangkok: B. Lekagul, 1972.
2nd ed. 374p. col. illus.

This handy field guide contains descriptions of all Thailand's 829 known bird species. The authors have subsumed Herbert G. Deignan's *Checklist of the birds of Thailand* (Smithsonian Institution, 1963). Cf. also Herbert G. Deignan, 'Birds of northern Thailand', *Bulletin of the United States National Museum*, vol. 186 (1945), 615p.

167 **Field guide to the butterflies of Thailand.**
Boonsong Lekagul, Karen Askins, Jarujinta Nabhitabata, Arun Samruadkit. Bangkok: Association for the Conservation of Wildlife, 1977. 260p. map. bibliog. illus.

A useful pocket field guide with an endpaper picture-chart of Thailand's butterfly species for easy identification. The text carries names and descriptions in English and Thai, with colour photographs. Being in the transition zone of Indian and Sundaic fauna, Thailand has an exceptionally rich and varied butterfly population, consisting of over 800 species within numerous geographical sub-regions. The book gives hints on when and where to look for them, and how to use bait.

168 **Mammals of Thailand.**
Boonsong Lekagul, Jeffrey A. McNeely, chapters on Muridae by Joe T. Marshall and Sciuridae by Robert Askins, contributions by Harold Jefferson, C. Coolidge. Bangkok: Kuruspita, 1977. 691p. bibliog. glossary. illus.

This is a definitive large-format mammalia of Thailand, with full descriptive, historical and zoological material in English; includes an exhaustive bibliography and profuse illustrations (black-and-white photographs). It is published in a limited edition under the auspices of the Association for the Conservation of Wildlife.

169 **List of reference collection of algae, sea grasses, marine inverte-brates and vertebrates.**
Phuket Marine Biological Research Centre Research Bulletin, no. 28 (1981). 86p. Special publication.

This special publication which marks the 10th anniversary of Thai-Danish co-operation at the Marine Biological Research Centre at Phuket, provides an analytical checklist of the centre's reference collection from the island coastal waters of eastern peninsular Thailand.

170 **Wildlife management in Southeast Asia: proceedings of the Biotrop symposium on animal populations and wildlife management in Southeast Asia, Bogor, 1978.**
Edited by Jeffrey A. McNeely, Dioscoro S. Rabor, Effendy A. Sumardja. Bogor, Indonesia: Regional Center for Tropical Biology (Southeast Asian Ministers of Education on Organization —SEAMEO). 1978. 236p. (Biotrop Special Publication, no. 8).

The subject-matter of papers of specifically Thai interest presented to this symposium included: elephant management (Jeffrey A. McNeely); and grassland food preferences of the sambar in the Khao Yai National Park (Chompol Ngampongsai).

171 **The species of gibbons of Thailand.**
Joe T. Marshall, Bruce A. Ross, Swart Chantharojvong. *Journal of Mammalogy,* vol. 53, no. 3 (1972), p. 479-86. map. bibliog. photos.

This paper describes the gibbons whose whooping call gives them the common name 'Wa-Wa'. They are among the most attractive and engaging members of the Thai forest fauna. The breeding and behavioural studies of some species were carried out on Ko Klet Kaeo Island in 1968 by the Applied Science Research Corporation of Thailand in collaboration with the Royal Thai Navy and SEATO. Cf. 'Breeding and behavioural studies of primates', (ASRCT Project no. 26/1. Report nos. 1, 2 & 3), by Gershon Berkson, Joe T. Marshall and Bruce A. Ross, which discusses the propagational behaviour, laboratory breeding, habitat and description of gibbons.

172 **Cone shells of Thailand.**
A. da Motta. Bangkok: Graphic Art Company, 1979. 20p. endpaper map. col. illus.

This publication is of interest for the illustrations of Thai cone shells, and contains descriptive information.

173 **The turtles of Thailand.**
Wirot Nutaphand, translated from the Thai by Visnu Conqsiri. Bangkok: Siam Farm Zoological Garden, 1979. 222p. illus. (some col.).

The Siam Farm is a valued contributor to the literature on the aquatic fauna of the country and gives information on the availability of specimens.

174 **Butterflies in Thailand.**
Brother Amnuai Pinratana, book 1 is translated and produced by
F. A. Degeorges. Bangkok: Viratham, 1975-81. 4 vols. maps.
bibliogs. col. plates.

This sequence of volumes constitutes the major published source on Thailand's
butterflies. The first section, consisting of two separate, pocket-sized, illustrated
handbooks, appeared from 1975 respectively in a French translation (72 plates,
colour photographs) and an English translation (63 plates) from the Thai; volumes
2, 3 and 4 are large-format books in English, also carrying fine sets of plates of
colour photographs. Volume one is in two parts; book 1 in French and book 2
in English. Subjects covered are – vol. 1: Papilionidae, Danaidae; vol. 2: Pieridae,
Amathusildae; vol. 3: Nymphalidae; and vol. 4: Lycaenidae.

175 **Fossils of Thailand III.**
Kaset Pitakpaivan, R. Ingavat, P. Pariwatworn. Bangkok:
Department of Mineral Resources, 1969. 41p.

This is the concluding report on fossil finds by the Mineral Resources Department
of Thailand. Cf. also T. Kobayashi, F. Takai and I. Hayami, 'On some mesozoic
fossils from the Korat region of east Thailand', *Japan Journal of Geology and
Geography* (1963), p. 181-86; and G. H. R. von Koenigswald, 'A mastodon and
other fossil mammals from Thailand' (Bangkok: Royal Department of Mines,
Report Investments no. 2, [1959], p. 25-34).

176 **A revision of the spider genus Liphistius (*Araneae mesothelae*).**
Norman I. Platnik. *American Museum Novitates*, paper no. 2781
(Feb. 1984). 31p. 87 figs.

The paper, published individually, describes an interesting type of 'archaeological'
spider – a left-over genus of primitive segmented trap-door spiders, found only in
a belt stretching southwards from Upper Burma through western and pensinsular
Thailand and Malaysia.

177 **Common snakes of Southeast Asia and Hong Kong.**
Frank F. Reitinger, contributions and photographs by Jerry
K. S. Lee. Hong Kong: Heinemann, 1978. 114p. 16p. col. plates.

A useful, concise, illustrated field guide to snakes found in Thailand and mainland
Southeast Asia.

178 **Gibbon and siamang I: evolution, ecology, behavior and captive
maintenance.**
Edited by D. Rumbaugh. Basel: S. Kager, 1972. 263p.

This volume and its companion (cf. entry below), provide a general description of
the zoological, management and behavioural features of the gibbons, which are a
family of particular interest in Thai forest fauna.

179 **Gibbon and siamang III: natural history, social behavior, reproduction, vocalizations, prehension.**
Edited by D. Rumbaugh. Basel: S. Karger, 1974. 209p.
A companion volume to the previous entry.

180 **An annotated checklist of the anopheles of Thailand.**
John E. Scanlon, E. L. Peyton, Douglas J. Gould. Bangkok: Applied Scientific Research Corporation of Thailand, 1968. 35p. bibliog. (Thai National Scientific Papers, Fauna Series).
This paper gives a taxonomic listing of anopheles mosquitoes found in Thailand; it includes comments and locations.

181 **General survey of crabs in Thailand.**
Raoul Serene. Bangkok: Applied Science Research Corporation of Thailand, 1966. 13p. (Research Paper no. 18/1).
The author, based on the Unesco Regional Centre in Singapore, lists some 400 species of brachyura in Thailand. The project was concerned with economic aspects. Cf. also Raoul Serene, C. L. Soh, 'Brachyura collected during the Thai-Danish expedition (1966)', *PMBC Research Bulletin*, no. 12 (1976), 37p. 9 plates. bibliog.

182 **Checklist of the aquatic fauna of Siam (excluding fishes).**
Chote Suvatti. Bangkok: Bureau of Fisheries, 1937. 116p.
This checklist in parallel English and Thai includes molluscs, Crustacea and Malacostraca (prawns and shrimps).

183 **Fauna of Thailand.**
Chote Suvatti. Bangkok: Thailand Department of Fisheries, 1950. 1,100p. bibliog.
Provides a full taxonomic listing in English and Thai with an exhaustive bibliography of publications in both languages (p. 665-929), arranged both chronologically (from 1770-1950) and alphabetically by author.

184 **An illustrated checklist of marine shelled gastropods from Phuket Island, adjacent mainland and offshore islands, western peninsula Thailand.**
Ratsuda Tantanasiriwong. *Phuket Marine Biological Centre, Research Bulletin*, no. 21 (1978), 22p. 21 plates. bibliog.
This checklist of shelled gastropods includes an excellent set of plates of drawings showing the whorled cone shells.

185 **The amphibian fauna of Thailand.**
Edward H. Taylor. *University of Kansas Scientific Bulletin,*
vol. 43 (1962), p. 265-599. plates.
This article provides a complete, illustrated, descriptive listing of specimens of a
hundred species and subspecies of amphibians, including several new ones,
collected by the author during expeditions in Thailand between 1957 and 1960.

186 **The lizards of Thailand.**
Edward H. Taylor. *University of Kansas Scientific Bulletin*,
vol. 44 (Sept. 1963), p. 687-1,077. plates.
Part of the author's series on Thailand's herpetological fauna which deals with
lizards.

187 **Serpents of Thailand and adjacent waters.**
Edward H. Taylor. *University of Kansas Science Bulletin*, vol. 45
(June 1965), p. 609-1,096. plates.
This report is one of a series on the herpetological fauna of Thailand collected
during expeditions between 1957 and 1960. It describes the serpent species, and
is illustrated with black-and-white plates.

188 **The turtles and crocodiles of Thailand and adjacent waters,**
with a synoptic herpetological bibliography.
Edward H. Taylor. *University of Kansas Scientific Bulletin,*
vol. 49, no. 3 (1970), p. 87-179. map. plates. synoptic bibliography.
This is a descriptive list of Testudines and Loricata observed during a 26-month
tour in Thailand, taking into account specimens from collections in the country
and at the University of Kansas. The report comprises the entire, known croco-
dile and turtle fauna of Thailand and adjacent waters, arranged in families, genera
and species. The bibliography (p. 166-79) covers four articles on aquatic fauna,
of which this is the fourth (cf. the previous three entries).

189 **Fishes of Thailand: their English, scientific and Thai names.**
J. Thiemmedh. *Fisheries Research Bulletin, Kasetsart University,*
no. 4 (1966), 112p. plate.
Kasetsart is the agricultural university of Bangkok; this publication is a useful,
comparative nomenclature of fish.

190 The history of mammalogy in Thailand.
Kitti Thonglongya. *Natural History Bulletin of the Siam Society,* vol. 25 nos. 3 & 4 (Dec. 1974), p. 54-67. bibliog.

This article consists of a discursive bibliography of records of the mosaic of wildlife which Thailand has inherited from several converging faunal regions. Records mentioned include Dr. Finlayson's report of 1821; Sir Robert Schomburgk's report during his consulate of 1869 of the deer named after him which is peculiar to Thailand and is now thought to be extinct; and reports compiled by SEATO (South-East Asia Treaty Organization) and the Thai Royal Forestry Department in 1958.

191 Common Malaysian beetles.
Vincent Weng-yu Tung. Kuala Lumpur: Longman, 1983. 142p. bibliog. 32p. of plates. (Malaysian Nature Handbooks).

A good handbook on beetles. Species found in Thailand, and elsewhere in the neighbouring Asian tropics, are indicated in the habitat notes.

192 Jungle prison.
Leigh Williams. London: Andrew Melrose, 1954. rev. ed. 196p. map. photos.

This is a conversational first-hand account of the author's twenty years' experience of working with elephants in the teak forests of northern Thailand and northern Burma. His reminiscences include the jungle tribes, and character studies of some of the elephants (such as a wily old bull elephant called the 'Trade Unionist'). The author also sketches in the historical backgrounds of Lopburi and other regional centres of central and northern Thailand which he visited. The book was first published as *Green prison* in 1941, and also includes a glossary of elephant terms.

Prehistory and Archaeology

193   Ancient cities in Thailand.
Abha Bhamarabutr.   Bangkok: Muang Boran, 1981. 85p. 8 col.
plates.
This is one of the English-language occasional publications of the archaeological
publishers in Bangkok, illustrating some of the principal archaeological sites.

194   Thailand.
Pisit Charoenwongse, M. C. Subhandradis Diskul, series director
Jean Marcade.   Geneva: Nagel, 1978. 256p. endpaper maps.
bibliog. illus. (Archaeologia Mundi Series).
The series director is professor of archaeology at the University of Bordeaux. The
general plan consists of collections of plates, many in colour, illustrating the
archaeology and prehistory of individual countries, with annexed captions and a
general text in various Western languages – English in this edition. The introductory text reviews recent additions to the archaeology of Thailand, with comments
on some resulting re-classification of the earlier art periods. Architecture, painting,
gold and other artefacts, especially those recently discovered at Ayudhya, are well
illustrated in the plates, making this reasonably handy volume a valuable adjunct
to standard guidebooks for the tourist interested in a deeper background to the
religious art of the classical sites of Thailand.

195   The significance of clay rollers of the Ban Chiang culture,
Thailand.
William J. Folan, Burma H. Hyde.   Asian Perspectives, vol. 23,
no. 2 (1980), p. 153-63. 6p. of photos. bibliog.
Prompted by the speculative interpretation in the article by van Esterik and Kress
in a previous issue of Asian Perspectives, vol. 21 (q.v.), this article sums up suggestions made so far as to the significance of the ceramic (or clay) rollers of Ban
Chiang. One suggestion is that they were ideographic symbols used by a pre-literate
people, and goes on to propose an alternative: that (on a parallel with similar
discoveries in Iran), they were tokens of account in a fairly advanced system of
rice cultivation. A further set of photographs provides an interesting addition to
those in the previous article.

196 **Thailand's Ban Chieng: the birthplace of civilisation?**
R. S. Griffin. *Arts of Asia*, vol. 3, no. 6 (Nov.-Dec. 1973),
p. 31-34.
Contributes to the debate on the dating of artefacts found at Ban Chiang in
northeast Thailand.

197 **Provisional classification of painted pottery from Ban Chieng.**
Piriya Krairiksh. *Artibus Asiae*, vol. 35 (1973), p. 145-62. illus.
The discovery of large deposits of superb, whorl-patterned and cord-marked
pottery, together with prehistoric burial sites, jewellery and other artefacts, at the
archaeological site of Ban Chiang (a village near the Mekong River in northeast
Thailand), created a furore among archaeologists in the 1960s. The earliest, now
controversial, datings suggested a revolution in theories concerning the origins of
metallurgy and of rice cultivation. Thermoluminescence tests have since been
going on at Oxford University and the University of Pennsylvania. The pottery
and other finds are well represented in Bangkok at the National Museum, and at
Wang Suan Pakkad, the private museum of Princess Chumbhot na Nagara Svarga-
vard, to which visitors are welcomed.

198 **The Bang site, Thailand: an alternative analysis.**
William K. Macdonald. *Asian Perspectives*, vol. 21, no. 1 (1978),
p. 30-51. bibliog.
This article analyses the spatial orientations of the principal excavation site at
Ban Chiang, with figure-maps, and concludes that sub-village organization (cf.
S. J. Tambiah, *Buddhism and the spirit cults in northeast Thailand* [q.v.]), was
a factor in the arrangement of the burials. A useful bibliography is appended,
summing up previous writings on various aspects of the Ban Chiang discoveries.

199 **Palaeontological investigations of the Thai-American expedition
in north Thailand (1978-80): an interim report.**
Geoffrey O. Pope, David W. Freyer, Malai Liangcharoen, Pinit
Kulasing, Sukaborn Nakabanlang. *Asian Perspectives*, vol. 21,
no. 2 (1978), p. 147-63. map. bibliog. illus.
This is a preliminary report of an expedition in Thailand designed to investigate
the distribution and migration routes of Asian hominids in the early Pleistocene
period.

Prehistory and Archaeology

200 **Archaeological excavations in Thailand: vol. 3: Ban-Kao: part 2: the prehistoric Thai skeletons.**
Sood Sangvichien, Potal Sirigaroon, J. Bouslev-Jörgensen, appendix on mesolithic skeletons by Teuke Jacob. Copenhagen: Munksgaard, 1969. 67p. 47p. of plates.

This volume continues the reporting of the joint Thai-Danish archaeological expeditions of 1960-62, describing and illustrating skeletons found at the Ban-Kao site. Further publications were planned. The expeditions sparked off some discussion, and subsequently developed sites have provided material which tends to suggest modifications of some of their conclusions; meanwhile these volumes present an excellently illustrated impression of the archaeological potential of Thailand for the general reader.

201 **Early Southeast Asia: essays in archaeology, history and historical geography.**
Edited by Ronald B. Smith, William Watson. New York, Kuala Lumpur: Oxford University Press, 1979. 561p. maps.

This is a compilation of papers submitted to a colloquium held in 1973 at the School of Oriental and African Studies at the University of London, covering the first millennium BC and the first millennium AD in Southeast Asia. The new researches outlined in the papers constitute an updating in significant respects of material in previous standard textbooks on the prehistory and early history of the region. Contributions included on Thailand are in two parts; part 1 deals with archaeological matters: T. Bayard and W. Watson on prehistoric and early metallurgy; I. R. Selimkhanov and R. B. Smith on Non Nok Tha archaeological site; Nikom Suthiragsa on Ban Chiang; W. G. Solheim and M. Ayres on Pimai; part 2 deals with matters affecting art history: Bennet Bronson on Chansen; H. H. E. Loofs on U Thong; Elizabeth Lyons and M. C. Subhandradis Diskul on Dvaravati.

202 **Asian Perspectives: Journal of Archaeology and Prehistory of Asia and the Pacific.**
Edited by W. G. Solheim II. Honolulu: University of Hawaii, 1958- . annual or less often.

The editor of this periodical on archaeology has specialized in Thai prehistory, and this journal has tended to concentrate on Thai themes, though it also publishes contributions on general matters of Asian ethno-archaeology and linguistics, and occasional special-subject volumes with guest editors. Publication dates of volumes may run up to two years later than volume-reference years.

203 **Archaeological excavations in Thailand: vol. 2: Ban-Kao: part 1: prehistoric settlement with cemeteries: burials.**
Per Sorensen, with a contribution by Tove Hatting. Copenhagen: Munksgaard, 1967. 164p. 140p. of plates.

This continued publication on the joint Thai-Danish expeditions records discoveries at neolithic burial sites in Kanchanaburi province.

204 **The flaming torch of priceless culture and Ban Chiang.**
Bangkok: Praepittaya International Press, 1975. 83p. illus.
This pocket-sized volume has a short description and an excellent set of colour plates of the archaeological site, burials, and pottery found at Ban Chiang.

205 **An interpretation of Ban Chiang rollers: experiment and speculation.**
Penelope van Esterik, Nancy Kress. *Asian Perspectives*, vol. 21 (1978), p. 52-57. bibliog. plates.
Proposes speculative interpretations of the cylindrical ceramic rollers found at Ban Chiang; one suggestion was that they were used to mark cloth, or the body, perhaps as indications of status or type of activity.

206 **Archaeological excavations in Thailand: vol. 1: Sai-Yok: Stone Age settlement in the Kanchanaburi Province.**
H. R. van Heekeren, Count Egil Knuth. Copenhagen: Munksgaard, 1967. 129p. 23p. of b/w plates.
This is the first of a series of four handsomely-produced, large-format volumes recording the results of the joint Thai-Danish archaeological expeditions of 1959-62. This volume describes and illustrates pebble-tool and neolithic implements and artefacts discovered at the Sai-Yok site near Kanchanaburi.

History

General

207 **A short introduction to the history and politics of Southeast Asia.**
Sir Richard Allen. London: Oxford University Press, 1968.
306p. map. bibliog.

This book is based on a series of lectures delivered by the author for the Virginia Colleges Consortium for Asian Studies in 1968, designed for pre-university level. The author contrasts the development of mainland and archipelago Southeast Asia, mentioning the pre-Thai kingdom of Champa, and Siam's early contacts with France. The book makes a useful and easily assimilated preliminary study of the formative history of Thailand.

208 **The world of Southeast Asia: selected historical readings.**
Harry J. Benda, John A. Larkin. New York: Harper & Row, 1967. 331p.

This is an anthology of brief extracts from documents illustrating the history of Southeast Asia in general; there are several extracts on Thailand, from its discovery by travellers and local or foreign observers like the 4th-century Chinese Buddhist pilgrim Fa Hsien, to politicians and notables in modern Bangkok. The compilers add introductory notes placing the selected passages in historical context. The book could make a useful secondary-school level introduction to primary source materials.

209 **Les cycles chronologiques dans les inscriptions thaïes.** (The chronological cycles in Thai inscriptions.)
Roger Billard. *Bulletin de l'Ecole Française d'Extrême-Orient,* vol. 51 (1963), p. 403-31.

This article traces some interesting comparisons between 10th-century Khmer and 14th-century Thai usages of Indian, Chinese, and north Indochinese calendrical cycles for days, weeks and months, and use of Chinese 12-animal cycles for years. Lü Thai (Sukhothai, 1357) adopted an entirely Chinese-derived system for days and months.

50

210 Southeast Asia: its historical development.
John F. Cady. New York: McGraw-Hill, 1964. 637p. maps.
bibliog. chronology.
This is a comprehensive study of regional history, with a good picture of the
effect of European commerce, and of the pre-war trends of reform and revival in
Thailand. The author follows these trends through to see how they affected
Thailand's response to the coming of the Second World War to Southeast Asia.

211 Thailand, Burma, Laos, Cambodia.
John F. Cady. Englewood Cliffs, New Jersey: Prentice-Hall,
1966. 152p. bibliog. (A Spectrum Book).
A concise handbook, treating the four Theravada Buddhist countries of Southeast
Asia as a whole rather than one by one, and illustrating shared elements in their
Indian heritages, for instance, the spread of Gupta art forms.

212 Fields from the sea: Chinese junk trade with Siam during the late 18th and early 19th centuries.
Jennifer Wayne Cushman. Ann Arbor, Michigan: University
Microfilms International, 1975. 253p. map. bibliog. (PhD thesis
for Cornell University).
This thesis, covering additional aspects of the Chinese junk trade, may be read in
conjunction with Sarasin Viraphol's *Tribute and profit* (q.v.).

213 Historical retrospect of Junckceylon Island.
Colonel G. E. Gerini. *Journal of the Siam Society*, vol. 2, part 2
(July 1905), p. 121-227.
The material adduced in this article is of interest in view of, both the historical
incidences of the island (alias Thalang, or later Phuket), and of its current promi-
nence as an idyllic tourist as well as maritime research centre. The article lists
historical references to the island from the 13th century (Kedah annals) to the
French concerns of 1685, and the Burmese invasion of 1809, and contains
Captain Low's descriptive account of his visit in 1824, cf. E. H. S. Simmonds,
Francis Light and the ladies of Thalang (q.v.).

214 A history of Southeast Asia.
D. G. E. Hall. London: Macmillan, 1981. 4th ed. 1,070p. maps.
bibliog.
Though in some respects overtaken by more recent research since its original
publication in 1955, this history of Southeast Asia, updated through several
editions, remains the best general overview. It treats the region as a whole as well
as by individual countries, and considers external influences acting upon it as
well as evolutionary forces active within it. The author's general theme is to show
how the Tai and other individual nations emerged from the membership of
primitive empires having Chinese or Indian contacts, through changes brought
about by conquest, trade or colonization, and into their formation of modern
political entities.

215 **A history of Southeast Asia since 1500.**
   Gilbert Khoo. Kuala Lumpur: Oxford University Press, 1970.
   188p. (Oxford Progressive History Series).

This is a history of individual countries of Southeast Asia ('Thailand' p. 92-119)
and also describes external influences acting on the area as a whole (East India
Companies). The material is specially arranged for secondary educational purposes,
with test questions at each stage.

216 **Siam in transition.**
   Kenneth Perry Landon. London: Oxford University Press, 1969.
   328p. foldout map. bibliog.

Examines the principal factors of change in Thai history. The author considers
two in particular: first, Ayudhya's wide foreign contacts, and especially, those
facilitated by her possession of Mergui, with French and other traders, adventurers, and guards (Japanese); second, the political, economic and ethnic problems
of adjustment in the five years following the coup introducing constitutional
monarchy in 1932, with resultant changes in arts, crafts, recreation and family
life.

217 **L'introduction d'Islam au Champa.** (The introduction of Islam
   into Champa.)
   Pierre Yves Manguin. *Bulletin de l'Ecole Française d'Extrême-
   Orient*, vol. 66 (1979), p. 258-87. bibliog. (Champa Studies
   vol. 2).

This article gives a good description of the slow tide of Islamic conversion in the
region of the pre-Thai kingdom of Champa by Arab and Persian traders from the
10th century onwards. The bibliography in Western languages affords a useful
extension of the subject.

218 **Proceedings of the 7th IAHA conference held in Bangkok, 22-26
   August 1977.**
   Bangkok: Chulalongkorn University Press, 1979. 2 vols.

These well-produced, substantial volumes contain a large number of papers by
members of the International Association of Historians of Asia (IAHA), arranged
under five principal headings, dealing with problems and prospects for modern
Asia, the impact of historical heritage on modernization, value systems and
ideologies, the role of women, and historiography and archaeology. The meeting,
having been held in Bangkok, was well represented by Thai specialists and the
mass of material produced valuable contributions on a variety of historical and
developmental themes of Thai as well as of regional interest.

219 **Sino-Siamese tributary relations 1282-1853.**
Suebsaeng Promboon. Ann Arbor, Michigan: University Microfilms International, 1977. 358p. bibliog. (PhD thesis for Wisconsin University).

This thesis covers tributary relationships between Sukhothai and the Yüan Dynasty; between Ayudhya and the Ming Dynasty; and between Bangkok and the Ch'ing Dynasty. The conclusion is that privileged trading conditions always formed a more significant element than suzerainty, which was a purely nominal component of the tribute missions; they were eclipsed as a result of the Western trade incursions into China in the mid-19th century. The author provides a good annotated bibliography of Chinese and Western source materials.

220 **A history of east Asian civilization.**
Edwin O. Reischauer, John K. Fairbank, Albert M. Craig.
London: Allen & Unwin, 1960 (vol. 1) & 1965 (vol. 2). 2 vols.
maps. bibliogs. illus.

These two fine and profusely illustrated volumes — *East Asia: the great tradition,* and *East Asia: the modern transformation* — are the product of collaborative studies begun at Harvard in the late 1930s. They are essentially disparate in their treatment of the growth of east Asian civilization; together, they illuminate a single, vast historical panorama, but from the standpoint of two distinct phases; the first centred on China, and the second dealing with changes brought about by the European confrontation with China and with the principal intermediate region of Sino-Indian influence — Southeast Asia. Thailand's involvement provides important sub-themes in both volumes. Volume one includes a map showing the kingdom of Nan-chao (seen as a key point in the Tai migration southwards) in the T'ang period; volume two gives substantial consideration to the emergence of the Thai state in conflict with Burma, and at a crossroad of European trade transit aimed towards China.

221 **The traditional trade of Asia.**
C. G. F. Simkin. Kuala Lumpur: Oxford University Press, 1968.
417p. maps. bibliog. plates.

Presents a good account of early trade contacts in Southeast Asia, mentioning Ralph Fitch, a visitor to Ayudhya in the 16th century, and other travellers, such as Barbosa, whose records are of interest. It includes an illustration of one of the Arab ships involved.

222 **A concise history of Southeast Asia.**
Nicholas Tarling. Singapore: Donald Moore; New York: Praeger, 1967. 354p. bibliographic notes.

This concise appreciation of regional history, from an Australian viewpoint, takes three development periods: up to 1760; 1760-1942; and since 1942. The author considers political and economic pressures which cause social change, and suggests reasons why there is relatively less of such change in Thailand.

History. General

223 The Thai states: Thailand and Laos.
D. J. M. Tate. In: *The making of modern Southeast Asia, vol. 1.*
Kuala Lumpur: Oxford University Press, 1977. rev. ed.
p. 483-510. maps.

This section of the comprehensive work on Southeast Asia's modern history provides a useful introduction to the Thai and Lao sectors on either bank of the Mekong River. The two states, Thailand and Laos, have evolved considerably divergent political shapes, but underlying ethnic and cultural affinities remain, making northeast Thailand a distinctive sub-region.

224 Tribute and profit: Sino-Siamese trade, 1652-1853.
Sarasin Viraphol. Cambridge, Massachusetts: Harvard University Press, 1977. 419p. endpaper maps. bibliog. (Harvard East Asia Monographs, no. 76).

The book covers a vital sector of the history of Siam's international relations, in which the country occupied a nodal position in trade exchanges involving Japan as well as China, and also Portugal, the Netherlands, England, France and the East Indies. The Chinese junk trade was an early and enduring element in this pattern of long-haul trade; but, as the title of the book implies, 'tribute', in this context, tended to confer a profitable rather than vassal status on China's trading partners. Cf. the author's note on the political significance of Taksin's tribute mission to Peking in 1780, and of the degree of Rama II's dependence on the junk trade for revenue. The volume includes a useful glossary and a list of Chinese and Thai dynastic and reign names with Chinese and Thai vernacular equivalents.

225 Ancient Southeast Asian warfare.
H. G. Quaritch Wales. London: Bernard Quaritch, 1952. 206p.

The author, a specialist in Thai religious and court procedures, discusses early methods of warfare and their implications for the ethics of militarism in Buddhist societies.

226 Thailand: a handbook of historical statistics.
Constance M. Wilson. Boston, Massachusetts: G. K. Hall, 1983. 366p.

This substantial work depicts the history of Thailand's economic, political and social development in statistical terms.

227 Historical patterns of tax administration in Thailand.
Wira Wimoniti. Bangkok: Thammasat University, 1961. 184p. bibliog. (PhD thesis for the Faculty of Administration).

Analyses the origination and development of the national tax structure and its administration, from tax farming and practice in the Sukhothai era, to the first budget, under Western influence connected with the railway loan of 1875.

228 **A history of Siam.**
W. A. R. Wood. London: Unwin, 1926. 294p. map. bibliog. illus.

The author died in Chiang Mai, his chosen city of residence, in 1970 at the age of ninety-two. He was appointed British Consul cf. *Consul in paradise* (q.v.). His history of Siam from the earliest times up to the end of the absolute monarchy is a fairly brief sketch, drawn largely from Thai sources. It predates the post-war flow of modern scholarship and was for some time the only available monograph in English. Its main value today lies in its impressions of the early period and in its charm of approach and readability.

229 **Thailand: a short history.**
David K. Wyatt. New Haven, Connecticut: Yale University Press, 1982. 351p. maps. bibliog. illus.

This is a major new history of Thailand, within a reasonable compass and by an acknowledged authority. It is presented in a clear style, and makes compelling reading for the general reader as well as a valuable source for specialists. The central theme, Thailand from its earliest beginnings, is set in an imaginatively expanded geographical and cultural context. In comparison with earlier histories, the opening and closing parts of the book are of particular interest. The first chapters reconsider the indeterminate and sparsely-documented antecedents of the Tai linguistic and national group from which the Thai emerged to occupy the present Thailand. This section includes a new look at the controversial question of the presumed origins of the Thai in the 10th-century kingdom of Nan-chao in Yunnan. The latter part of the book connects up the early period of the constitutional monarchy (1932-1945) with the revolutionary politics of the three decades following the Second World War. The book provides useful reference tables of rulers. The discursive bibliography is the best available introduction to the historiography of Thailand in English and some other Western languages, and includes a guide to primary sources.

Pre-Thai (-1200 AD)

The Tai, Nan-chao and the classical empires
(from their beginnings to 1200 AD)

230 **The Nan-chao kingdom and China's northwestern frontier.**
Charles Backus. Cambridge, England: Cambridge University
Press, 1981. 224p. maps. bibliog. glossary (Cambridge Studies in
Chinese History, Literature and Institutions).

Presents a useful, short history of the kingdom of Nan-chao from the Chinese
standpoint, describing its gradual rise to a position of power in the 8th-9th
centuries by counterbalancing Tibet against China. In 866AD a Chinese army had
to drive Nan-chao forces from Hanoi; Nan-chao's threats hastened the fall of the
T'ang empire, but it was itself exhausted four years before that, in 902AD.

231 **The ancient Khmer empire.**
Lawrence Palmer Briggs. Philadelphia: Transactions of the
American Philosophical Society, 1951. 295p. bibliog.

This volume, one of the special-subject publications of the American Philosophical
Society, is a valuable background study. It contributes to an understanding of the
Saivite and Mahayanist civilization of the Khmer empire, from which the early
Thai states broke away, to evolve gradually to their own softer and more delicate
Theravadist cultural ethos.

232 **Angkor: an introduction.**
George Coedès. Hong Kong: Oxford University Press, 1975. 6th
imprint. 118p. foldout maps. bibliog. endpaper plan.

This deceptively small, well-illustrated handbook introduces the great temple
complex of Angkor Wat. Further than that, it amounts in effect to a learned
discussion of the historical and ideological basis of the Khmer civilization which
sent imperial offshoots into northeast Thailand in about the 12th century, in the
course of which its ruling dynasty built the important temple complex at the
town now known as Phimai. The book accordingly constitutes an excellent introduction not only to Angkor, but also to Phimai.

History. Pre-Thai (-1200 AD). The Tai, Nan-chao and the classical
empires (from their beginnings to 1200 AD)

233   **The Indianized states of Southeast Asia.**
George Cœdès, edited by Walter F. Vella, translated from the
French by Susan Brown Cowing. Honolulu: East-West Center
Press, 1968. 403p.

This classic study of the spread of Indian influence throughout the continental
and archipelago regions to the east and southeast was published in French as
Les états hindouisés d'Indochine et d'Indonésie, in 1948. It remains essential
reading for an understanding of the cultural and political evolution of the entire
region – sometimes called 'Further India'. The formative stages in the diffusion
of Indian religion occurred in the first half of the 1st millennium AD, especially
in the kingdoms of Funan and Champa, and as affecting China and the diaspora of
Tai peoples. The author considers the limiting influences resulting from the
Islamic influxes into the region; the book concludes with the decline of direct
Indian influence by the 14th century. The material includes summaries of the
effects of contacts with India and Sri Lanka on the early Thai kingdoms.

234   **The making of Southeast Asia.**
George Cœdès, translated from the French by H. M. Wright.
Berkeley, California: University of California Press, 1966. 268p.
bibliog.

The author, a specialist in the documentation of the early period in Indochina
and Thailand, summarizes the historical evolution of Southeast Asia, leading up
to the period of state formation in 13th-century Thailand.

235   **Cultural and geographical observations made in the Tali-Yunnan
region with special regard to the Nanchao problem.**
Willhelm Credner, translated from the German by Eric Seidenfaden. Bangkok: Siam Society, 1935. map. 20p.

The ancient empire of Nan-chao in the Yunnan dominated the Han Chinese
caravan route leading to Burma and gives access to immigration routes used by the
Tai for migrations into the Mekong and Chao Phraya River basins. Recent historiography has disputed the definitive role assigned to this tribal centre as a principal
source of the populations of the early kingdoms in northern Thailand from about
the 10th century AD. This first-hand study of the geographical, demographic and
linguisitic features of this mountainous region is therefore of more than usual
interest.

236   **Shan and Siam.**
G. E. Gerini. *Imperial and Asiatic Quarterly Review*, 3rd series,
vol. 5, nos. 9-10 (Jan.-April 1898), p. 145-63.

Examines some implications of the terminology and early history of Tai migrations
from Nan-chao.

History. Pre-Thai (-1200 AD). The Tai, Nan-chao and the classical empires (from their beginnings to 1200 AD)

237 **The travels of Fa Hsien (399-414 A.D.); or a record of the Buddhist kingdoms.**
Re-translated by Herbert Allen Giles. Cambridge, England: Cambridge University Press, 1923. Reprinted, London: Kegan Paul, 1959. endpaper map. plate. 96p.

Many of the first records of the Thai and adjoining regions consist of the accounts of Chinese pilgrims, of whom Fa Hsien is one of the earliest and most important. The author of this small volume was professor of Chinese at Cambridge University, and compiler of a well-known and respected Chinese-English dictionary. Fa Hsien's account of his overland route to the Indian Buddhist sites via Champa and some thirty other countries was published at different times under different titles (hence the alternative title of this book); and once in the T'ang period under the name Fa-ming, because the emperor had appropriated the character Hsien and this character became taboo. For a fuller account of Buddhist pilgrimages via Champa to India, cf. Stanislas Aignan Julien, *Mémoires sur les contrées occidentales traduit du Sanskrit en Chinois en l'an 648 par Hiouen Thsang* (Paris: Imprimerie Imperiale, 1856, 2 vols. (being vols. 2 & 3 of 'Voyages des Pélérins Buddhistes'). Volume 2 has an excellent foldout map, drawn in Japan in 1710, showing the routes of Fa Hsien and Hiouen Thsang. The plate in H. A. Giles' book is a delicate drawing of three horse-drawn carts by Nan-yü (ca1560) — an allegory of the Buddhist *tripitaka* (three canonical vehicles).

238 **The early Syam in Burma's history.**
Gordon H. Luce. *Journal of the Siam Society,* vol. 46, part 2 (Nov. 1958), p. 123-214 (with foldout map) & vol. 47, part 1 (June 1959), p. 59-101.

The first of these two articles consists of a general discussion of the provenance of Shan-Tai peoples in the area of northern Burma and northern Thailand with notes and an extensive bibliography of Chinese, Shan and Old Thai sources (p. 173-214); the second, of supplementary observations based on further examination of Chinese source material, principally the Yüan-shih (chronicle of the Yüan dynasty, 1271-1368). The word 'Syam' (first found in Khmer inscriptions at Angkor) gives rise to 'Shan', and also to 'Assam' and 'Sayam' (Siam). The articles — rightly characterized by David K. Wyatt as magisterial in *Thailand: a short history* (q.v.) — describe the tribal migrations and linguistic and cultural spread of these peoples, in which a significant landmark was the capture of Tali, the capital of Nan-chao, by Kublai Khan in 1253. With reference to the Kara-Khitai (Qara-Khitay), to whom the author refers, cf. also Karl A Wittfogel and Feng Chia-sheng, 'History of Chinese society: Liao (907-1125)', *Transactions of the American Philosophical Society,* vol. 36 (1946), new series, appendix 5, p. 619-73 and bibliog. p. 684-95; and Edwin O. Reischauer, *A history of east Asian civilization* (q.v.) vol. 1, chart p. 245 and map p. 268.

239 **An introduction to the history of Southeast Asia.**
B. R. Pearn. Kuala Lumpur: Longmans Malaysia, 1969. 244p.
maps. bibliog. illus.

This concise introduction to Southeast Asian history gives a useful account of the early ethnic movements of the mainland. The author introduces the early empires of Funan, Srivijaya, Majapahit, and Thaton (the early Mon city in Burma, from which the Mon spread northwards to Pagan, and eastwards into Thailand). The book ends with the growth of modern nationalisms, and the coming of the Second World War to Southeast Asia.

240 **Siam, or the history of the Thais from the earliest times to 1569 A.D.**
Ronald Bishop Smith. Bethesda, Maryland: Decatur Press, 1966. 109p. maps. bibliog.

A concise, simple exposition of the traditionally accepted pattern of successive early Thai state formations, with particular reference to Chinese sources.

Dvaravati (ca 600-1200 AD)

241 **L'archéologie mône de Dvaravati.** (The Mon archaeology of Dvaravati.)
Pierre Dupont. Paris: Ecole Française d'Extrême-Orient, 1959. 2 vols. (vol. 1 – 329p. & vol. 2 – 152p. b/w plates.) bibliog.

This is a magnificent study, splendidly illustrated in a separate, large-format volume, of the vital Mon element in the introduction and formative period of Buddhist religion and religious art in Thailand around the middle of the 1st millennium AD. The ruins of the main, 6th-century temple sites in the vicinity of Nakhon Pathom (Wat Phra Men and several others nearby) are scrutinized in detail. The giant 19th-century reconstruction of Wat Phra Pathom now occupies the main site. The author outlines the Mon history of Lower Burma and Siam, and analyses the iconography of standing and seated Buddha images, including those seated on coiled nagas, in a sequence of separate chapters.

242 **Old Burma – early Pagan.**
Gordon H. Luce. Locust Valley, New York: Augustin, 1969-70, for *Artibus Asiae* and Institute of Fine Arts (New York University), 3 vols. bibliog. illus.

This work is a masterpiece of historiography, religious art, and iconography, and a fine example of large-format book production. The subject is the first phase of the Burmese capital, Pagan, in the 11th and 12th centuries. The main sources are the difficult Mon chronicles, and the visual evidence, superbly presented in photographic detail, of the city's innumerable buddhist temples. The author points out that the work is a torso – headless and without feet. The missing head is the pre-Mon and early Mon history of Burma (which is to an extent also that of Thailand) – too complex for inclusion even in such a massive history as this is. The missing feet comprise the exclusively Burmese phase after Singhalese invasions in the 12th century led to a Mon-Burmese split. What remains is the heyday of Pagan's Theravadist construction during approximately the century from 1060 AD, to which Thai religion and art became deeply indebted. A map of the Pagan empire at this period shows its links with the civilizations of Haripunjaya and Dvaravati in present-day Thailand, east and southeast of Pagan. Volume 1 (422p.) contains two parts, history and iconography; volume 2 contains a substantial bibliography (p. 213-30), and maps (in pocket); volume 3 consists entirely of fine monochrome plates.

243 **Dvaravati: the earliest kingdom of Siam.**
H. G. Quaritch Wales. London: Bernard Quaritch, 1969. 149p. bibliog. illus.

With the aid of numerous plates, the author elaborates evidence from recent archaeological sites to give a revised interpretation of the earliest Indian-influenced empire, which had spread over most of the territory of present-day Thailand by the end of the 1st millennium AD.

The era of Lan Na and Sukhothai (ca 1200-1350 AD)

244 Sukhothai-Monghol relations: a note on relevant Chinese and Thai sources (with translations).
E. Thadeus Flood. *Journal of the Siam Society*, vol. 57, part 2 (July 1969), p. 201-58.

The documents itemized in this article shed some further light on the question of Sukhothai's contacts with the Mongol court (Yüan) in China during the key period of flux in the region at the end of the 13th and beginning of the 14th centuries. Students of Chinese and of Thai will find the illustrated and translated excerpts from contemporary annals in both those languages useful.

245 **The epigraphy of Mahadharmaraja I at Sukhodaya.**
A. B. Griswold, Prasert na Nagara. *Journal of the Siam Society,*
vol. 61, part 1 (Jan. 1973), p. 71-178. plates. (Epigraphic and
Historical Studies, no. 11, part 1).

King Lü Thai (Sanskrit title Mahadharmaraja I) is credited with the compilation
of the principal Theravada canonical scriptures of Thailand in 1345, while he was
viceroy of Sri Sajjanalai. He acceded to the throne of Sukhothai, probably in
the following year, and was responsible during the next twelve years for a
Buddhist reorganization and six further sets of inscriptions, some in Khmer and
some in Thai. This excellent study, explains their provenance, and provides translated texts with illustrative plates.

246 **The Ramkamhaeng stele.**
A. B. Griswold, Prasert na Nagara. In: *Collected articles in*
memory of Prince Wan Waithayakorn. Bangkok: Siam Society,
1976. p. 177-244. illus.

The stele inscribed by King Ramkhamhaeng, bearing the first record in Thai script,
dates from 1292 AD and forms an outstanding document in the history of the
first Thai kingdom, Sukhothai. This article comments on the translation of the
inscription into French by George Coedès (1924), supplies a translation into
English with annotations, and gives a facsimile reproduction of the original text.

247 **Annales du Siam, t. III: chronique de Xieng Mai.** (Annals of Siam,
vol. III: the Chiang Mai chronicle.)
Translated by Camille Notton. Paris: Paul Geuthner, 1932.
287p.

The Notton translations into French of the annals of Siam, consists of four
volumes: three published in Paris, 1926-32, and a fourth entitled *Légendes sur le*
Siam et le Cambodge (Bangkok, 1939), are a much cited source for primary
materials. Further comparative research is beginning to reveal some variations or
lacunae in the versions available to Notton cf. David K. Wyatt, *Thailand: a short*
history (q.v.). Volume two includes the chronicle of Haripunjaya, the last
Dvaravati outpost kingdom in the north, conquered by the Chiang Mai dynasty
in the late 13th century. Volume three is of particular interest for the chronicle
of Chiang Mai itself, relating to that dynasty, and especially King Tiloka (1441-87),
who had an important influence on the spread of Theravada Buddhism in the
northern kingdom of Lan Na.

248 **Ancient Siamese government and administration.**
H. G. Quaritch Wales. London: Bernard Quaritch, 1934. 206p.
bibliog.

This recommended study by a specialist in religious and court practice considers
the factors which led to the emergence in Thailand in the 13th century of a state
system linking monarch and monkhood, people and army, centre and provinces.

The empire of Ayudhya (1351-1767 AD)

249 **Mémoire du père de Bèze sur la vie de Constance Phaulkon, premier ministre du roi de Siam, Phra Narai, et de sa triste fin.**
(Memoir by Father de Bèze of Constance Phaulkon, prime minister to the king of Siam, Phra Narai, and of his sad end.) Annotated by Jean Drans, Henri Bernard. Tokyo: Presses Salesiennes, 1947. 282p.

An interesting contemporary collection by Father de Bèze of letters and documents of Constance (or Constantin) Phaulkon.

250 **Translation of events in Ayudhya, 686-966.**
O. Frankfurter. *Journal of the Siam Society*, vol. 6, part 3 (1909), p. 1-21.

This article translates one of the important shorter versions of the Ayudhya chronicles. The dates covered (given in the title as the current Ayudhyan calendric form) correspond to 1304-1604 AD. A feature of the chronicles is that they show evidence of Hindu practices, e.g. the presence of statues of Brahman gods in processions.

251 **The natural and political history of the kingdom of Siam.**
Nicolas Gervaise, translated from the French by H. S. O'Neill.
Bangkok: Siam Observer Press, 1928. 324p. foldout map.

The original publication in Paris of this contemporary handbook took place in 1688, a fateful year for Ayudhya, and for the French interest there which the book represented. The four parts deal with the country (including flora), its customs, religion and court. The author describes King Narai (who died in the year of publication) from personal acquaintance.

252 **A critical analysis of van Vliet's historical account of Siam in the 17th century.**
Francis H. Giles. *Journal of the Siam Society*, vol. 30, part 2 (1958), p. 155-240, part 3 p. 271-380.

The author cites Ravenswaay's translation of van Vliet's treatise of 1647 (JSS vol. 7, part 2 [July 1910]) in a critical comparison with other sources. The article (in two parts) is, in effect, a reconstruction of the history of the Dutch East India Company in Siam; its first factory post at Patani on the Gulf of Thailand being established in 1602, and in 1604, that at Ayudhya (of which Schouten and subsequently van Vliet were residents between 1624 and 1634). The author lists the dramatis personae involved, of whom one of the more interesting is Ieyasu, who extended Japan's trading interests abroad, including those of Ayudhya.

253 **Adventurers in Siam in the 17th century.**
E. W. Hutchinson. London: Royal Asiatic Society, 1940. 283p.
maps. bibliog. illus.

Hutchinson spent some years in Chiang Mai before 1930, and subsequently became intrigued with the personality of Constantine Phaulkon (the Greek adventurer). This led him to 17th-century contemporary materials in Europe, Tokyo and elsewhere. The volume discusses the results of his enquiries concerning Phaulkon, the French missions to King Narai (including that of the Chevalier de Chaumont, recounted by the 'boudoir Abbé de Choisy', of whom the author gives details), and the eventual fall of Phaulkon, the king, and of French Jesuit hopes. The book makes a good approach to primary sources, woven into a running story of this part of Ayudhya's fortunes, with relevant bibliographic notes, and also a summary of earlier Portuguese, Dutch and English contacts with Ayudhya in the 17th century.

254 **The history of Japan, together with a description of the kingdom of Siam 1690-1692.**
Engelbert Kaempfer, translated from the German by J. G. Scheuchzer. Glasgow: James Maclehose, 1971. reprinted. 3 vols.

The original of this work was published in New York (M. S. Press, 1906). In the Thai part, it deals with the little-covered period after the fall of King Narai, when the succession of the kingdom of Ayudhya had fallen into some doubt and contention and most foreign contacts, including the Japanese (who had supplied the royal guard), were excluded.

255 **The rise of Ayudhya: a history of Siam in the 14th and 15th centuries.**
Charnvit Kasetsiri. Kuala Lumpur: Oxford University Press, 1976. 194p. map. bibliog. (Oxford in Asia Historical Monographs).

This book, from the author's original thesis presented to Cornell University (1973), offers a new hypothesis on the origins of the Ayudhya kingdom. It suggests that it was rather a natural coalescence of minor fiefdoms extant in the mid-14th century than, as hitherto assumed, the result of a conscious political decision, prompted by disease or other calamity, to move the capital from U Thong.

256 **Southeast Asia in the eyes of Europe in the 16th century.**
Donald F. Lach. Chicago: University of Chicago Press, 1968. 130p. (Reprinted from vol. 1, book 2, ch. VII, of *Asia in the making of Europe*).

This reprint is from part of a major study of the impact on European thought of the first contacts with Asia – in this section, Southeast Asia – by mariners in search of new trade goods. The entire, two-volume work, five books in all (Chicago: 1965-77), consists of a fundamental re-assessment in terms of European culture of the literary record and repercussions of the voyages of discovery. Cf. vol. 1, book two, p. 76, which lists books on Asia in sixty 16th-century collections.

257 **The mandarin road to old Hue: narrative of Anglo-Vietnamese diplomacy from the 17th century to the eve of the French conquest.**
Alastair Lamb. London: Chatto & Windus, 1970. 349p. bibliog.

This is a compilation of contemporary documents relating to the period of Anglo-French rivalry for the control of trade routes via Siam and Indochina to China. Included are reports by Sir John Bowring, Dr. John Crawfurd and others. The introduction gives a synopsis of Anglo-Siamese contacts of this period.

258 **The Padaeng chronicle and the Jengtung state chronicle translated.**
Sao Saimong Mangrai. Ann Arbor, Michigan: University of Michigan, Center for South East Asian Studies, 1981. 301p. map.

These Shan chronicles concerned with Lan Na (north Thailand) and Kengtung, hitherto neglected owing to difficulties of dating and interpretation, are of the *tamnan* genre, dealing with Thai religious history and state formation. In particular, this new translation sheds light on the religious policy problems of King Tiloka (1441-87) resulting from the sectarian split between the 'garden' and 'forest' Buddhist sects of his day.

259 **The ship of Sulaiman.**
Translated from the Persian by John O'Kane. New York: Columbia University Press; London: Routledge & Kegan Paul, 1972. 250p. (Persian Heritage Series, no. 11).

The recent discovery of this Persian account of Ayudhya, resulting from a mission undertaken by Shah Sulaiman of Persia in 1685, adds a new dimension to the knowledge of Muslim religious pressures as well as long-standing trading interests at Ayudhya.

260 **Chroniques royales du Cambodge 1594-1677.** (The royal chronicles of Cambodia 1594-1677.)
Edited and translated by Man Phoeun. Paris: Ecole Française d'Extrême Orient, 1981. 524p. map. (Texts and Documents on Indochina, no. 13).

This massive collection of the Khmer chronicles relates to a period of eclipse of the Khmer empire, when Cambodia was undergoing constant friction with her Thai neighbour.

261 **Inscription dite de Brai Svay ou 'bois des manguiers' de Sukhoday.**
(The Brai Svay or 'mango grove' inscription of Sukhothai.)
Saveros Pou. *Bulletin de l'Ecole Française d'Extrême-Orient,*
vol. 65, part 2 (1978), p. 333-60. plates.
This article sums up the translation and interpretative work done by successive
scholars, especially A. B. Griswold and Prasert na Nagara in 'The epigraphy of
Mahadharmaraja I of Sukhodaya', JSS, vol. 61, part 1 (Jan. 1973), p. 71-178
(q.v.), on the inscription, in Khmer, on a 14th-century stele found at the 'mango
grove' monastery of Sukhothai. The author analyses elements of the Khmer text
with illustrative script and a plate showing part of the inscription, which can be
compared to the first Thai script on the Ramkhamhaeng stele cf. A. B. Griswold
and Prasert na Nagara, 'The Ramkhamhaeng stele' (q.v.). Inscriptions in Khmer
and Thai ran *pari passu* for some time during this period, and during the reigns
of Ramkhamhaeng and his grandson, Lü Thai (up to ca1370).

262 **The world encompassed: the first European maritime empires
c. 800-1650.**
Geoffrey V. Scammell. London: Methuen, 1981. 538p. bibliog.
Ayudhya (often in contemporary literature referred to simply as 'Siam') became
in the 17th century the cosmopolitan nexus of an impressive assembly of foreign
trading companies' posts and shipping from both East and West. It owed much of
its pre-eminence, as the most important royal capital in Southeast Asia, to its
central position on the trade routes between Europe and China. This book is
recommended as an imaginative general introduction to the provenance, purposes
and life of these maritime traders and the ships which brought them so far to
form an unmistakable feature of Ayudhya's skyline, mingling masts and rigging
with the capital's temple spires. The author is Chairman of the British Commission
of the International Commission for Maritime History; his illustrated booklet,
The English chartered trading companies and the sea (Greenwich, England:
National Maritime Museum, 1983) is also recommended as a short, illustrated
guide to the English ships of the time and their charter conditions.

263 **The Dutch in 17th-century Thailand.**
George Vinal Smith, introduction by Constance M. Wilson.
De Kalb, Illinois: Northern University Press, 1977. 200p. bibliog.
(Center for Southeast Asian Studies, Special Report, no. 16).
The depiction of the cosmopolitan society of 17th-century Ayudhya and the
early history of the VOC (Dutch East India Company) are substantially advanced
by this study. The book spans the years between 1604 and 1700 and deals with
the company itself, with its European competitors (French, English and Danish)
and with the regional (in part Muslim) trading environment of its activities in
the East, and of its factory at Ayudhya, which acted as a staging post for trade as
far as Japan. The author's principal researches were of the VOC's voluminous
records at The Hague, and for non-readers of Dutch his work provides a useful
précis of relevant archival and secondary material in that language; he also
supplies a glossary of contemporary Thai and Dutch terminology and lists
Thai and Dutch leaders concerned.

264 **History of Siam in the reign of H. M. Somdetch Pra Narai and other kings.**
Translated from the French by Samuel J. Smith. Bangkok: S. J. Smith, 1880. 115p.

This is a compilation of translated materials represented as contemporary French accounts of episodes from the late Ayudhya period. It is of interest particularly for an almost blow-by-blow description of the Burmese attack on, and shelling, looting and burning of the city in 1767.

265 **Beschrijvinge van de Oost Indische Compagnie.** (The records of the East India Company.)
Pieter van Dam, edited by F. W. Stapel, Baron van Boetzelaer van Asperen en Dubbeldam. The Hague: Rijks Geschiedkundige Publicatien, 1927-54. 4 parts in 7 vols.

Dutch trade relations with Ayudhya reached their zenith with the trade treaty of 1664, preceding by nearly two centuries the treaty concluded for the English East India Company with King Mongkut in Bangkok by Sir John Bowring, in 1855. These voluminous papers by van Dam represent the major record of the VOC's (Dutch East India Company's) transactions in the East Indies and Siam in the 17th century.

266 **A new Tamnan about Ayudhya.**
Michael Vickery. *Journal of the Siam Society,* vol. 63, part 2 (July 1975), p. 123-86. bibliog.

This extensive review article re-examines the primary source material on Ayudhya and offers an alternative interpretation to that advanced by Charnvit Kasetsiri in *The rise of Ayudhya* (q.v.).

267 **The 2/k 125 fragment: a lost chronicle of Ayudhya.**
Michael Vickery. *Journal of the Siam Society*, vol. 65, part 1 (Jan. 1977), p. 1-80. illus.

This article relates to the discovery by the author of what appears to be a new fragment of the Ayudhya chronicles. The article gives the text, with a photograph of part of the original fragment, and includes a translation and a commentary, in which he postulates Angkor as an economic rival to early 14th-century Ayudhya. The power of Angkor was a result of its advantageous position as a trading centre at the four-river confluence of the Mekong River near Phnom Penh.

268 **Ayudhya and the rearward part of the world.**
O. W. Wolters. *Journal of the Royal Asiatic Society* (1968, parts 3 & 4), p. 167-78. bibliog.

The article deals with problems facing King Naresvara (Naresuan, 1590-1605) at Ayudhya in the critical year 1592, and the bold and statesman-like strokes by which he evaded several warlike threats — especially by sending a tribute mission to Peking to neutralize pressure from the 'Napoleon of Japan', Hideyoshi. Bibliographic notes suggest further reading on both the historical and the poetic literary heritage of the period.

269 **The abridged royal chronicle of Ayudhya of Prince Paramanuchit-chinorot.**
David K. Wyatt. *Journal of the Siam Society*, vol. 61, part 1 (Jan. 1973), p. 25-50.

Translates one of the important short versions of the Ayudhya chronicles. The abridged text, prepared by Rama III in 1810, is reproduced in this article.

Transitional: King Taksin and Thonburi (1767-82)

270 **Somdet Phra Chao Tak Sin, le roi de Thonburi.** (Somdet Phra Chao Tak Sin, the king of Thonburi.)
Jacqueline de Fels. Paris: Sorbonne University, 1976. 2 vols. bibliog. microfiche.

This mass of documentation interpreted by the author in French deals with Taksin's régime at Thonburi in the disturbed but artistically important interim between the kingdoms of Ayudhya and Bangkok.

271 **Kingship and political integration in traditional Siam, 1767-1824.**
Lorraine Marie Gesick. Ann Arbor, Michigan: University Microfilms International, 1976. 198p. maps. bibliog. (PhD thesis for Cornell University).

This thesis deals with the role of Taksin, within the traditional conceptions of kingship in Thailand, in the evolution of the new administrative structure of the kingdom which was eventually enacted at Thonburi following the fall of Ayudhya in 1767. The author overlaps this fragmented interim with a comparative study of the legal system of Ayudhya, the efforts of Taksin to legitimize his own application of this to the new situation, and the more flexible interpretation of the Buddhist principle of kingship (*dhamma*) by Rama I in the new capital of Bangkok after Taksin's failure to establish himself at Thonburi. An interesting sub-theme is the interplay of centralism and regionalism (*muang*) during the period.

272 **The Thai monarchy in the Ban Phlu Luang period 1688-1767.**
   Busakorn Lailert. Ann Arbor, Michigan: University Microfilms International, 1972. 386p. bibliog. (PhD thesis for the University of London).

This thesis covers the closed period of Ayudhya's history, when foreign influences were excluded following the death of King Narai. The research and bibliography provide a useful contribution by filling an otherwise little-documented gap in the historical picture of the declining phase of King Narai's empire.

273 **A history of modern Thailand, 1767-1942.**
   Barend Jan Terwiel. St. Lucia, Australia: University of Queensland Press, 1983. 379p. maps. bibliog. glossary.

This short history performs a service in the opening sequence by condensing a wide selection of primary and secondary materials dealing with the fragmented period following the fall of Ayudhya in 1767. The author includes a character study of Taksin, the protagonist of this period, and offsets the conciseness of the text with detailed explanatory and bibliographic notes. The book deals in similar vein, reign by reign, with the more reliably documented era of the Chakri dynasty founded at Bangkok in 1782, and concludes with the pre-war, military-political power struggles initiated by the coup of 1932. The Bangkok period is well covered elsewhere, but the author's straightforward narrative style makes this volume a useful short, general introduction to Thailand's modern history, and especially her customs; it should be read in conjunction with the political interpretations of fuller accounts.

The Bangkok period (1782-)

The Chakri (Rama) dynasty: I (1782-1851)

274 **Cambodia before the French: politics in a tributary kingdom 1794-1848.**
   David P. Chandler. Ann Arbor, Michigan: University Microfilms International, 1973. 212p. bibliog. (PhD thesis for the University of Michigan).

The author combed Cambodian, Thai and Vietnamese sources for this analysis of Siam's attitude to Cambodia during the pre-modern Bangkok period. The border situation was as yet uncomplicated by the emergence of the French interest in Indochina. The Cambodians, squeezed between the powerful Vietnamese Emperor Gia Long to the east and avuncular Siamese neighbours to the west, proved unruly enough to avoid becoming a wholly client tributary state for much of the time.

275   **Cambodia's relations with Siam in the early Bangkok period:
the politics of a tributary state.**
David P. Chandler. *Journal of the Siam Society*, vol. 60, part 1
(Jan. 1972), p. 153-69.
This article is a shorter version of the author's thesis (q.v.).

276   **Journal of an embassy to the courts of Siam and Cochin China.**
John Crawfurd, introduction by David K. Wyatt.   Kuala
Lumpur: Oxford University Press, 1969. 598p. (Oxford in Asia
Reprints).

This is the author's account, originally published in two editions in 1828, of his
mission on behalf of the government of British India to Siam and Cochin China in
1822. The mission did not achieve a great deal, but it set the scene for subsequent
negotiations culminating in the important treaty of 1855, and Dr. Crawfurd's
observations themselves form an indispensable corpus of contemporary record.
The handsome 'Oxford in Asia' volume includes the original drawings and Thai
and tribal-language vocabulary. A short introduction by David K. Wyatt has been
added, with bibliographic notes.

277   **The mission to Siam and Hue, the capital of Cochin China,
in the years 1821-22.**
George Finlayson.   London: John Murray, 1826. 427p. plate.
The author accompanied John Crawfurd as surgeon and naturalist on this mission
during the early 1820s. This account consists of Finlayson's journal, which was
published posthumously. It contains an interesting description of contemporary
Bangkok and its people. Finlayson found Bangkok still very much an aquatic city,
resembling present-day riverside villages, and almost entirely lacking the modern
development of houses built of brick, except for temples and monasteries. He
describes the wooden houses, which either float at the river or canal edges and are
moveable, or are built along the banks on stilts. The book has a frontispiece
consisting of a contemporary engraving of Bangkok by Edward Emden, and an
introduction and memoir of the author by Sir Thomas Stamford Raffles.

278   **Henry Burney: a political biography.**
D. G. E. Hall.   London: Oxford University Press, for the School
of Oriental and African Studies (University of London), 1974.
330p. bibliog.

In this book the author fills in much of the family and personal background of
Henry Burney, the military secretary at Penang, who was charged with the crucial
and delicate diplomatic negotiations with Thailand in 1825-27. Burney's brief was
to protect British interests in Perak and Selangor following the Thai invasion of
Kedah in 1821. He was later appointed as British resident at Ava, the then
Burmese capital; the book contributes material required to relate the Thai and
Burmese aspects of the historically important Burney papers (q.v.) and to assess
the impact of Burney's personality on the negotiations.

History. The Bangkok period (1782-). The Chakri (Rama)
dynasty: I (1782-1851)

279 **The organisation of Thai society in the early Bangkok period,
1782-1873.**
Akin Rabibhadana. Ithaca, New York: Cornell University Press,
1969. bibliog. (Southeast Asis Program Data Paper, no. 74).
This detailed study examines the concepts of kinship, kingship and administration
in the early Bangkok period. The author shows how the division of society
into noble (*nai*), commoner (*phrai*) and slave (*that*) classes, with closely defined
individual superior-to-inferior regulations, was used to overcome the perennial
manpower shortage – until this system began to be eroded by the influx of
Chinese labour.

280 **Francis Light and the ladies of Thalang.**
E. H. S. Simmonds. *Journal of the Malaysian Branch of the
Royal Asiatic Society*, vol. 38, no. 2 (1965), p. 213-28.
This paper presents an intriguing part of the story of Captain Light's acquaintance
with Thai personalities at a time when the country was at war with Burma over
the area including Kedah and the islands, out of which Light selected Penang as an
East India Company trading base with the agreement of Warren Hastings. The
author gives further references to contemporary materials. Penang, or Prince of
Wales Island, was the first British settlement of Malaya, and the East India
Company struck a coinage for it cf. *Coins and coinages of the Straits Settlements
and British Malaya*, by F. Pridmore (Singapore, 1955); the Royal Mint was later
responsible for providing the coinage of Siam cf. *The coinage of Siam*, by R. Le
May (q.v.).

281 **Siam under Rama III, 1824-51.**
Walter Francis Vella. New York: Augustin, 1957. 180p.
chronology. maps. bibliog. (Monographs of the Association for
Asian Studies, 4).
The reign of Rama III completed the re-formation of the traditional Thai state
after the Burmese sacking of Ayudhya in 1767. The author describes the new
stable, unitary state, based on close and direct links between king, people, monkhood and an administration not yet expanded, and possessng a wide area of vassal
and diplomatic contacts, some of which concerned Britain and the northern
Malay states, Kedah, Kelantan, Pattani and Trengganu. The period covered by this
volume includes the treaty negotiated by Henry Burney on behalf of the government of India cf. *The Burney papers* (q.v.).

282 **The restoration of Thailand under Rama I, 1782-1809.**
Klaus Wenk, translated from the German by Gresley Stahl.
Tucson, Arizona: University of Arizona Press, 1968. 149p.
bibliog. (Association for Asian Studies Monographs and Papers,
no. 24).

This is an analysis of Thai source material with comments based on various
external writings, which are listed in a comprehensive bibliography comprising
both types of material. Among the problems for the new capital was the securing
of the western frontier, which was one of the reasons for moving the capital
across the river. Further Burmese invasions did in fact have to be met during the
period covered by the book. It provides a useful introduction to the contemporary
chronicles, and to the circumstances of the new foundation at Bangkok.

The Chakri (Rama) dynasty: II (1851-1932)

283 **The accession of King Mongkut.**
William L. Bradley. *Journal of the Siam Society*, vol. 57, part 1
(Jan. 1969), p. 149-62.

The author deals with the succession crisis at the end of the third reign of the
Chakri dynasty, which led to the accession of King Mongkut.

284 **Louis and the king of Siam.**
William S. Bristowe. London: Chatto & Windus, 1976. 160p.
map. illus.

This is a delightful and very readable piece of research on the life and times of the
son, Louis, of Anna Leonowens. Louis grew up alongside the young King Chulalongkorn, whose tutor was Anna, and Louis remained his close friend. Most of his
working years, the 1880s to early 1900s, were spent in the teak area of Chiang
Mai and northern Thailand, then a boisterous and unruly region under local *chaos*
(chieftains); in the absence of the modern roads this area was a fortnight's journey
by boat and elephant from Bangkok. This distance led to Louis acting in some
degree as a local free agent of the king; on one occasion, armed with hunting
rifles, he and a few business companions defended the ancient walls of Lampang
against a posse of Shan raiders. The author's information was culled partly from
interviews with servants and others, with living memory of the people and events
concerned. A hobby of the author's, during his own working life in Thailand, was
spiders, of which he was inordinately fond, and on which his papers earned him
distinction through much of his lifetime (1901-79).

History. The Bangkok period (1782-). The Chakri (Rama)
dynasty: II (1851-1932)

285 **The provincial administration of Siam, 1892-1945.**
Tej Bunnag. Kuala Lumpur: Oxford University Press, 1977.
322p. map. bibliog.

This study analyses the functioning of the important Ministry of the Interior
under Prince Damrong during the key period of administrative reform initiated
by King Chulalongkorn. It contains a good account of the evolution of the
country's provincial administrative system.

286 **Lords of life; a history of the kings of Thailand.**
Prince Chula Chakrabongse, introduction by H. R. Trevor-Roper.
Bangkok: DD Books, 1982. 3rd rev. ed. 353p. bibliog. foldout
map. bibliog. photos.

This revised edition of the original work of 1960 adds a short summary of the
earlier periods to preface the main subject, which is the Chakri dynasty of the
Bangkok period. Written with charm and from the inside sources of a member of
that dynastic family, the account concentrates on the constitutional phase within
living memory. It includes numerous portrait photographs.

287 **Les relations entre la France et la Thaïlande (Siam) au XIXème
siècle d'après les archives des affaires étrangères.** (Relations
between France and Thailand [Siam] in the 19th century with
reference to the archives of foreign affairs.)
Pensri (Suvanij) Duke. Bangkok: Chalermnit, 1962. 328p.
maps. bibliog.

The author, a professor of history at the Sorbonne and Chulalongkorn universities,
has compiled a valuable monograph outlining the complexities of Franco-Thai
relations during the period of Siam's modernization and renewal of contacts with
Western powers, up to the end of King Chulalongkorn's reign. The first phase
results in the treaties of 1856, 1863 and 1867; a second phase in the fraught
treaty of 1893, and a third phase in three further accords during the first decade
of the 20th century – the book appends these treaties, and provides useful maps
showing the disputed frontier areas on the Mekong River. Cf. also the author's
*La politique étrangère du Siam, Thaïlande, pendant la première période du minis-
tère du Prince Devawongse 1885-1900* (Paris: International Federation of University Graduates, 104 folios typescript [n.p., n.d.]. bibliog.)

288 **Franco-British rivalry over Siam 1896-1904.**
M. F. Goldman. *Journal of Southeast Asian Studies*, vol. 3,
no. 2 (1972), p. 210-28.

Deals with the protracted negotiations over French legal and territorial claims
in the trans-Mekong region around the ancient kingdom of Luang Prabang (Laos),
which culminated in concessions by Siam in the Franco-Siamese treaty of 1904.

289 **The contest for Siam, 1889-1902: a study in diplomatic rivalry.**
Chandran Jeshurun. Kuala Lumpur: University of Malaysia
Press, 1977. 383p. map. bibliog.
This study makes extensive use of contemporary, private, diplomatic papers to
provide a deeper analysis of the unexpected crisis in Anglo-French relations over
the upper Mekong and Siam in 1893. The book quotes from contemporary
Foreign Office records and from the private papers of Lord Rosebery, who was
foreign secretary from 1892-94, and Lord Salisbury, who was the then prime
minister. British ministers felt that French penetration into the sensitive region
near China's border with Burma prejudiced Britain's Monroe Doctrine policy in
relation to India. The British concern was the French threat to Burma following
the annexation of the kingdom of Ava in 1886. The author exposes a new view of
British foreign policy at the time; his account makes exciting reading of the inner
story of a moment of wide and acute international tension which came close to
dissolving Siam's long-preserved independence from colonialism.

290 **Hikayat Patani: the story of Patani.**
A. Leeuw, David K. Wyatt. The Hague: Martinus Nijhoff, 1970.
2 vols. (Biblioteka Indonesia Series, no. 5). maps. bibliog.
The Abdullah *hikayat* (chronicle) was recently rediscovered although its existence
in the Malacca sultanate has been known since 1883. These two volumes relate
the story of its provenance, fill in the historical setting of the foundation of the
Malay state of Patani on the Gulf of Thailand, and give a text translated from the
Malay followed by a commentary and conclusions. A facsimile of part of the
Malay text is also given. Though its historical precision is not vouched for in
detail, the *hikayat* is of considerable interest for the light which it sheds on Patani,
which was still largely a Malay province of southern Thailand and on the sultanate
itself and its relationship with this region in earlier times.

291 **History of Wat Pavaraniveça.**
Robert Lingat. *Journal of the Siam Society*, vol. 26 (1933),
p. 73-102. photos. pullout plan.
This article hinges on the appointment, in 1837, of the future King Mongkut as
abbot to a monastery which played an important part in the process of law
formation in early modern Thailand, both under Mongkut when he became king,
and under his successor, King Chulalongkorn. The author discusses the careers of
some noted leaders of the *sangha* (monkhood), and supplies portrait photographs.

292 **Mongkut: the king of Siam.**
Abbot Low Moffat. Ithaca, New York: Cornell University Press,
1961. 254p. bibliog.
This book, by an abbot, is an interesting and thorough account of the life and
times of King Mongkut (Rama IV, 1851-68), who was himself a former abbot.
Mongkut began the modernization of Siam, instituted contacts with Queen
Victoria and appointed as governess at his own court, Anna Leonowens, whose
largely fictitious memoirs, *The English governess at the Siamese court* (q.v.), is
counteracted by this volume.

293   **Socio-economic institutions and cultural change in Siam 1851-1910: a documentary survey.**
Edited by Chatthip Nartsupha, Suthy Prasartset.   Singapore: Institute of Southeast Asian Studies & Social Science Association of Thailand, 1977. 80p. glossary.

This compilation consists of translations from twenty-one contemporary documentary sources relating to such matters as marriage, elopement and abduction; *corvée* labour and administrative tattooing; digging *klongs* (canals); rice cultivation; and training of goldsmiths.

294   **River road to China: the Mekong River expedition, 1866-1873.**
Milton E. Osborne.   New York: Liveright, 1975. 249p. maps. illus.

This study gathers together primary source material on Siam's relations with Laos and France in the reign of King Mongkut. In particular, the book describes the exacerbatory effect of the exploratory expedition of 1866-68 led by Lagrée-Garnier. The purpose of the expedition was to consolidate French interests in Cambodia, and it traversed Thai territory bordering the Mekong River between Phnom Penh and Chiang Hung.

295   **Siam: treaties with foreign powers, 1920-27.**
Edited by Francis B. Sayre.   Bangkok: Royal Thai Government, 1928. 280p.

The publication deals, from a legal standpoint, with treaties between Siam and Japan as well as Western countries during the 1920s.

296   **Siam and Sir James Brooke.**
Nicholas Tarling.   *Journal of the Siam Society*, vol. 48, no. 2 (Nov. 1960), p. 43-72.

Describes negotiations conducted by Sir James Brooke towards the treaty which was concluded by Sir John Bowring in Bangkok in 1855. To avoid encouragement of the mounting French pressures in Indochina, the British side in the negotiations moderated its demands for the return of the Malayan provinces.

297 **The dynastic chronicle, Bangkok era, the fourth reign B.E.
2394-2411 (1851-1868).**
Chao Phraya Thipakorawong, translated by Chadin Flood,
E. Thadeus Flood. Tokyo: Centre for Asian Cultural Studies,
1965-74. vols. 1-5.

These five volumes constitute a massive work of editing and translation from the
Bangkok chronicle of Chao Phraya Thipakorawong (Kham Bunnag), relating to
the reign of King Mongkut (Rama IV). The title gives both the Buddha Era dates
and their conversion to AD. The text is contained in volumes 1 and 2; volumes 3
and 4 consist of annotations and commentaries with a bibliography; volume 5 is
the general index.

298 **Chaiyo! King Vajiravudh and the development of Thai
nationalism.**
Walter Francis Vella, Dorothy B. Vella. Honolulu: University
Press of Hawaii, 1978. 347p. bibliog. illus.

Chaiyo! (victory) was a rallying cry coined by King Vajiravudh (Rama VI,
1910-25) as part of his mission to rouse the nation from lethargy to nationalistic
fervour. The policy was based on reviving the army, and the king's personal guards
(the 'Wild Tiger' Corps), achieved some notoriety. Vajiravudh died in 1925 at the
early age of forty-four, but the militarist and nationalist mood which he inspired
persisted, and led, after the military coup against his successor in 1932, to the
army-based dictatorship of Field Marshal Phibul Songkhram in 1938. The book
deals with this historical phase in readable form, relating fascinating vignettes to
illuminate the author's thoughtful interpretation of a significant aspect of the
origin of contemporary Thai political life.

299 **The impact of the West on government in Thailand.**
Walter Francis Vella. Berkeley, California: University of
California Press, 1955. 410p. bibliog.

This is a comparative study, in which the author argues from considerable
personal experience in Thailand, that the past century of contacts with the West,
which he examines in detail, has resulted in relatively little enduring influence on
the country's style of government.

300 **State and society in the reign of Mongkut 1851-1868: Thailand on the eve of modernization.**
Constance M. Wilson. Ann Arbor, Michigan: University Microfilms International, 1971. 2 vols. bibliog. (PhD thesis for Cornell University).

This massive integration of material builds up the most complete picture available of the transformation of Siamese society under King Mongkut into a state capable of the take-off into modernity which took place in the reign of his successor, King Chulalongkorn, in the last quarter of the 19th century and the first decade of the 20th century. The thesis includes an exhaustive bibliography, and should be of particular value to scholars interested in the social foundations of Thailand's modern economy.

The Chakri (Rama) dynasty: III: Constitutional monarchy (1932-42)

301 **Ma vie mouvementée et mes 21 ans d'exile en Chine populaire.**
(My life of ups and downs and my twenty-one years of exile in People's China.)
Pridi Banomyong (Luang Pradist Manudharm). Paris: P. Banomyong, 1972. 320p. map. plate.

An exceptionally interesting volume, not only (as David K. Wyatt comments in *Thailand: a short history* [q.v.]), for what it says, but also for what it does not. Nai Pridi Phanomyong (thus usually transliterated, or simply 'Pridi') is one of the most remarkable figures of the constitutional period of Thai politics: progenitor of Thai socialism; political architect behind the coup of 1932 and ensuing constitutional changes; regent; prime minister; leader of the Free Thai resistance movement, and ultimately an exile in Peking. From there, he returned to live in Paris (where he was educated), still a significant influence for Thai intellectuals. Pridi twice left the country in circumstances of political confusion, bound up with repercussions after the death of of King Ananda in 1946 (cf. Rayne Kruger, *The devil's discus* [q.v.]), and the coup of 1947. The book is in a sense the author's political testament. It covers the international and internal situation in relation to the coming to Thailand of the Second World War; immediate post-war events; the United Nations; and developments in the People's Republic of China. The frontispiece is a colour plate of *Cheopsis aurifrons pridii*, a new sub-species of bird named after Pridi as leader of the Free Thais (cf. Smithsonian Miscellaneous Collections, vol. 106).

302 **The end of the absolute monarchy in Siam.**
Benjamin A. Batson. Singapore: Oxford University Press, 1984.
372p. bibliog.

Batson traces the evolution of modern Thai politics in the pre-war period. The book is of particular interest for its treatment of King Prajadhipok's abortive attempts, prior to his abdication in 1935, to reconcile the emergent civilian administrative structure of constitutional monarchy with the country's conservative military establishment.

303 **Siam: the crossroads.**
Sir Josiah Crosby. London: Hollis & Carter, 1945. 174p.
endpaper maps.

Crosby was British ambassador in Bangkok at the outset of the war. The book gives percipient first-hand impressions of the institution of constitutional monarchy in the immediate aftermath of the coup of 1932. It also describes the then Thai government's interest in regaining territory ceded to France in 1893 as a factor in its acceptance of Japanese demands accompanying the landings in 1941.

304 **L'évolution de la Thaïlande contemporaine.** (The emergence of modern Thailand.)
Pierre Fistie. Paris: Armand Colin, 1967. 390p. map. bibliog.

The author, a French specialist in Thai political history, outlines the traditional administration of the country and then compares this with the emergent officialdom of the civil service and the military during the early stages of constitutional monarchy.

305 **Japan's relations with Thailand 1928-41.**
Edward Thadeus Flood. Ann Arbor, Michigan: University Microfilms International, 1968. 2 vols. bibliog. (PhD thesis for the University of Washington).

This thesis is of particular interest for its meticulous piecing together of the story of Japan's intervention and mediation in 1940-41 in the Thai-French affair over trans-Mekong territorial rights. The author discusses the strategic implications of Japan's lend-leasing of bomber aircraft to Thailand, and of the extension of runways for these. He compares French, Japanese and Thai accounts of the Thai-French naval engagement of Ho Chang on the Mekong (July 1941) — (incidentally characterizing Sivaram's presentation of the outcome of the battle in *Mekong clash and Far East crisis* as 'distorted'). Among the author's many conclusions, one is an exposition of the non-affinity resulting from the Thai and Japanese backgrounds.

306 **Power and Parliament in Thailand: the futile challenge 1968-71.**
   David L. Morell. Ann Arbor, Michigan: University Microfilms
   International, 1974. 2 vols. bibliog. (PhD thesis for Princeton
   University).

This exhaustive study, supported by a valuable bibliography, examines the
structure of political power in Thailand in relation to the constitution of
1968. The author assesses the effectiveness of the constitution in face of the
debilitating alternation of extra-parliamentary forces exercised by the monarchy,
the bureaucracy and the mechanism of military rule.

307 **The modernization of a bureaucratic polity.**
   Fred W. Riggs. Honolulu: East-West Center Press, 1967. 470p.
   bibliog.

This is a very thorough and well-presented study of the gradual evolution of
Thailand's modern administrative system. The author traces the process from the
time when European-headed boards were set up during the absolute monarchy
in 1892; via the 1932 coup by foreign-educated middle officers which set up the
first constitution, and into the post-war phase of uneasy compromise between
intermittent Western-style party politics and intervening coups by various military-
backed power cliques.

308 **Years of blindness.**
   H. G. Quaritch Wales. New York: Thomas Y. Crowell, 1943.
   332p. bibliog.

Examines the immediate antecedents of the coup of 1932, which ended the
absolute monarchy in Thailand and instituted the period of constitutional
monarchy.

World War II (1942-45)

The Thai resistance movement

309 **The Southeast Asian world.**
   John F. Cady. St. Louis, Missouri: Forum Press, 1977. 80p.
   (The World of Asia Series).

This concise overview contains a summary of the course and effect of the Second
World War in Southeast Asia (p. 50-70).

310 **S.O.E. in the Far East.**
   Charles Cruikshank. London: Oxford University Press, 1983.
   285p.

An account of the clandestine missions in Thailand and elsewhere in the Far
East of the SOE (Special Operations Executive) of the Allies during the Second
World War.

311 **Bangkok top secret.**
Andrew Gilchrist. London: Hutchinson, 1970. 231p. maps.
photos.

Frustration is an inevitable theme in this diary of the efforts of the members of Force 136 to establish clandestine bases in remote areas of Thailand, as a prelude to the planned invasion by a British task force in 1945 which never took place. The author, Sir Andrew Gilchrist, was an officer in pre-war Thailand in the Foreign Service, in which he went on to make a distinguished career after the end of the war. His memoirs of his temporary service as a soldier in India and Ceylon, of his Thai friends in the force, of its leader, Peter Pointon, and of its activities in wartime Thailand, are of interest for their immediacy. Although published twenty-five years after the recorded events, the author wrote this diary while in hospital within months of the end of the war. The book is also of value for its contemporary photographs, and for its documentation of the author's contacts with General Hamada, and with the derelict remnants of the coolie labour force sent by the Japanese army to the Kra Isthmus in 1945.

312 **The Thai resistance movement during the Second World War.**
John B. Haseman, with an introduction by Frank C. Darling.
De Kalb, Illinois: Northern Illinois University, 1978. 192p.
maps. bibliog. (Special reports, no. 17).

This is a carefully researched account of resistance operations connected with Thailand during the Second World War, referring to OSS Force 136 and Free Thai contacts with British and American forces. The author exonerates Marshal Phibul Songkhram (the then war-time prime minister), from charges that he went further in his attitude to the Japanese occupiers than his country's best interests could justify.

313 **Siam and World War II.**
Direk Jayanama, English edition by Jane Godfrey Keyes.
Bangkok: Social Science Association of Thailand Press, 1966.
358p.

By the time Thailand became involved in the war the author, a university professor, judge, and government minister, was in an exceptional position to have an inside knowledge of the circumstances and the ensuing events. His reminiscences of these, and of personalities concerned with the Free Thai movement like Pridi Phanomyong and Puey Ungphakorn (the latter visited London during the war), make this book one of the significant documents of the period.

314 **The first Phibun government and its involvement in World War II.**
Charnvit Kasetsiri. *Journal of the Siam Society*, vol. 62, part 2
(1974), p. 25-88.

The paper assesses the role of Marshal Phibul Songkhram during the period of the Japanese occupation of Thailand, following the invasion of 1941.

315 **Southeast Asia under Japanese occupation.**
Edited by Alfred W. McCoy. New Haven, Connecticut: Yale
University Press, 1980. 302p. maps. (Yale University Southeast
Asia Studies Monographs, no. 2).

A general account of Japanese war-time activities in Southeast Asia, including
Thailand.

316 **Modern Far Eastern International relations.**
Harley F. MacNair, Donald F. Lach. New York: Van Nostrand;
London: Macmillan, 1950. 681p. maps. illus.

This is a massive study of the incidence and antecedents of the Second World War
in the Far East against a backcloth of American, Chinese and Japanese interests
in the arena of hostilities. See chapter 19 on 'Southeast Asia and Oceania' (p. 567-
606), containing an account of the arrival of the war and reactions in Thailand.
The book provides a striking aerial picture of the Burma road (p. 570).

317 **Thailand: the Japanese presence 1941-45.**
Chamsook Numnonda. Singapore: Institute of Southeast Asian
Studies, 1977. 142p. bibliog. (Research Notes and Discussions
Series, no. 6).

The author has compiled a detailed account and estimation, mainly from Thai
sources, of the Japanese occupation of Thailand, of the economic conditions
prevalent at the time, and of the Thai response to the occupation. He gives a
profile of the Thai resistance movement and the personnel involved, including
those trained in Britain and the USA, with a 'Who's who' guide to the key figures
in the Thai government and Free Thai movement. Texts of relevant historical
documents are appended.

318 **Into Siam: underground kingdom.**
Nicol Smith, Blake Clark. Indianapolis, Indiana: Bobbs-Merrill,
1946. 315p. endpaper maps.

A first-hand account of Thai resistance activities in the field during the Second
World War.

319 **Land of the moonflower.**
Gerald Sparrow. London: Elek, 1955. 242p. portrait photos.

Sparrow was a legal representative in Bangkok at the outbreak of war, and was
interned for its duration. The book contains his reminiscences of this time and
impressions of some leading personalities with whom he came into contact.

Allied prisoners-of-war; the Burma-Siam railway

320 Bamboo and bushido.
A. G. Allbury. London: Hale, 1955. Reprinted Corgi, 1975.
170p. drawings.

The author gives a graphic and grim account of his experiences as a prisoner-of-war
of the Japanese at Changi, in Singapore, and then at camps along the Burma-Siam
railway in Thailand such as Tarsao and Chungkai. The story ends with the author
being torpedoed in a Japanese troopship *en route* for Japan, and picked up by an
Allied submarine. *Bushido* of the title is the spirit of the warrior code, which
inspired the Imperial Japanese Army, and which some of its members expected
would also inspire the prisoners to make greater efforts towards building the
railway.

321 Return from the River Kwai.
Joan Blair, Clay Blair. London, Sydney: Macdonald & Jane's,
1979. 338p. endpaper maps. photos.

This book is a good read. Meticulously researched from official and naval sources,
the book tells the story of a group of Allied prisoners-of-war shipped by the
Japanese from Tamarkan camp on the Kwai River to work in Japan. The most
terrifying episodes transpire during the voyage, when the prisoners find themselves
sunk, alongside their Japanese captors, in the South China Sea.

322 Towards the setting sun: an escape from the Thailand-Burma railway, 1943.
James Bradley. London: Phillimore, 1982. 139p. maps. photos.

The circumstances of the prisoners-of-war working on the Burma-Siam railway
made it almost unthinkable to attempt to escape. The only feasible route lay
through hundreds of miles of hostile, malarial, virtually foodless jungle, with a
good chance of betrayal to the Japanese if any villagers were encountered *en
route*. From the diary of one of a party of ten officers who tried to make the
break from a cholera isolation camp, this book tells a gripping story of the escape,
and of its aftermath. The first third of the text describes the fate of the army
captured at Singapore and follows a party ('F force') sent to one of the worst
areas of railway construction; the final part describes the escape and how it
ended.

81

323 **Railroad of death.**
John Coast. London: Commodore Press, 1946. 256p. map.

Written shortly after the end of the war, this account is a close-up, diary-type
reminiscence by a discerning officer, who became a prisoner-of-war, and witnessed
the railway construction in jungle camps as far 'up-river' as Chungkai; at the same
time he made contact with Thai resistance workers (like 'Boon Pong' to whom he
dedicates the book), who helped the prisoners with supplies and information. The
author has painstakingly made his story as accurate and balanced an account of
reactions to military and human stresses on all sides, as available records would
permit.

324 **Miracle on the River Kwai.**
Ernest Gordon. Glasgow: Collins, 1963. 108p. Reprinted,
London: Fontana, 1977.

The author recounts personal reminiscences, recollected a few years after his
release, of experiences building the Burma-Siam railway as a prisoner-of-war of
the Japanese. In describing his reactions to the hardships he endured in the jungle
camps which the prisoners built and occupied, the author stresses the importance
which he attached to his religious belief.

325 **War dead of the British Commonwealth 1939-45 buried at
Kanchanaburi War Cemetery.**
Great Britain Commonwealth War Graves Commission. Maiden-
head, England: The Commission, 1983. 50p. amended. map. plan.

This register is one of two recording the names of the Commonwealth soldiers
buried at the main camps occupied by Allied prisoners-of-war, who were engaged
in building the Burma-Siam railway. The volume contains an amended list (part 1,
Abb-Coz). The previous edition of the register was published in 1958.

326 **The Burma-Siam railway: the secret diary of Dr. Robert Hardie,
1942-45.**
Robert Hardie. London: Imperial War Museum, 1983. 192p.
maps. illus.

The author was a medical officer with the FMS Volunteer Force and became a
prisoner-of-war after the fall of Singapore. During the subsequent three-and-a-
half years he accompanied groups of Allied prisoners to jungle camps like
Takanun, Chungkai and Tamuang, performing the difficult and, at times,
harrowing professional task of preserving the health and lives of the prisoners, as
far as conditions and supplies permitted. This book consists of the diaries which
he kept throughout this period; at a crucial stage he buried them in the Chungkai
cemetery to avoid their confiscation by the Japanese camp guards. The diaries
form a vivid and valuable war record, augmented by the author's own sketches
and accurately-observed water-colours.

327 **Death railway.**

Clifford Kinvig, introduction by Russell Braddon, sketches by John Batchelor. London: Pan, 1973. 160p. short bibliog. illus.

This is one of the liberally-illustrated popular war histories published for Ballantine. It presents a detailed description of the building of the Burma-Siam railway, including the Burma side, aided by war photographs and whole-page sketches reconstructing episodes from camp life, and work in the jungle. The effect is to produce a somewhat sensational impression, based on collected stories of experiences on the railway.

328 **Bricks without straw.**

Michael S. Watts. In: *Convoy*, no. 4. Edited by Robin Maugham. London: Collins, 1946. p. 28-40.

This article consists of the author's reflections and recollections, written while fresh in his mind, of his experiences as an officer in charge of working parties, cookhouses, concert parties, and at times grave-diggers, as a prisoner-of-war in Thailand, 1942-45. The implication of the title, 'Bricks without straw', is a tribute to the ingenuity of the prisoners in creating a semblance of normality out of rather sparse material resources.

Population and Minorities

General

329 **Asia-Pacific Population Programme News.**
     Bangkok: Economic and Social Commission for Asia and the
     Pacific, Population Division. ca 1950- . quarterly.
This magazine-type UN publication includes general regional population programme surveys, with occasional features on progress and planning in Thailand.

330 **The fertility of Thai women.**
     John E. Knodel, Visid Prachuabmoh. Bankok: Institute of
     Population Studies, Chulalongkorn University, 1973. 87p.
     bibliog.
This report embodies the results of the first rounds of the longitudinal rural and
urban study of social, economic and demographic change in Thailand.

331 **Thailand's population: facts, trends, problems and policies.**
     Ralph Thomlinson. Bangkok: R. Thomlinson, 1971. 118p.
     maps. bibliog. tables.
A good, general overview of Thailand's population including specific treatment of
urban Chinese, southern Malay-speaking Muslim, and other minority groups, and
of official policies relating to population problems. The author notes some
differences concerning the latter over the 1970 census (q.v.), which had a gestation
period of seven years before publication.

The tribes

332 **Akha and Miao: problems of applied anthropology in Further India.**
Hugo Adolf Bernatzik, translated from the German by Alois Nagler. New Haven, Connecticut: Human Relations Area Files, 1970. 2 vols. bibliog. illus.

The large group of Akha and Meo tribes, whose origins, precise nomenclature and transliterations are subjects of variant interpretation by anthropologists cited by the author, are described in these two volumes in an encyclopaedic manner. The work (originally published in 1947, and therefore without the findings of subsequent field researches) gives a total picture of the traditional life and customs of these tribes in the context of their cross-border habitats; migrants into Thai areas have since been coming under pressure of incalculable change. The work examines kingship and kinship affinities and terminology, spirit beliefs, effects of missionary activity and of Thai government policy, and contains numerous illustrations of tribal types, arts and crafts, and an extensive general anthropological bibliography in Western languages.

333 **The spirits of the yellow leaves.**
Hugo Adolf Bernatzik, with the collaboration of Emmy Bernatzik, translated from the German by E. W. Dickes. London: Robert Hale, 1958. 222p. photos.

The author who is an anthropologist, assisted by his wife, set out to discover the original inhabitants of the arena of Southeast Asia where the influx of Indian and Chinese cultural influences stimulated most tribal migration and change. The book describes their findings in a readable and engaging manner, introducing the reader to primitive peoples from the seagoing Semang of Mergui to the Phi Tong Luang of the inner jungle – the picturesquely named tribe of the title in Thai and Lao, translated as 'spirits of the yellow leaves', thus called because of their extreme evasiveness; the only trace the seeker will find of them is the yellowing banana leaves of their abandoned beds.

334 **Paysans de la forêt.** (Farmers of the forest.)
Louis Bouchet. Paris: Ecole Française d'Extrême-Orient, 1975. vol. 105. 150p. 6 maps. 30 plates.

This is a somewhat sentimental exegesis on the *swidden* (slash-and-burn) farmers of the mountainous regions of Indochina. Though the author collected relatively little material specifically on northern Thailand, the same culture and tribes are to a large extent common to the region as a whole, and indeed more widely through the Indonesian archipelago. The book is therefore of interest in relation to Thailand, because it demonstrates the extension of this tribal system; it includes a wealth of plates which show a people who, in the author's estimation, deserve to be left to carry on with their traditional methods of agriculture, undragooned by central authorities, as social changes may do irreparable damage to their lifestyle.

335 **The Southeast Asian Negrito; further notes on the Negrito of south Thailand.**
John H. Brandt. *Journal of the Siam Society*, vol. 52, no. 2 (July 1964), p. 27-43. photos.

This article adduces further information on the Semang of peninsular Malaya and Thailand, including the 'sea gypsies' of Thailand's west coastal area, and provides photographs of Negrito types and also of blow-pipe weapons. The effects of separation along the Wallace line are illustrated.

336 **Eléments comparatifs sur les habitations des ethnies de langues Thaï.** (Comparative elements in dwelling houses of Tai-speaking tribes.)
Sophie Charpentier, Pierre Clement. Paris: Institut de l'Environnement, 1978. 258p. bibliog. illus. (Centre d'Etudes et de Recherches Architecturales ENSBA).

Numerous large drawings of tribal dwelling houses form a most interesting element in this large-format report of a comparative ethno-architectural study of spatial construction through a wide variety of tribal areas speaking Tai-based languages. The volume contains a useful bibliography on relevant tribal matters in Western languages.

337 **Muang metaphysics: a study of northern Thai myth and ritual.**
Richard Davis. PhD thesis for Sydney University, 1974. 467p. bibliog. (Unpublished, available from Sydney University).

The Muang of this thesis are the northern Thai people (the word in standard Thai refers to country or state). The study deals in depth with the ethos of villagers living near the Nan River in northern Thailand: their life cycle (birth, marriage and death ceremonies), the annual agricultural cycle, and their system of beliefs. The author deals in particular with the uses of the calendar; the putrefaction and the princeliness associated with the New Year; and rites connected with clan and tribal mythology.

338 **The T'in (Mal), dry rice cultivators of northern Thailand and northern Laos.**
William Y. Dessaint. *Journal of the Siam Society*, vol. 69 parts 1 & 2 (Jan. & July 1981), p. 107-37. bibliog. photos.

The T'in (or Mal) are the third most numerous hilltribe of the northern regions, after the Karen and Hmong (or Meo). This illustrated anthropological study describes the linguistic (Lawa or Mon-Khmer) and demographic features of the tribe, as well as its methods of dry rice cultivation.

339 **Agricultural products and household budgets in a Shan peasant village in northwest Thailand: a quantitative description.**
E. Paul Durrenberger. Athens, Ohio: Ohio University Press, 1978. 142p. bibliog. (Center for International Studies, Southeast Asia Series, no. 49).

This paper is a close-up study of a Shan village, its family and financial arrangements and cropping system. The bibliography contains further useful material on the lowland tribes inhabiting the border region near Burma.

340 **A history of Assam.**
Sir Edward Gait, revised and enlarged by B. K. Barua, H. V. S. Murthy. Calcutta, India: Thacker & Spink, 1963. 3rd rev. ed. 427p. maps (one pullout). bibliog. notes.

Originally published in 1906 (2nd rev. ed. in 1926), this history gives a good account of the Ahom branch of the Tai who migrated to Assam and developed an Indic-based script of their own, which they used to record a chronicle on tablets prepared from the aloes-wood bark.

341 **Migrants of the mountains: the cultural ecology of the Blue Miao.**
William Robert Geddes. London: Oxford University Press, 1976. 274p. bibliog. photos.

Presents an interesting and readable description of the ancient origin (in southern China) and way of life of a tribe, known as the Blue Miao, a branch of the widely dispersed Miao (Meo or Hmong, as they prefer to be called) of northern Thailand. The author accomplishes a dual purpose, analysing the social customs of the tribe, its marriage, clan, working, agricultural and landholding (or shifting) systems, and at the same time offering an estimate of the ecological effect of its main crop, opium, on its present and future society.

342 **Maternity and its rituals in Bang Chan.**
Jane Richardson Hanks. Ithaca, New York: Cornell University Press, 1964. 128p. bibliog. (Southeast Asia Program Data Paper, no. 51).

A distinguished American anthropologist reports in this paper the findings of a field study, in 1953-54, of village attitudes to maternity. The author considers ritual and custom in relation to the whole cycle of conception, pregnancy, midwifery, and the image of the male, in a village society.

343 **Children of the Meo hilltribes.**
Frances Hawker, Bruce Campbell. London: Evans, 1982. 28p. map. (Kids in Other Countries Series).

This is a book for children, showing how children live in a Meo hilltribe village.

344 **Men of the sea: coastal tribes of southern Thailand's west coast.**
David W. Hogan. *Journal of the Siam Society*, vol. 60, part 1 (1972), p. 205-34. bibliog.

Deals with the coastal Semang Negrito of the west coast of peninsular Thailand.

345 **Rorschach test in farming villages in north Thailand.**
Yosinaru Huzioka. *Nature and Life in Southeast Asia*, vol. 2 (1962), p. 139-273.

This report from the Osaka University expedition, in 1957-58, shows the detailed replies given by forty-eight male heads of households in villages in north Thailand, giving their interpretations of standard Rorschach prints. The replies provide an interesting impression of their mental furniture and interests. The article is accompanied by photographs of the villages in 8 leaves of captioned plates.

346 **South Indians on the plantation frontier in Malaya.**
Ravindra K. Jain. New Haven, Connecticut: Yale University Press, 1970. 460p. bibliog.

This book gives a detailed history of the Tamil *Pal Melayu* (rubber estate) labourers brought into Malaya from the early days of the plantations. The author's account includes the drafting, often with their leaders' coercive collaboration, of labour from these estate settlements by the Japanese during the Second World War in large numbers to supplement working parties on the Burma-Siam railway. This influx may have proved impermanent; but the proximity of Thailand's southern provinces to the big Tamil minorities in northern Malaya may account for a significant Indian minority as traders in Bangkok and other centres in Thailand, whose origins and customs the author describes.

347 **Some social and religious institutions of the Lawa.**
H. E. Kauffmann. *Journal of the Siam Society*, vol. 60, part 1 (Jan. 1972), p. 237-306. bibliog. foldout map.

An initial, close-up report of the Lawa, based on an anthropological trip in northern Thailand; the itinerary is shown on the map provided.

348 **Ethnic adaptation and identity: the Karen on the Thai frontier with Burma.**
Edited by Charles Fenton Keyes. Philadelphia: Institute for the Study of Human Issues, 1979. 278p. maps. photos.

The Karen are an interesting and numerous group of tribes inhabiting the cross-border regions of north and west Thailand with Burma. Their origins and identity have been something of a puzzle, and they may be among the earliest settled inhabitants of their present areas in Thailand, extending nearly as far south as the Malay border, and including the lowland valley as well as upland territory. This study, the result of fieldwork from 1967 by the editor and co-anthropologists Peter Kunstadter, David H. Marlowe, Peter Hinton and F. K. Lehman, distinguishes Sgar, Pwo, and Kayah Karen, and examines aspects of their environmental adaptation and ethnic variation.

349 **Isan: regionalism in northeast Thailand.**
Charles Fenton Keyes. Ithaca, New York: Cornell University
Press, 1967. 86p. maps. bibliog. (Southeast Asia Program Data
Paper, no. 65).

This large lobe of the northeastern plateau of Thailand adjoining the Mekong
River is inhabited by three times as many Lao people as there are in Laos itself.
This anthropological and behavioural study examines the interrelation of the Isan,
as the northeastern people are known in Thailand, with the rest of the country
and shows (e.g. from electoral statistics) that the relationship can be uneasy,
perhaps even intermittently ominous.

350 **Southeast Asian tribes, minorities and nations.**
Edited by Peter Kunstadter. London: Oxford University Press,
1967. 2 vols. maps. bibliog.

Seven of the twenty-one chapters in this compilation deal with tribal minorities
of Thailand. The Meo, in particular, are considered in relation to their wide
dispersal among the uplands of countries bordering Thailand's northern provinces.
Contributions cover questions of cultural and economic accommodation among
migrating tribal groups and main populations in this area.

351 **Peoples of the golden triangle: six tribes in Thailand.**
Paul W. Lewis. London: Thames & Hudson, 1984. 300p. maps.
bibliog. illus.

The six tribes shown are: Karen, Hmong, Mien, Akha, Lahu, and Lisu. The book
is profusely illustrated with numerous colour plates.

352 **Highlanders of Thailand.**
Edited by John McKinnon, Wanat Bhruksasri. Kuala Lumpur:
Oxford University Press, 1983. 358p. maps. bibliogs. illus.

This is a well-informed, illustrated cultural guide to the hilltribes of northern
Thailand, with numerous plates, some coloured.

353 **Elephant kingdom.**
H. N. Marshall. London: Robert Hale, 1958. 190p. map. photos.

The author of this diary, which covers seven years in the northern Thai jungle,
was a member of a dying breed – the European 'teak wallah', a product of British
enterprise introduced into northern Burma and northern Thailand in the late
19th century. The book describes experiences with elephants, with the jungle, and
also with the jungle tribespeople, who hunted with poisoned bamboo darts fired
from crossbows. It also includes a glossary of terms used in elephant handling.

354 **Cultivated plants in some ethnic communities of northwest Thailand.**
Michio Matsuoka, Tatuo Kira. *Nature and Life in Southeast Asia*, vol. 4 (1965), p. 81-109. map. illus.

This report from the Osaka University expedition of 1961-62 provides a detailed analysis of seeds recovered in Thai Yai (Shan), Thai Lü, Ho, and six other hilltribe villages. Crops examined were: rice, maize, soya, groundnut, gourd and squash.

355 **The bronze drums of Shizhai shan, their social and ritual significance.**
Michele Pirazzoli-T'serstevens. In: *Early Southeast Asia.* Edited by R. B. Smith, W. Watson. London, New York, Kuala Lumpur: Oxford University Press, 1979. p. 125-36. plate.

This article is abstracted from the author's *La civilisation du royaume de Dian à l'époque Han* (Paris: Ecole Française d'Extrême-Orient, 1974), for the purpose of the symposium in which it appears; it draws interesting inferences from bronze drums found between 1955 and 1960 near Tali, the capital of Nan-chao in Yunnan. The tombsites where the drums were found date from the Dian (Tien) civilization of the last two centuries of the 1st millennium BC; the decorations on the drums consisting of frogs and other symbols suggest magic uses for simulating thunder, water and crop controls, and uses for tribal and village authority, which can be related to similar uses among the Shan, Karen and Meo peoples of Burma, Thailand and Indochina originating in the same region.

356 **Die Negrito Asiens.** (The Negrito of Asia.)
Paul Schebesta. Vienna: Gabriel Verlag, 1957. 2 vols. bibliog. photos. (Studia Institute Anthropos).

Presents an important anthropological treatise on the Negrito of the Malay peninsula. The Negrito of Thailand form part of a northward tribal migration, distinct from the main drift southward from China of the hilltribes of the north, and from the Karen, who appear to have been static in the Burma border regions from very early times. Relevant Negrito types include the Andaman islanders, the Semang of the eastern peninsula coast, and a few in the north, pejoratively referred to in Thai folklore as *ngo*, a small, delicious but ugly and hairy fruit (Malay: *rambutan*); this was a disguise by which Prince Sang Thong, in a much loved pseudo-jataka story (depicted in murals at Wat Phra Singh in Chiang Mai), secretly enters the palace of a neighbouring king to court his daughter. The author deals very thoroughly with the anthropology, ethnography and sociology (vol. 2, part 1), and religion and mythology (vol. 2, part 2), of the Andaman, Aeta and Semang Negrito. The work is lavishly illustrated with photographs of the housing, implements, weapons (blow-pipes), and daily life of the tribes, and includes an extensive bibliography in Western languages.

357 **Bang Chan: social history of a rural community in Thailand.**
Lauriston Sharp, Lucien M. Hanks. Ithaca, New York: Cornell
University Press, 1978. 314p. maps. bibliog. (Cornell Studies in
Anthropology).

This readable study of a Thai village society, written by originators of Cornell
University's Southeast Asia Program project, broadens the story of one community
into an essay in the country's anthropological history.

358 **Village Mons of Bangkok.**
Michael Smithies. *Journal of the Siam Society*, vol. 60, part 1
(Jan. 1972), p. 307-32. photos.

The early Mon migrations from Burma left pockets of communities which can in
a sense be considered 'stateless', or having a dual culture. The article, illustrated
with numerous photographs, discusses the village life and beliefs of these Mon
communities in Bangkok, who live to some extent in a separate world of Brah-
ninical and animist spirits and taboos.

359 **Shifting cultivation in Southeast Asia.**
Joseph E. Spencer. Berkeley, California: University of California
Press, 1966. 247p. bibliog.

This is a definitive study of the method of shifting agricultural cultivation, sometimes (unjustifiably, in the author's opinion) referred to as *swidden*. Though
typical of the hilltribes of Thailand and adjoining uplands, the method is not
dictated by either location or height of dwelling, but is rather a once universal
form of neolithic culture, retained by tribes (including 'sea gypsies') who have not
learned alternative agricultural techniques to supersede it. The author discusses
other factors making for uniformity of upland village cultures.

360 **The Tai of Assam.**
Barend Jan Terwiel. *Southeast Asian Review*, vol. 4, no. 1 (Aug.
1979) & no. 2 (Feb. 1980); vol. 6, nos. 1 & 2 (Dec./Jan. 1981).
bibliog.

These numbers of the *Southeast Asian Review* (Gaya) constitute a monographic
study in two volumes on the customs of the Tai of Assam. Volume one *The Tai
of Assam and their life-cycle ceremonies*, examines the retention of ancient
(pre-migratory) customs, and the involvement of the Ahom in Assam, with a map
showing the distribution of the Tai in mainland Southeast Asia (including
Thailand). Volume two *The Tai of Assam: sacrifice and time reckoning*, deals
with human and other sacrificial rites (feasting the spirits on the eve of the
monsoon), and with the calendar and time cycle measurements. The study
includes a wide variety of hill and lowland tribes: White, Red and Black Tai;
Khmer and Pear; Hmong and Karen; Ahom and Shan; Thai and Lao. Life-cycle
ceremonies mentioned include white cotton wrist-ties, *khwan* therapy and vitali-
zation of people and rice; and stroking away of disease. The author notes differences from Chinese soul-summoning ceremonies: he proposes a regional origin in
Han times (ca 200 BC-200 AD) for the Tai peoples in the Kwangsi and Tongking
warm lowlands as being consistent with their wet-rice culture.

361 **Peoples of the earth, vol. 11: Southeast Asia.**
Volume editor Andrew Turton. Verona, Italy: Europa Verlag,
1973. 144p. maps. col. illus.

This large-format, excellently presented and illustrated volume probably provides
the best available general introduction and conspectus of the tribes of Thailand
and adjacent areas. It has the advantage of dealing with the entire population
spectrum of the region as a whole, thus making it easier to understand how
Thailand's peoples fit into the country itself and the extent to which they merge
into neighbouring territories, and share linguistic and cultural origins with tribes
whose migrations have taken them mainly to areas beyond Thailand's present
borders. The volume has separate chapters on 'Unwritten literature' (Ruth
Finnegan); 'Peoples of Southeast Asia' (Andrew Turton); 'Buddhism' (H. Ingaki)
'People of Thailand' (Andrew Turton); and six of the principal individual tribal
groups of particular Thai interest (Yao, Meo, Lua, Karen, Shan, Negrito).

362 **Aw-ha hku ve: the Lahu Nyi (Red Lahu) rite for the recall of
a wandering soul.**
Anthony R. Walker. *Journal of the Royal Asiatic Society*,
vol. 1 (1972), p. 16-29.

This article is the first part of a report of an anthropological field study in
northern Thailand. This part describes the complex pattern of soul beliefs and
associated ceremonies among the Red Lahu.

363 **Farmers in the hills: upland peoples of north Thailand.**
Anthony R. Walker. Taipeh: Chinese Association for Folklore,
1981. 211p. maps. photos. (Asian Folklore and Social Life
Monographs).

The report of a visit to north Thailand by a team of the School of Comparative
Social Science at the University of Malaysia. It includes accounts of several tribes
and gives some translations of Yao documents in Chinese characters.

364 **Three Lahu Nyi (Red Lahu) marriage prayers: Lahu texts and
ethnographic notes.**
Anthony R. Walker. *Journal of the Royal Asiatic Society*, vol. 2
(1974), p. 43-49.

This article is the second part of a description, from an anthropological field
study, of tribal ceremonies in northern Thailand. This part gives texts and translations of songs used in marriage ceremonies.

365 **The hilltribes of northern Thailand: a socio-ethnological report.**
Gordon Young. Bangkok: Siam Society, 1974. 5th ed. 96p.
photos.

A popular, illustrated study of the northern hilltribes. It stimulated a review
article, expanding the anthropological themes, by Anthony R. Walker cf. JSS,
vol. 63, part 2 (July 1975), p. 355-70.

366   **Tracks of an intruder.**
      Gordon Young. London: Souvenir Press, 1967. 191p.
This book tells the story of the author's hunting expeditions in northern Thailand, where his companions were from the Lahu and other local tribes.

The Chinese

367   **The Chinese in Bangkok: a study in cultural persistence.**
      Richard J. Coughlin. Ann Arbor, Michigan: University Micro-
      films International, 1969. 615p. maps. bibliog. (PhD thesis for
      Yale University, 1953).
Presents a sociological study in historical perspective of Chinese immigration into Bangkok, starting with relevant material on the southern Chinese provinces of origin, and examining the communities in the city and some of the barriers to their assimilation into it. The material argument of this thesis can also be found in the author's *Double identity: Chinese in modern Thailand* (Hong Kong: Oxford University Press, 1960. 223p. map. bibliog.).

368   **Ethnicity and work culture in Thailand: a comparison of Thai
      and Thai-Chinese white-collar workers.**
      Frederic C. Deyo. *Journal of Asian Studies*, vol. 34, no. 4
      (Aug. 1975), p. 995-1015. bibliog.
This article compares and discusses the findings on Thai and Thai-Chinese workers' activities and conditions in various fields in Thailand by several well-known authors on Chinese in Thailand and Southeast Asia. Apart from the author's own conclusions, the article is useful in calling attention to the range of these works and others in the form of bibliographic notes.

369   **The third China: the Chinese community in Southeast Asia.**
      C. P. Fitzgerald. Melbourne: Cheshire, 1966. 109p.
This work, by an acknowledged expert on Chinese and Southeast Asian affairs, is a thumbnail sketch of the Overseas Chinese, their background, and ways in which they have developed distinctive communities in the southern ocean lands over many centuries.

370 **Chinese-Thai differential assimilation in Bangkok: an exploratory study.**
Boonsanong Punyodyana. Ithaca, New York: Cornell University Press, 1971. 117p. bibliog. (Southeast Asia Program Data Paper, no. 79).

An analytical, tabulated study exhibiting opportunities and reactions among the Chinese community in Bangkok and concluding, for instance, that they expect little change of government service employment.

371 **Chinese society in Thailand: an analytical history.**
G. William Skinner. Ithaca, New York: Cornell University Press, 1957. 459p. bibliog.

The author's treatment of Sino-Thai relations in the 17th and 18th centuries, and subsequent Chinese settlement in Thailand, has stood the test of time. The book deals with the effects of Thai immigration policies: the 'open door' policy ended in 1917; the author itemizes subsequent demographic trends and the rate of assimilation of the Chinese population up to 1955. Other themes of the book include some anti-Chinese policy phases, such as F. M. Phibul's repression, and later changes in government policy on education in Chinese.

372 **Leadership and power in the Chinese community of Thailand.**
G. William Skinner. Ithaca, New York: Cornell University Press, 1958. 363p. (Monographs of the Association for Asian Studies, no. 111).

Skinner was director of the Cornell Research Center in Bangkok. This study examines with the aid of charts the organization of Chinese communities in Thailand from the standpoints of clan and origin, leadership status, and business and political activity. He also offers conclusions on the extent to which expediency plays a part in the Chinese acceptance of assimilation in the Thai community.

373 **The future of the overseas Chinese in Southeast Asia.**
Lea E. Williams. New York: McGraw-Hill, 1966. 143p. bibliog. (US and China in World Affairs Series).

This essay highlights the diversity of the overseas Chinese and of the factors of change in progress amongst them, from communism to nationalism, and gives an estimate of future trends.

Muslims and Malays

374 Islam in Southeast Asia.
Edited by Michael Barry Hooker. Leiden, The Netherlands: Brill, 1983. 262p. bibliog.

Presents an overview of Islam in Indonesia, Malaysia, the Philippines and Thailand (specifically covered in p. 211-12). The book provides a good background of the state, ethics, philosophy and law of the Islamic countries of ASEAN (Malaysia and Indonesia), with which Thailand is either in immediate contact, or has frequent diplomatic and political touch, and has a long background of historical interchanges. The Moro problem in the Philippines (a third ASEAN partner) is also covered.

375 Islam in Thailand before the Bangkok period.
Raymond Scupin. *Journal of the Siam Society*, vol. 68, part 1 (Jan. 1980), p. 55-71. bibliog.

This article considers the relatively successful diffusion of Islam into southern Thailand via the trade ports in the 13th century, as against its less successful attempts at establishment in the central area; it also touches on the different type of Islam in the north under Chinese (Haw and other tribal) Muslim influences from Yunnan. The extensive bibliography will be of value.

376 Islamic reformation in Thailand.
Raymond Scupin. *Journal of the Siam Society*, vol. 68, part 2 (July 1980), p. 1-10. bibliographic notes.

Deals with Islamic reformist organizations in Bangkok, and argues that the religion, at least in its modern form in Bangkok, tends to be syncretic.

377 Thai Muslims.
Bangkok: Ministry of Foreign Affairs, 1979. 24p. photos.

This is a short official account of the present situation and location of the Muslim population centres and mosques of Thailand. It includes a historical review, and deals with the southern provinces, education, economic factors, and relations with the Thais.

378 Political violence in the Muslim provinces of southern Thailand.
M. Ladd Thomas. Singapore: Institute of Southeast Asian Studies, 1975. 27p. (ISEAS Occasional Paper, no. 28).

This paper gives an account of the disturbed conditions pertaining in the southern provinces as a result of friction between the local Muslim leaders and the Thai central government authorities. The main town of the area, Yala, has a sullen atmosphere, disposed towards violence in the face of causes, which the author examines, such as dismissals of Muslim headmen. The author refers to the question of relations between Bangkok and the Malaysian authorities in relation to separatist tendencies in the Muslim provinces of southern Thailand.

Language and Literature

Textbooks and grammars

379 **The vowels and tones of standard Thai: acoustical measurements
and experiments.**
Arthur S. Abramson. *International Journal of American
Linguistics*, vol. 28, no. 2, part 3 (1962), 146p. bibliog. (Indiana
University Research Center in Anthropology, Folklore and
Linguistics, Occasional Paper).

Tones are an indispensable element of the Thai language, inherent in its orthography as well as in the intonation of its spoken vowels. They may be historically,
regionally or dialectically variant, or current features of the language. This study,
a revised version of the author's dissertation presented to Columbia University in
1960, contains notes based on critical comments by George L. Trager. In addition
to a full description of the tonal element of spoken Thai, it provides a typical
analysis of problems and methodology involved in researching tonal linguistic
structures. The useful bibliography lists materials on Thai and general tonal
linguistics, including the dissertation (Yale, 1947) and other work by William J.
Gedney (q.v.).

380 **Modern Thai.**
Gordon H. Allison. Bangkok: Nibondh, 1959. 252p.

The author, teaching at a Thai school, gives a systematic course of lessons with
exercises, answer keys and vocabulary.

381 **Foundations of Thai.**
Edward M. Anthony, Debrah P. French, Udom Warotamasikkhadit. Ann Arbor, Michigan: University of Michigan, 1968. 551p. tapes.

This is a thorough groundwork in usage, grammar and lexicon of Thai, with tapes available in support of speech learning; the text is, however, in transliterated form only. For a recommended shorter groundwork with Thai script cf. Stuart Campbell, Chuan Shaweevongse *The fundamentals of the Thai language,* 4th ed. (Bangkok, 1968).

382 **Linguaphone Thai course.**
Manas Chitakasem. London: Linguaphone Institute, 1984. Handbook, 284p. 4 cassettes.

The Thai script is a transitional alphabet. It has 44 consonants, around which vowels and tone-marks are written; some vowel sounds are inherent (unwritten). The allocation of consonants (of which in some cases up to six alternatives may be available for a single basic consonantal sound), also helps to indicate spoken tones. The script, derived from Sanskrit via Khmer, is unique, and in addition to exceptional intrinsic beauty, possesses the capability of reproducing the spoken language much more efficiently than any of the several roman transliterations which have been devised for it. For all these reasons, it is desirable to acquire familiarity with it as early as possible in any serious study of the language. This Linguaphone course is designed to fulfil this intention; it provides sound, grammar and orthography in a related sequence of lessons from the beginning. There is no better way to learn the language, for whatever ultimate purpose, and the course is highly recommended. For a description of transitional alphabets cf. David Diringer, *The alphabet; a key to the history of mankind* (London: Hutchinson, 1968, 2 vols. 3rd rev. ed., with Reinhold Regensburger). This is a remarkable work, well worth reading for its own sake.

383 **Thai reader.**
Mary R. Haas. Washington, DC: American Council of Learned Societies, 1954. 220p. map.

A useful general reader, with graduated lessons in Thai and accompanied by vocabulary notes in English and pronunciation guidance, taking the student who can already read Thai up to ordinary family conversation and newspaper level.

384 **Introduction to Thai literature.**
Robert B. Jones, Ruchira C. Mendiones. Ithaca, New York: Cornell University Press, 1970. 563p.

This general, introductory selection of Thai literature, from the classical court style to a poetic and modern short story style, is for advanced readers. It should preferably be used in conjunction with McFarland's dictionary.

385 **Thai cultural reader.**
Robert H. Jones, Ruchira C. Mendiones. Ithaca, New York: Cornell University Press, 1969. 791p. (Southeast Asia Program).

This collection of Thai texts, for advanced readers, is arranged according to topics and periods with English vocabulary.

386 **Quelques cas complexes de dérivation en cambodgien.** (Some complex cases of derivation in Cambodian.)
S. Lewitz. *Journal of the Royal Asiatic Society*, no. 1 (1969), p. 39-48.

Discusses orthographic and semantic evidence for various types of linguistic link between Mon-Khmer and Thai, whose alphabet is derived from Sanskrit via Khmer. Bibliographic notes provide suggestions for further study in Thai, Russian, German, French and English.

387 **Thai reference grammar.**
Richard B. Noss. Washington, DC: Foreign Service Institute, Department of State, 1964. 254p.

This is an excellent analysis of the phonemic and tonal structure and morphology of spoken Thai, arranged in progressive lessons. The material is devised to familiarize students with problems presented by the unfamiliar idea-formulation and sentence-construction of colloquial Thai. The book does not deal with Thai script, but is couched in an effective transliteration system including tones.

Dictionaries

388 **Thai-English student's dictionary.**
Compiled by Mary R. Haas. Kuala Lumpur: Oxford University Press, 1966. reprinted. 638p.

This is the best general student's dictionary (indexed in Thai only). The volume begins with a comprehensive grammatical description of the language and of its orthography, and indicates an effective, complex transliteration system appropriate for Western technical linguistic purposes.

389   **English-Thai dictionary.**
M. L. Manich Jumsai. Bangkok: Chalermnit, 1963. 724p.
This medium, pocket-sized dictionary contains an everyday English vocabulary, well-spaced out and clearly printed. Equivalent words or explanations are given in Thai script only, with pronunciation of the English words in Thai transliteration, for which the author suggests a system of conversion in the preface; it does not include an English transliteration of the Thai equivalents. For the visitor who has acquired a reasonable familiarity with the Thai script, it is an invaluable companion.

390   **New model English-Thai dictionary.**
So Sethaputra. Samud Prakan, Thailand: S. Sethaputra, 1961. 3rd ed. library edition. 1,677p.
This beautifully printed dictionary is indispensable for the advanced student. Indexed in English only, it includes modern English coinages, usages and acronyms. It pursues English words and compounds through wide varieties of alternative meanings in sentences in English with equivalents in Thai.

391   **Hobson-Jobson; a glossary of Anglo-Indian words and phrases.**
Colonel Henry Yule, A. C. Burnell, new edition edited by William Crooke. New Delhi: Munshiram Manuharial, 1984. reprinted. 1,021p.
In addition to loanwords from Buddhist texts in Sanskrit and Pali, the Thai language has acquired a further stock of loanwords from Indian or Persian sources as a result of early trade contacts, in particular those with British India; this stock of words occurs frequently in writings in English concerning such contacts. *Hobson-Jobson*, originally published in 1886, provides a unique and delightul etymological discussion of this genre of terminology compiled by authors who pioneered the relative trade researches cf. *Cathay and the way thither*, by Henry Yule (1896). It is recommended as a companion reference work, especially for readers for whom an interest in Thailand is also an introduction to Indianized Southeast Asia and to early trade exchanges with this region. Another interesting book on this subject is *Thai painting by Jean Boisselier* (q.v.) or, for a fuller listing with Chinese parallels *A dictionary of Chinese Buddhist terms*, by W. E. Soothill and L. Hodous (1937), reprinted in Taipei: 1976); this includes a Sanskrit-Pali index.

Classical and modern literature: translations

392 Letters from Thailand.
Botan, translated from the Thai by Susan Fulop Morell.
Bangkok: D. K. Book House, 1977. 391p.

The author of this novel uses a pen-name; in form, the novel purports to consist of the letters home of a Chinese immigrant businessman, Tan Suang U, who takes up residence in Bangkok, and there is no explicit evidence to show whether or not it is fiction. The book was awarded the SEATO prize for Thai literature when it was originally published in 1967, and was later adopted by the Thai Ministry of Education as standard reading to promote Thai and Thai-Chinese understanding. Its style is reminiscent of G. Lowes Dickinson's *Letters from John Chinaman* (an attempt to mitigate anti-Chinese feeling at the time of the Boxer rising); in content, it is a family saga portraying the ordinary people's way of life, in a manner which has been compared to that of Thomas Mann. The translator explains that, in selecting the volume, she felt it should stand on its own merit, and would last, as an exceptionally finely-observed mirror-portrait of the country during the mid-20th century.

393 Sug, the trickster who fooled the monk: a northern Thai tale with vocabulary.
Viggo Brun. London: Curzon Press, 1976. 191p. (Scandinavian Institute of Asian Studies Monograph, no. 27).

This book reproduces and translates a cycle of some twenty-seven exploits of a popular droll, collected by the author during a research project in villages in the north of Thailand. The exposition serves three quite different useful purposes: as a delightful rehearsal of typical tales passed on in the oral tradition; as an account of the villages themselves and the methods the author used to gather this unique record of what threatens to be a disappearing form of regional popular entertainment; and as a linguistic analysis of relevant elements of the local dialect.

394 The emergence and development of the nirat genre of Thai poetry.
Manas Chitakasem. *Journal of the Siam Society*, vol. 60, part 2 (July 1972), p. 135-68.

This article outlines the emergence and nature of the genre of Thai poetry known as *nirat*, a favourite form of which was known at the court of King Narai of Ayudhya in the 17th century. It expresses the pangs of the lovelorn traveller or expeditionary prince. The author gives examples of its modern development, including some where the verses are compiled in alternating fashion as a parlour-game. For a fuller treatment of the subject, with bibliography, cf. the author's doctoral thesis of 1974 (University of London, thesis no. 914, 414p.).

395 **The short story in Southeast Asia: aspects of a genre.**
Edited by Jeremy H. C. S. Davidson, Helen Cordell. London:
School of Oriental and African Studies, University of London,
1982. 270p. (Collected Papers in Oriental and African Studies).
This compilation deals with evolutions in Southeast Asian short story writing,
within which Thailand is considered in detail by Manas Chitakasem, who illustrates
the modern Thai element of the genere from stories taken from university life
abroad, or in the form of vignettes derived from newspaper stories.

396 **Das Nirat Müang Kläng von Sunthon Phu: Analyse und
Übersetzung eines thailändischen Reisegedichts.** (Sunthon Phu's
Nirat Muang Klaeng: analysis and translation of a Thai poem of
travel.)
Harald Hundius. Wiesbaden, GFR: Harrassowitz, 1976. 177p.
map. bibliog. facsimile plate. (Goethe University, Frankfurt-am-
Main, Southeast Asia Studies, vol. 5).
Nirat or poems conveying the erotic nostalgia of travellers temporarily separated
from their loved ones, comprise one of the favourite genres of Thai classical
literature. Cast in antiphonal form, they summon features of the passing landscape
to call to mind features of the absent beloved. Sunthon Phu (1786-1855) is the
most noted popular exponent of this genre; he wrote this poem, in 1807, at the
new court in Bangkok on his return from a journey, undertaken to escape royal
displeasure over an affair with a lady-in-waiting. His travel took him to Klaeng,
a southeastern country district on the Gulf of Thailand, where his father was an
abbot. Even students of Thai language and literature for whom German is not a
first or second language should find the translator's analysis, with a literary background and full text in Thai, an instructive and useful introduction to this poet
and the Thai poetic tradition.

397 **Siamese tales old and new: with some reflections on the tales.**
Reginald Le May. London: Noel Douglas, 1930. 192p.
The author, at the time a legal adviser in Bangkok, retells fifteen piquant traditional Thai tales, starting with the 'Four Riddles'. The book concludes with the
translator's extended reflections on the elements of family tradition shown in
the tales involving spirits, healing and necromancy.

398 **Les entretiens de Nang Tantrai.** (The communications of
Nang Tantrai.)
Translated by Edward Lorgeou, engravings by L. P. Cosyns.
Paris: Bossard, 1924. 257p.
An attractively illustrated series of tales by the lady Tantrai written along the
lines of the Arabian nights.

399 **King Vajiravudh and Phra Ruang.**
Umavijani Montri. Bangkok: Siriporn Press, 1981. 9p.
Gives some examples of royal poetry by king Vajiravudh (1910-25).

400 **The reluctant princess; a legend of love of Siam.**
Retold by Mom Dusdi Paribatra, illustrated by Sukit Chuthama.
Rutland, Vermont: Tuttle, 1963. 61p. colour drawings. large
format.
The tale of the weaver birds is a traditional Thai fairy story, retold in this delight-
fully illustrated volume. Two amorous weaver birds perish, only to resume their
flirtatious activities as reincarnated princelings in a tale of love, mystery and
magic.

401 **Four reigns.** (Si phaen din.)
Kukrit Pramoj, translated from the Thai by Tulachandra.
Bangkok: D. K. Book House, 1985 (vol. 2). 2 vols (vol. 1 in
preparation).
This novel, now available in English, is the most important novel published in
Thailand since the war. The author — himself an urbane collector, dilettante and
sometime prime minister — unfolds in Galsworthian style a fascinating social and
élitist panorama covering four reigns of the Chakri dynasty, from Chulalongkorn
to Ananda. The heroine, Ploi, is a favourite Thai literary figure, conveying experience of high life both within and outside the protective walls of the palace.

402 **Sunthon Phu: the story of Pha Abhai Mani.**
Prem Chaya (Prince Prem Purachatra). Bangkok: Chatra Books,
1952. 141p.
An example of several explanatory stories re-told by the same author derived
from leading exponents of the poetic corpus of Thai theatrical art forms.

403 **Essays on Thai folklore.**
Phya Anuman Rajadhon. Bangkok: Social Science Association
of Thailand, 1968. 383p.
These essays cover superstitions related to trees and plants; the family and
marriage; rites, rituals and poisons.

404 **Etude sur la littérature siamoise.** (A study of Siamese literature.)
P. Schweizguth. Paris: Imprimerie Nationale, 1951. 409p.
pullout map. bibliog. (American and Oriental Library).
This is an excellent, general account of Thai literature and literary history,
including legends and folk tales, drama and poetry. It has a full bibliography of
Western and Thai works (Thai script), both listed under Roman alphabetical order.
Recensions of the *Ramakien* are separately tabulated.

405 **Contes et légendes de Thaïlande.** (Tales and legends of Thailand.)
Jit-kasem Sibunruang. Bangkok: Phraepittaya, 1976. 231p.
illus. (Chulalongkorn University Institut des Etudes Asiatiques).

This small volume contains fifteen folk tales of Thailand, simply told, and
evocatively illustrated with drawings. Number 15 (p. 201-31) is the story of
Prince Sang Thong cf. *Die Negrito Thailands* (q.v.).

406 **Khun Chang, Khun Phèn: la femme, le héros et le vilain: poème
populaire thaï.** (*Khun Chang, Khun Phaen*: the lady, the hero
and the villain: a popular Thai poem.)
Translated by Jit-Kasem Sibunruang. Paris: Presses Universitaires
de France, 1960. 159p. (French Ministry of Education. Musée
Guimet Series, vol. 65).

This epic poem is one of the best-known and loved of the Thai literary tradition
of Ayudhya. The translator, professor of French at the Chulalongkorn University
in Bangkok, provides a background setting, notes and an extensive glossary of
Thai, Sanskrit and Pali terms. Cf. also H. H. Prince Bidya, *Sebha recitation and
the story of Khun Chang, Khun Phan*, JSS (JTRS), vol. 33, no. 1 (March 1941),
p. 1-22.

407 **Siamese folk tales.**
Jit-Kasem Sibunruang, illustrated by Saeng Arun Rataksikorn,
Bangkok: Don Busco Technical School and Orphanage, 1954.
86p. (Distributed by Cellar Bookshop, Michigan).

Includes five well-known Thai folk tales narrated in English.

408 **Texts from an episode from *Khun Chang, Khun Phaen*.**
E. H. S. Simmonds. *Asia Major*, vol. 10, no. 2 (1964), new series,
p. 279-94.

In this article the author, a leading modern English exponent of Thai poetic literary
forms, provides parallel texts in Thai and English from *Khun Chang, Khun Phaen*,
a favourite epic of the late 15th and early 16th centuries, proclaiming deeds from
the dynastic conflicts between Ayudhya and Luang Prabang (the royal capital of
Laos, which was then another principality), and the sacking of Chiang Mai.

409 **The Rama story in Thai cultural tradition.**
S. Singaravelu. *Southeast Asian Review*, vol. 5, no. 2 (Dec.
1980), p. 31-48.

This article, one of many dealing entirely with the *Ramayana* in Southeast Asia,
provides a useful, short account of its literary evolution in Thailand.

410 **The politician and other stories.**
Khamsong Srinawak (Lao Khamhawn), translated from the Thai
by Damnern Garden, edited and introduced by Michael Smithies
Kuala Lumpur: Oxford University Press, 1973. 101p.

These modern, Thai short stories illustrate the interplay of tradition, regimentatio
and character in Thai village life. The translation loses little of the charm an
subtlety of this new genre of stories dealing with personal relationships.

411 **The story of Prince Rama.**
Brian Thompson, drawings by Jeroo Roy. Harmondsworth,
England: Penguin, 1980. 64p. (Kestrel Books).

This large-format, slim volume presents, in a manner suitable for children an
others, a beautifully-illustrated account of the Indian story of Prince Rama, th
Ramayana, the origin of one of the fundamental mythological bases of Th:
culture and art. Of the many Sanskrit recensions of the epic, that used in Th:
literature, the *Ramakirti* (or *Ramakien* in Thai), developed a wide cycle of su
stories which provide the subject matter of an entire branch of Thai dance dram
and painting, whose sources may be more readily appreciated by a compariso
with a background treatment such as that in this volume. For a more scholar
analysis of some further recensions of the *Ramayana* and their religious signif
cance, cf. *Religious attitudes in Valmiki's Ramayana*, by J. L. Brockington (q.v.

412 **Ein Lehrgedicht für junge Frauen – Suphasit Son Ying – des
Sunthon Phu.** (A moral poem for young ladies – *Suphasit Son
Ying* – by Sunthon Phu.)
Klaus Wenk. *Oriens Extremus*, vol. 12, no. 1 (1965), p. 65-106.

This is a further example (in this case untranslated from the German) of th
author's expositions of the *suphasit* (moral tale) Thai literary genre, using a poer
by its best-known and loved exponent, Sunthon Phy (ca 1820).

413 **Die Metrik in thailändischer Dichtung.** (Metric form in Thai
poetry.)
Klaus Wenk. *Mitteilungen der Gesellschaft für Natur- und
Völkerkunde Ostasiens* (OAG), vol. 41 (1961), 160p.

In this publication the author explains the distinctive metric system of Th:
poetry, which, in oral or written form, contains much of the country's early an
regional cultural record.

14   **Phali teaches the young: a literary and sociological analysis of
     the Thai poem *Phali son nong.***
     Klaus Wenk, translated from the German by Volkmar Zühlsdorff.
     Honolulu: University of Hawaii, 1980. 218p. bibliog. (Southeast
     Asia Paper no. 18).

he original of this study by one of the most distinguished German scholars of
hai language, art and culture, was published by Hamburg University in 1977.
he 'teacher' whose precepts are the subject of the poem is the monkey king from
ıe *Ramakien*, the recension of the Indian *Ramayana* epic whose adaptation into
'hai forms a main element in Thai culture. The poem is given in the original
hai with translation, in successive versions made from traditional sources,
nder court patronage at Ayudhya and in the early Bangkok period. It belongs
ɔ the *suphasit* (moral tale) genre developed from Indian models at Sukhothai
ı the 14th century. The author's comments provide insights into the royal as
ᵛell as the literary traditions associated with the genre: the 'young' of the title
the king's younger brothers) implies junior status, in the sense of all the king's
ıbject classes, both at court and in the citizenry outside it, whose behaviour can
arn them merit and freedom from punishment.

Minority languages

15   **A new look at the history and classification of the Tai languages.**
     James R. Chamberlain.   In: *Studies in Tai linguistics in honour
     of William J. Gedney.* Edited by Jimmy G. Harris, James R.
     Chamberlain. Bangkok: Central Institute of English, Office of
     State Universities, 1975. p. 49-66.

he author takes a new look at the history and classification of the Tai language
roup, and thus provides a useful conspectus of their extent and interrelations.

16   **A Tai festschrift for William J. Gedney on the occasion of his
     fifth cycle of life birthday anniversary, April 4 1975.**
     Edited by Thomas G. Gething.   Honolulu: University of Hawaii,
     1975. 183p. bibliog. (Southeast Asia Study Program Working
     Paper).

his compilation, containing ten papers by specialist associates of the dedicatee
ın aspects of Thai and related languages, sums up published material in a con-
ɔniently accessible form and also provides a useful bibliography on Tai language
roup linguistic studies.

417 **Studies in Tai linguistics in honour of William J. Gedney.**
Edited by Jimmy G. Harris, James R. Chamberlain. Bangkok:
Central Institute of English Language, Office of State Univer-
sities, 1975. 419p.

This compilation consists of twenty-four papers (four in Thai) on Tai linguistics
For the advanced student, it contains much excellent and stimulating materia
some of it being concerned with the Thai language itself.

418 **A model for the alignment of dialects in southwestern Tai.**
John F. Hartmann. *Journal of the Siam Society*, vol. 68, part 1
(Jan. 1980), p. 71-86. maps.

This linguistic overview gives an illuminating explanation of the interrelation o
the Tai, Shan, and Ahom group of dialects of the northwestern Thai-Burmes
border region.

419 **Vocabulaire français-thay blanc et éléments du grammaire.**
(French-White Thai vocabulary and elements of the grammar.)
George Minot. Paris: Ecole d'Extrême-Orient, 1949. 2 vols.

The vocabulary and grammar deals with the White Thai branch of the hilltribe
of northern Thailand.

420 **White Hmong language lessons.**
Doris Whitelock. Minneapolis, Minnesota: University of
Minnesota Press, 1982. 126p. (Minneapolis Center for Urban and
Regional Affairs, Southeast Asia Refugee Studies, Occasional
Papers no. 2).

The Hmong, or Meo, occupy sporadic villages in the highlands of Thailand an
adjoining countries south of China. This language-study course prepared i
1966-68 for the Overseas Missionary Fellowship, deals with one group, the Whi
Hmong. The colour-nomenclature in several of the hilltribes refers to the
prevailing costume colours.

106

Fiction

421   **The bridge on the River Kwai.**
Pierre Boulle, translated from the French by Xan Fielding.
London: Fontana, 1978. 157p. Reprinted, London: Viaduct,
1982. 64p. (Complete Bestsellers Series).

Pierre Boulle's novel was originally published in 1952 and was translated in 1954. The book was turned into a highly successful film which made the story world-famous. It is set in a prisoner-of-war camp beside the River Kwai, where the bridge provided a crossing for the railway which the Japanese Army required the Allied prisoners, both officers and men, to build. The river is, in fact, the Mae Nam Khwae Noi, or 'lesser tributary', but since the film it has been named River Kwai on Thai maps in English, and the site, with a new hotel, has become a tourist attraction. The metal bridge which, in fact, carried the railway is still to be seen, with one new square span replacing a round one which was knocked out by the RAF in a hazardous low-level bombing raid in 1945 — the only destruction of the bridge which really took place. The book and film are not historically accurate as they show the prisoners both designing and building a wooden bridge, which a land party blows up, much to the chagrin of the British colonel (played in the film by Alec Guinness). In reality, the prisoners built a wooden supply bridge which was made to Japanese design. A justifiable artistic licence has been used in the novel to support a gripping tale and it gives a remarkably authentic impression of everyday life in the camps and on the 'death railway'.

422   **King rat.**
James Clavell.   London: Coronet, 1962. 320p.

This is a gripping and exciting tale, based on the author's personal experience of the prisoner-of-war camp set up by the Japanese Army at Changi after the fall of Singapore in 1942. The story shows how the prisoners who remained in this camp for some three-and-a-half years reacted to its conditions of deprivation and claustrophobia. An interesting comparison can be made with *The bridge on the River Kwai* (q.v.), which, though with an equally authentic background, fiction-alizes in many ways quite different experiences of prisoners who were moved out of Changi and into the Thai jungle within a few months, to build the railway across the mountainous region leading to Burma. There, though with the same Korean and Japanese guards, they faced a different set of privations, and of challenges. The author, expanding his knowledge of the Japanese, later wrote *Shogun*; both titles have been made into successful films.

423 Siamese White.
Maurice Collis. London: Faber & Faber, 1936. 230p.

Though the book is fiction, the author bases it on reliable sources and it amounts to a readable historical essay. The story recounts the adventures of Samuel White, an East India Company man. White's Far Eastern forays bring him to the scintillating court of Ayudhya, where he becomes acquainted with Constantin Phaulkon, a Greek mariner in the service of Louis XIV, who later became prime minister to King Narai.

424 Siamese counterpart.
Elizabeth Lake. London: Cresset, 1958. 263p.

This love story is set in a provincial Thai hospital, where a clash occurs between Thai and Western social mores, arising from the situation where a Western 'counterpart' works alongside a Thai equivalent in order to transfer expertise.

425 Fanny and the Regent of Siam.
R. J. Minney. London: Collins, 1962. 383p. map.

A readable narrative, in the form of a novel with dialogue, of events surrounding the love affair of the young King Chulalongkorn and Fanny, the daughter of Sir Thomas Knox who was Britain's consul-general in Bangkok from 1864 to 1879. The book was conceived in association with Dr. Bristowe, author of *Louis and the King of Siam* (q.v.). Concerning Sir Thomas Knox as a conservative opponent of the young King Chulalongkorn, cf. *Thailand: a short history* (q.v.).

426 A woman of Bangkok.
Jack Reynolds. London: Pan, 1959; New York: Ballantine, 1956. 313p.

This love story — described by the publishers as 'brutal, frank and enthralling' — is a human, and at times poignant tale of an English visitor's infatuation for a dance-hall girl of Bangkok. Also published under the title *A sort of beauty* (London: Secker & Warburg, 1956).

427 Novels set in Thailand.
David K. Wyatt. Ithaca, New York: D. Wyatt, Cornell University, 1973. 3p. mimeographed.

This bibliography lists fifty novels, set in Thailand, in English or French.

Religion and Spirit Beliefs

Theravada Buddhism

428 The wheel of the law: Buddhism illustrated from Siamese sources.
Henry Alabaster. London: Trübner, 1871. 323p. Facsimile
reprint, Farnborough, England: Gregg International, 1971.

A seminal work on Theravada Buddhism, which was acquired by Burma and
Thailand from Sri Lanka soon after the formation of the state in each of those
countries. In Thailand, Buddhism borrowed substantially, not only directly
from Sri Lanka but also indirectly from Singhalese sources at Pagan in Burma.
Previous bibliographic references are summed up discursively in the preface of
this book. The author, who was interpreter to the British consul-general in
Bangkok, considers this religion in general as well as in relation to its observance
in Thailand; he also notes the roles played by animism and superstition.

**429 The world of Buddhism: Buddhist monks and nuns in society
and culture.**
Heinz Bechert, Richard Gombrich. London: Thames & Hudson,
1984. 198p. illus.

This large-format, coffee-table style book is a beautifully illusrated general guide
to the spread of the Buddhist religion and culture to all the countries including
the United States, where it has taken root. This volume covers some of the early
Indian, Chinese and Tibetan Buddhist literature and deals with the Buddhist
tradition in Sri Lanka — the source of Thai Theravada Buddhism. The section on
'Thailand, Laos and Cambodia' is by Jane Bunnag.

Religion and Spirit Beliefs. Theravada Buddhism

430   **Religious attitudes in Valmiki's Ramayana.**
       J. L. Brockington. *Journal of the Royal Asiatic Society*, no. 2
       (1976), p. 108-29. bibliog.

The original epic of Prince Rama, the *Ramayana*, which was set to verse by the
hermit poet Valmiki, unfolded the story of the court of Ayodhya in northern
India, somewhat in the manner we would now associate with a multi-part television
soap opera drama serial. In the same manner, innumerable additions and variations
were inserted over many years partly to suit the particular ethos of Burma or
Thailand, countries to which the story had spread from India, thus exercizing
enormous artistic and religious influences. Some of the additions involved the
assumption that Rama was in fact a god – an incarnation, or *avatar*, of the
Hindu god Viṣṇu. In this article Professor Brockington makes an interesting
analysis of the resultant blurring of secular and religious aspects in successive
Indian recensions of the epic.

431   *Ramakien*: **the Thai epic. Illustrated with bas-reliefs from Wat**
       Phra Jetupon, Bangkok.
       J. M. Cadet. Tokyo: Kodansha, 1971. 256p. bibliog.

The photographs from Wat Phra Jetupon (Wat Po) are a particularly attractive
element of this work, which is the Thai version of the Indian epic, the *Ramayana*.
It is presented in a popular, coffee-table format and style.

432   **Les trois mondes (Traibhumi brah r'van).** (The three worlds:
       the *Traibhum* of Phra Ruang.)
       George Coedès. Paris: Ecole Française d'Extrême-Orient,
       publications vol. 89 (1973), 294p.

This is a translation into French of the *Traibhum*, or 'Three Worlds' (variant
transliterations occur). The *Traibhum* is a compilation of Hindu-Buddhist texts
originating in Sri Lanka. The first Thai compilation of the *Traibhum* was reputedly
made in 1345 by King Lü Thai of Sukhothai, who was then viceroy of the
adjacent vassal state of Sajjanalai. The compilation, illustrated by specimen
paintings for murals together with captions and instruction, was reconstructed as
a principal document of state by successive monarchs, and latterly by King Taksin
at his new capital, Thonburi, in the late 1770s, following the destruction of
most state archives in the sacking of Ayudhya by the Burmese in 1767. The
'Three Worlds' represent tangible and intangible (*rupa* and *arupa*) elements of the
Buddhist cosmology, containing in all some thirty-two planes of existence on
earth or in various heavens or hells, in which reincarnation may occur. The
present volume includes canonical texts which formed the basis of the original
compilation.

110

33 **Selfless persons: imagery and thought in Theravada Buddhism.**
Stephen Collins. Cambridge, England: Cambridge University
Press, 1982. 323p.

his book provides an interesting and easily intelligible analysis of the trend in
'edic and Buddhist scripture towards selflessness, or asceticism, which gave rise
● central teachings in the Theravada doctrine in Sri Lanka, and passed from there
〉 Burma, Thailand and other neighbouring countries.

34 **Hinduism and Buddhism.**
Ananda K. Coomaraswamy. Westport, Connecticut: Greenwood
Press, 1971. reprint. 86p. bibliographic notes.

he essays in this slim volume constitute an excellent introductory analysis of the
●etaphysical basis of Eastern mystical religions, dealing separately with Brahman-
m or Hinduism, and Buddhism, and at the same time making clear their common
●ots.

35 **An introduction to Asia.**
Jean Herbert, translated from the French by M. Banerji.
London: Allen & Unwin, 1965. 410p. bibliog.

his is a profound, thought-provoking synthesis of the Asian attitude to life and
's environment. Many aspects of Thai custom and morality find reflections in it.
he author stresses the importance of the religious factor in the search for
armony between the self and the universe. He traces the evolution of religious
〉rms, including Theravada Buddhism, throughout the region stretching from the
liddle East to the Far East. He then considers Asian man and his expression in
〉ciety in relation to symbolism, attitudes to time, dream and reality, gods, the
lant kingdom and nature as a whole, his own person and pain, marriage, polite-
ess and morals, aversion to refusal and disagreement, the aims and inseparability
f art, wealth and poverty, work and the uses of knowledge, science and tech-
ology.

36 **Die Religionen Südostasiens.** (The religions of Southeast Asia.)
Andras Höfer, Gernot Prunner, Erika Kaneko, Louis Besacher,
Manuel Sarkisyanz. Stuttgart, GFR: Kohlhammer, 1975. 578p.
bibliogs. (Die Religionen der Menschheit, no. 23).

'or those who read German, this compendium will prove an invaluable source for
escriptions of the religious beliefs and practices in various parts of Thailand, and
t various stages in its history. The book also deals with neighbouring countries,
nd with tribes and minorities occupying borderlands spreading across other
ountries of Southeast Asia, including Negrito, Karen, Akha, Lahu, Meo, Yao
nd others. Some of these are collated according to the main languages, such as
lon-Khmer; the book also covers Confucianism, Taoism and other Chinese
ystems of belief common to South China and Taiwan.

Religion and Spirit Beliefs. Theravada Buddhism

437 **Understanding Thai Buddhism.**
M. L. Manich Jumsai. Bangkok: Chalermnit Press, 1973. 124p.

Jumsai, a distinguished compiler of general information on Thailand includi
an English-Thai dictionary (q.v.), uses his monastic name (Kulamanito) as th
anthologist of this short explanatory miscellany of material on Buddhism
professed in Thailand.

438 **Coomaraswamy. Vol. 1: selected papers: traditional art and
symbolism.**
Edited by Roger Lipsey. Princeton, New Jersey: Princeton
University Press, 1977. 580p. (Bollingen Series, no. 89).

The volume contains a selection from the large number of papers written by th
art historian Ananda K. Coomaraswamy when he was curator in the Departme
of Asian Art at the Boston Museum of Fine Arts. Dealing principally with origin
Indian source-concepts of Buddhist art and religious symbolism, the pape
selected range widely over subjects from the Tree of Life to the iconography
common utilitarian objects such as bowls or textiles. The volume is deep
thought-provoking in itself as to the foundations of the religious art acquired **b**
Thailand from India, and may also serve as an introduction to Coomaraswamy
massive monograph on symbolism in Buddhist art. The book contains usef
indexes of Greek, Sanskrit and Pali terms.

439 **Spirit of Asia.**
Michael Mackintyre. London: British Broadcasting Corporatior
1980. 288p.

This finely presented coffee-table volume is derived from the BBC televisic
series entitled 'Spirit of Asia', dealing with the spiritual and religious ethos, a
and practice of the Hindu and Buddhist countries, including Thailand. The maj
part of the book, with explanatory text from the series, consists of colo
pictures taken in the course of compiling the programmes, showing architectur
sculpture and scenes of religious occasions.

440 **Phra Lithai: Trai Phum Phra Ruang: three worlds according
to King Ruang. A Thai Buddhist cosmology.**
Translated from the Thai with an introduction and notes **b**
Frank E. Reynolds, Mani B. Reynolds. Berkeley, California:
University of California, 1982. 383p. 15 colour plates. (Berkeley
Buddhist Studies Series no. 4).

This is an English translation with commentary on the basic Thai Buddhist cano
the *Traibhum* (three worlds), as originally compiled in 1345 by King Lü Th
whilst still viceroy at Sajjanalai, before acceding to the throne of Sukhoth
Cf. also G. Cœdès, *Les trois mondes* (q.v.). The text rehearses the Buddhi
cosmology of the levels of existence or reincarnation, consisting of *karn*
(human experience and desire), *rupa* (form) and *arupa* (perfection devoid
form). These are split down into many sub-levels, including some thirty levels
hell with descriptions of punishments inflicted in these.

112

41 **World conqueror and world renouncer: a study in Buddhism and polity in Thailand against a historical background.**
Stanley Jeyaraja Tambiah. Cambridge, England: Cambridge University Press, 1976. 557p. bibliog.

'he author has a Sinhalese Tamil background and is an anthropologist as well as ₁ historian of Thailand. The subject matter of this profound, at times turgid and ifficult study is the relationship between church and state in post-Ayudhya 'hailand. The kernel of the argument is his concept of an alternating 'galactic olity'. He dissolves the sharp line of division between Hinduism and Buddhism in ħe religious interpretation of kingship, and explains how a Theravada monarch ttains the status of a world-conquering prince and, without relinquishing this, ssumes also the world-renouncing role of *bodhisattva*, thus combining the two pposite principles of *rajadhamma* and *dhammaraja*.

42 **A note on the date of the Traibhumikatha.**
M. Vickery. *Journal of the Siam Society*, vol. 62, part 2 (July 1974), p. 275-84.

'he *Traibhum* was re-compiled as a principal source of religious orthodoxy in uccessive Thai dynasties, the earliest (14th century) is not extant in its original orm cf. *Les trois mondes*, by George Coedès (q.v.). This paper calls attention to actors involved in dating early revisions of the compilation.

43 **The universe around them: cosmology and cosmic renewal in Indianized Southeast Asia.**
H. G. Quaritch Wales. London: Arthur Probsthain, 1977. 168p. bibliog.

pecialists in early religious evolution in Asia and its contrasting expression in ountries like Thailand and Bali will find this discussion of Hindu-Buddhist osmology and practice stimulating. The non-specialist reader may find the olume instructive in the extent to which it casts illustrative sidelights on the omplex matters raised in more generalized descriptions of the religious art and ractice of Indian-influenced Southeast Asia.

113

Buddhist practice and spirit cults

444 **Buddhist monk, Buddhist layman: a study of urban monastic organisation in central Thailand.**
Jane Bunnag. Cambridge, England: Cambridge University Press, 1973. 219p. bibliog. (Cambridge Studies in Social Anthropology.

This detailed anthropological study is the result of three years' research i Ayudhya, the largely ruined former capital, which is now the site of a considerab revival of urban life on a provincial scale. The study highlights the workin relationship between the abbots and the lay organizing committees which suppo the temples and monasteries. The author examines the balance between educatic in religious affairs, on the one hand, and personal charisma on the other, i obtaining advancement within the monastic establishments. Another theme is th role of monkhood and its lay supporters in the provision of opportunities fo merit-making for the general public.

445 **Les cetiya de sable au Laos et en Thaïlande: les textes.** (The san *chedis* of Laos and Thailand: texts.)
Louis Gabaude. Paris: Ecole Française d'Extrême-Orient, 1979. 336p. plates. (Publication of the EFEO, vol. 68).

Examines the Buddhist rites associated with the construction of sand *chea* (shrines) with elaborate bamboo and other decorations alongside both th Lao and the Thai banks of the Mekong River. Regional language students will fir the reproductions and translations of Lao and Thai texts valuable.

446 **A retrospective view and account of the That Maha Ch'at ceremony.**
G. E. Gerini. Bangkok: Bangkok Times, 1892. Reprinted, Bangkok: Sathirakoses-Nagapradipa Foundation, 1976. 69p. photographic plates.

The *Maha Ch'at* (Great Birth), or *Vessantara Jataka*, is the story of the last pr incarnation of Buddha. It is regarded as the most important of the *jatakas* observe in the Thai religious calendar, and is the inspiration for much religious literatu and art, of which kings were the patrons, or in some cases the originators. In th volume the author explains the story and significance of the *Vessantara Jatak* and quotes relevant poems, in vernacular and English translation, by King Sc Tham (1628-29) and others.

Religion and Spirit Beliefs. Buddhist practice and spirit cults

447 **The tonsure ceremony as performed in Siam.**
G. E. Gerini. Bangkok: Bangkok Times, 1895. 187p. plates.
The tonsure ceremony is still practised in Thailand as a religious initiation, equivalent to 'coming of age'. This detailed study of its background in Hindu and Pali canon describes the ceremony performed for King Vajiravudh in 1892, when he was Crown prince and about to leave for an European education. The ceremony, for Buddhist novices, involves reference to Hindu gods and the related Indian tradition of the topknot. This account traces its origins in Thailand to the *Traibhum* (q.v.) and notes its earliest records in respect of kings of the Ayudhya dynasty in the early 1600s including that of King Narai (1656-88) in 1642.

448 **Monks, merit and motivation: an exploratory study of the social functions of Buddhism in Thailand in processes of guided social change.**
J. A. Niels Mulder. De Kalb, Illinois: Northern Illinois University, 1969. 43p. (Center for Southeast Asian Studies Special Report no. 1).
This study examines the role of the *sangha* (monkhood) in relation to government, and to national and village power structures; it concludes that merit-making may be identified with motives of improvement and modernization.

449 **Introduction à la connaissance des Hlvn Ba de Thaïlande.**
(Introduction to the Hlvn Ba (Luang pho) of Thailand.)
Anatole-Roger Peltier. Paris: Ecole Française d'Extrême-Orient, 1977. 214p. 6 plates. bibliog. (Publications of the EFEO, vol. 115).
The Luang Pho are a sect of Buddhist monks which has gained a reputation among the people of the southwest Thai peninsular region near Songkhla as workers of magic and distributors of amulets, such as clay models of leading monks worn as necklets. This account of the sect carries interpretations of relevant Thai texts and photographs of monks and amulets.

450 **The Buddhist monkhood in 19th-century Thailand.**
Craig James Reynolds. Ann Arbor, Michigan: University Microfilms International, 1973. 307p. bibliog. (PhD thesis for Cornell University).
This thesis sets out to resolve a paradox: the monastic life involved the renunciation of the material world; yet the king's strength could depend on the support he afforded to the monasteries. The author considers the important political and educational role of the monasteries in the reform movement initiated by King Chulalongkorn in the late 19th century; he notes the value acquired by the monasteries through their historical contacts with the wider world – for instance, in early exchanges with Sri Lanka. For a discussion of the Supreme Patriarchate's temporal influence during the 19th century cf. the author's *Autobiography of Prince-Patriarch Vajiranana* (q.v.). Nevertheless the monkhood experienced conflicts, especially in the field of law, cf. R. Lingat, *Vinaya and lay laws* (q.v.).

451 **A village ordination.**
Thomas H. Silcock, introduction by Barend J. Terwiel. London:
Curzon Press; Bangkok: Craftsman Press, 1976. 93p. photos.
(Scandinavian Institute of Asian Studies Monograph Series).

This is a close translation into English of a Thai poem by a learned monk tracing
the life and ordination of a farmer's son who encounters the monastic life at the
age of seven as a boy server, returns to farm life for five years, and then chooses
to remain as a monk after his three months' stay in the monastery at the age of
twenty. The complete Thai text is interleaved with English, which reproduces
much of the form and manner of the original. The ordination ceremony is
illustrated with photographs. The work is of literary value and provides an
example of a familiar village ceremony primarily designed to make merit for the
ordinand's parents.

452 **Buddhism and the spirit cults in northeast Thailand.**
Stanley Jeyaraja Tambiah. Cambridge, England: Cambridge
University Press, 1970. Paperback editions 1975, 1977 & 1980.
388p. map. bibliog.

This work is a result of a sojourn in Thailand for Unesco in 1960-63; the study,
by an authority on Buddhism and anthropology, provides a detailed description
of practice in a particular village to exemplify the interaction of religion and spirit
cults. The book describes monastic life, its interconnection with the villagers, and
rituals and symbols such as those involved in *sukhwan* healing rites, exorcism and
invocation of guardian spirits.

453 **The Buddhist saints of the forest and the cult of amulets.**
Stanley Jeyaraja Tambiah. Cambridge, England: Cambridge
University Press, 1984. 417p. map. bibliog.

An anthropological study of Buddhist and spirit cult practice in forest monastic
communities.

454 **Monks and magic: an analysis of religious ceremonies in central
Thailand.**
Barend Jan Terwiel. London: Curzon Press, 1979. 2nd rev. ed.
296p. maps. illus. (Scandinavian Institute of Asian Studies
Monograph, no. 24).

A review of religious ceremonies in central Thailand written from an anthropological standpoint.

455 **The Tais and their belief in khwans.**
Barend Jan Terwiel. *Southeast Asian Review*, vol. 3, no. 1
(1978), p. 1-16.

The *khwan* is the immanent, invisible spirit which Thais believe inhabits all things
around them, and which must not be violated. This paper gives some examples of
the working of this belief, for instance in relation to ropes used to demarcate
land for tax purposes.

456 **Divination in Thailand; the hopes and fears of a Southeast Asian people.**
H. G. Quaritch Wales. London: Curzon Press, 1982. 145p.

In this addition to his earlier accounts of aspects of religious cults and ceremonial manifestations in Thailand, the author turns his attention to the relevance of psychic phenomena and divination.

Royal ceremonies and festivals

457 **The royal monasteries and their significance.**
A. B. Griswold. Bangkok: Fine Arts Department, 1958. 16p.
map. new series. (Thailand Culture, no. 2).

This useful pamphlet explains the differentiation of the monastic establishments of Thailand which, like the Temple of the Emerald Buddha in Bangkok, are under royal patronage.

458 **Conceptions of state and kingship in Southeast Asia.**
Robert Heine-Geldern. Ithaca, New York: Cornell University Press, 1963. 14p. (Southeast Asia Data Paper, no. 18).

Introduces the concepts of kingship derived from Hindu India and adapted during several dynastic periods in Thailand and neighbouring countries.

459 **Siamese state ceremonies: their history and function.**
H. G. Quaritch Wales. London: Bernard Quaritch, 1931. 326p.
bibliog.

This highly detailed study of the traditional royal ceremonies of Thailand is the fullest available account of the subject in English. The author spent some years as an adviser at the court in Bangkok. His account utilizes Thai classical sources, especially a massive compilation of these in Thai by King Chulalongkorn. The author illuminates specific aspects of the interaction of Hindu and Buddhist practice at the court, and in the discharge of the king's functions in society. The book describes coronation, funerary and other ceremonies conducted in the palace complex, and also those related to the calendar and to the annual cycle of agriculture. Cf. also the author's *Supplementary notes on Siamese state ceremonies* (1971).

Missionaries

460 **Siam then: the foreign colony in Bangkok before and after Anna.**
William L. Bradley. Pasadena, California: Wilfred Carey Library,
1981. 207p. maps. bibliog. photos.

Dan Beach Bradley (1804-73), one of a numerous family of American Protestant
missionaries, was a friend of King Mongkut; further evidence of the king's open-
mindedness towards Western ideas, whether representative of a foreign religion or
otherwise. This readable narrative by another member of the family consists of an
edition of Bradley's diaries, mentioning many of those present at the court,
including Anna who arrived in Bangkok in 1862.

461 **McFarland of Siam.**
Bertha Blount McFarland. New York: Vantage Press, 1958.
313p.

This is a biographical sketch of George Bradley McFarland, one of an important
American Protestant missionary family in Thailand, who edited the reminiscences
of earlier members of the family and also compiled an excellent Thai dictionary
specializing in forest products. The book describes the natural, educational and
social matters in which he interested himself during his work in the country in the
pre-war years.

462 **Historical sketch of Protestant missions in Siam, 1828-1928.**
Edited by George Bradley McFarland. Bangkok: Bangkok Times
Press, 1928. 386p.

This edition of records left by an important American Protestant missionary
family in Thailand includes reminiscences of Dan Beach Bradley, a friend and
confidant of King Mongkut.

463 **History of Protestant work in Thailand.**
Kenneth E. Wells. Bangkok: Church of Christ in Thailand, 1939.
213p.

The author's account of American Protestant missionary work in Thailand is
based on a pre-war decade in the country in that capacity.

464 **Thai Buddhism: its rites and activities.**
Kenneth E. Wells. Bangkok: Bangkok Times Press, 1939;
Reprinted, Bangkok Christian Bookstore, 1960. 320p.

This account by an American Protestant missionary gives his impressions of the
effect of Buddhist practice on everyday life in pre-war Thailand. The book
provides a basis for measuring changes which have, and have not appeared in life
today.

Society

465 **The folk religion of Ban Nai: a hamlet in central Thailand.**
Kingkeo Attagara. PhD thesis, Indiana University, 1967. 596p.
maps. bibliog. (Unpublished, available from the university).
The author describes shamanism, magic rites, spirits accepted by the families, and
the sense of the absurd in comic and obscene tales current among them. The bulk
of the material consists of texts in English of folklore tales and songs (p. 187-581).
This is a very interesting collection.

466 **Rusembilan: a Malay fishing village in southern Thailand.**
Thomas M. Fraser, Jr. Ithaca, New York: Cornell University
Press, 1960. 281p. bibliog. (Cornell Studies in Anthropology).
This is a good, all round account of life in a southern Thai fishing village. Themes
include internal and national organization; the mosque, religion and spirit cults;
the whole life cycle; and economics and work, both maritime and agricultural.

467 **Mensch und Gesellschaft.** (Man and society.)
Jürgen Hohnholz. In: *Thailand*. Edited by Jürgen Hohnholz.
Tübingen, GFR: Erdmann, 1980. p. 349-415. (Foreign Relations
Institute Country Studies, no. 13).
This section of a 'Country Study Handbook' on Thailand is a good, concise
account of the professional and social structure of the country, its urbanization
and administration, and the make-up of its society. It includes separate treatments
of the composition of its Chinese and Muslim elements.

468 **A behavioral study of rural modernization: social and economic
change in Thai villages.**
Charles A. Murray, foreword by Lucian W. Pye. New York,
London: Praeger, 1977. 149p. bibliog. (Praeger Special Studies
in International Economics and Development).
Murray introduces studies of rural village behaviour in Thailand to show changes
caused by modernization and development.

Society

469 The political economy of Siam.
Edited and introduced by Chatthip Nartsupha, Suthy Prasartset, with Montri Chen Vidyakorn. Bangkok: Social Science Association of Thailand, 1978 & 1981.

The two volumes cover the documentary history of the evolution of Thailand's social economy from the reign of King Mongkut to the end of the absolute monarchy. Volume one covers 1851-1910 and volume two covers 1910-32. Each volume is introduced with a short survey, and the documentary extracts quoted are set in their socio-economic perspective. Topics include: marriage and abduction, *corvée* labour and tattooing, *klong* digging, goldsmith training (vol. 1); and the activization of the tin industry (already a Chinese preserve), and the reasons for the failure of rice production methods to meet the rising demands of international trade (vol. 2).

470 The dynamics of politics and administration in rural Thailand.
Clark D. Neher. Athens, Ohio: Ohio Unversity Press, 1974. 105p. (Center for International Studies, Southeast Asia Region).

This short study gives an excellent picture of the village attitude to politics and patronage both within the village and its district and provincial peripheries. Villages show little regard for distant centres of national politics like Bangkok.

471 Modernizing Chiang Mai: a study of community élites in modern devolution.
Chakrit Noranitipadungkarn, A. Clarke Hagensick. Bangkok: National Institute of Development Administration, 1977. 120p.

Chiang Mai grew up with an independent existence to become, in effect, the 'capital of the north'. This short, statistical study examines the social changes which occurred as a result of its rapid modern development as an industrial and tourist centre, with luxury hotels and ugly one-storey clusters of shops jostling the monuments of its separate mediaeval monarchy.

472 Festivals and ceremonies of Thailand.
Raymond Pilon-Bernier, translated from the French by Joanne Elizabeth Soulier. Bangkok: Sangwan Surasawang, 1973. 173p. illus.

A short, simply told, illustrated story of the royal and other traditional festivals and ceremonies of Thailand, suitable for children and families.

473 Family life in a northern Thai village: a study in the structural significance of women.
Sulamith Heins Potter. Berkeley, California; London: University of California Press, 1977. 137p. bibliog.

This sociological study gives an outline and assessment of a wide variety of observed factors in the integration of women in family and economic life, in work and decision-making in northern Thailand.

474 **The life of the farmer in Thailand.**
Phya Anuman Rajadhon, translated from the Thai by William
J. Gedney. New Haven, Connecticut: Yale University Press,
1955. 60p. (Southeast Asia Studies Translation Series, no. 5).
By one of the most respected exponents of Thai life and customs, this is a simple
and detailed description of the daily life, work and preoccupations of Thai
farmers. It provides drawings of their implements.

475 **Trends in Thailand II: proceedings with background commentary
papers.**
Edited by Somporn Sangchai, Lim Joo-Jock. Singapore:
Institute for Southeast Asian Studies, 1976. 164p.
There are the edited papers from the proceedings of a seminar convened in 1976
at the ISEAS in Singapore, containing the views of a group of Thai authorities
on various socio-economic elements in Thailand; topics included are: mass media,
internal security and relations within ASEAN. An earlier compilation covered a
similar meeting in 1973.

476 **Thailand: social and economic studies in development.**
Edited by Thomas H. Silcock. Canberra: Australian National
University Press, 1967. 334p. bibliog.
This aggregation of studies remains an excellent basic account of the demographic,
economic and development structure of Thailand. Topics include banking and
payments, agricultural diversification, industrial finance, and the important
question of the rice export premium in relation to farming, trade patterns and
state policies affecting standards of living.

477 **Change and persistence in Thai society: essays in honor of
Lauriston Sharp.**
Edited by G. William Skinner, A. Thomas Kirsch. Ithaca,
New York: Cornell University Press, 1975. 387p. maps. bibliog.
This felicitation volume which is one of two such volumes, (the other being
Social organization and the applications of anthropology [q.v.], contains article
articles on aspects of Thai society from an anthropological standpoint; the volume
is in honour of Lauriston Sharp, a founder of Cornell University's post-war
'Southeast Asia Program of Research Papers'.

478 **Social organization and the applications of anthropology:
essays in honor of Lauriston Sharp.**
Edited by R. J. Smith. Ithaca, New York: Cornell University
Press, 1974. 337p.
One of two felicitation volumes cf. *Change and persistence in Thai society* (q.v.)
published in honour of Lauriston Sharp.

Society

479 From peasant to pedicab driver.
Robert B. Textor. New Haven, Connecticut: Yale University Press, 1961. 81p. (Southeast Asia Studies, no. 9).

This is a social study of northeast Thai farmers who have periodically migrated to Bangkok and become pedicab drivers to make some money for their families. The author examines factors which keep them so cheerful: kinship and group ties, which make them something of a Bangkok subculture; religion and magic; their economics, food, housing, clothing, health, and recreation; and their relations with the police.

480 Providence and prostitution: image and reality in Buddhist Thailand.
Khin Thitsa. London: Change, 1980. 28p. map. bibliog. (Change International Reports: Women and Society).

The object of 'Change Publications' is to promote research and reports on women's conditions and status worldwide. The author of this report, a Burmese woman educated and part-time resident in Thailand, argues that the prevailing combination of monk, monarch and militia in the country devalues the status of women, despite their record of 80 per cent labour participation. Prostitution in Bangkok is a result of the combination of a drift of young females to Bangkok from deprived agricultural communities seeking work to support their families, and the high rate of tourism from Japan and Europe; thus replacing the former American service demand for them.

481 A structural analysis of Thai economic history: case study of a northern Chao Phraya village.
Takashi Tomosugi. Tokyo: Institute of Development Economics, 1980. 190p. bibliog. glossary.

The author of this book studied behavioural patterns in a central Thai village from a philosophical standpoint, asking the question, 'What factors contribute to its cohesion as a village?' The answers are partly geographical, taking into account the necessity of mutual assistance in matters like rice production; with the modern decline of this necessity, traditional factors supervene, such as the spirit cults of place, and the need for fun (*sanuk*) and games. The book is arranged under anthropological description, theoretical framework and historical accounts. The full glossary of rural-social words and phrases will be found useful.

482 **Oriental despotism: a comparative study of total power.**
Karl A. Wittfogel. New Haven, Connecticut: Yale University
Press, 1973. 556p. bibliog.

This study has gained a considerable reputation since its original publication in
1957. The author interprets long-term social history in terms of hydraulic
societies, evolving administrative power structures as a result of their dependence
on large-scale water management. This applies especially to those, as in India or
China, with arid or humid climates and using major rivers for irrigation of wet
rice. In the case of Thailand, the author identifies the hydraulic element as the
underlying cause of the country's relatively static social and governmental
structure, capable of resisting, on the one hand, colonialism, and on the other,
effective democracy and the emergence of a powerful middle class.

Social Services and Public Health

483 **Statistical Report.**
Department of Medical Services, Thailand Ministry of Public
Health. Bangkok: The Ministry, 1964- . annually.
This is a complete departmental report on public health services of the country
with statistics and text in English.

484 **Community health and health motivation in Southeast Asia.**
Edited by Hans Jochen Diesfeld, Erich Kröger. Wiesbaden,
GFR: Steiner, 1974. 199p.
These are collected papers presented to an international seminar held in Berlin
on 22 Oct.-10 Nov. 1973 organized by the German Foundation for International
Development and the Institute of Tropical Hygiene and Public Health, South Asia
Institute, University of Heidelberg. Included is a report on the structure of the
public health service in Thailand, p. 148-54.

485 **Thailand: contraceptive prevalence survey.**
Family Health Division, National Institute of Development
Administration, Ministry of Public Health. Bangkok: Westing-
house Health Systems, The Institute, 1978. 31p. bibliog. refs.
This is a summary report, in English and Thai, on contraceptive prevalence, a sub-
ject of high priority in national public health policy.

486 **Medical problems in Southeast Asia.**
Edited by Noboru Higashi. Kyoto, Japan: Center for Southeast
Asian Studies, Kyoto University, 1968. 125p. (Symposium
Series, no. 4).
Papers contributed to this Kyoto symposium cover general incidence of major
regional diseases in Southeast Asia. Specific papers deal with treatment of leprosy
neurological and ophthalmological diseases in Thailand.

124

87 **Siam: general and medical.**
Ministry of Commerce and Communications. Bangkok: The
Ministry, 1930. 315p.

hough dated, this pre-war compendium of official information is still of value
or the material which it contains of archival interest relating to the end of the
eriod of absolute monarchy, and especially on public health matters. Cf. also
iam; nature and industry (q.v.).

88 **Public Health Statistics.**
Ministry of Public Health. Bangkok: The Ministry, 1965- .
annually.

he issue of 1976 has accumulated data for 1972-76 dealing with population,
ealth statistics, health services and administration, and various causes of death.

89 **Health and welfare survey.**
National Statistical Office. Bangkok: Office of the Prime
Minister, 1974- . annually.

his statistical report on public health, private and self-administered as well as
elfare services in the country as a whole is published annually in Thai and
nglish with text and tables.

Narcotics

490 L'affaire Marie-Andrée Leclerc. (The Marie-Andrée Leclerc case.)
Huguette Laprise. Montreal: Editions la Presse, 1977. 214p.
photos.

This is a vivid account by a Quebec journalist of her attempts to unravel a
complex series of international crimes, partly in India and partly in Thailand
involving murder and narcotics. The victim was a typist from Quebec. The author
visited Thailand twice, where she had access to confidential official and diplomatic
records in the course of her enquiries into the ramifications of the case.

491 Les chiens de Bangkok. (The dogs of Bangkok.)
Armand Lerco. Paris: Grasset, 1982. 252p.

Described by a reviewer as a 'terrible and magnificent' story, this is the account
of a 22-year-old adventurer in search of narcotics, who spends three years in a
Thai prison, to emerge into Bangkok only to become 'the prisoner of heroin'.

492 The politics of heroin in Southeast Asia.
Alfred W. McCoy, with Cathleen B. Read, Leonard P. Adams II.
New York: Harper & Row, 1973. 472p. illus. glossary.

A reviewer notes that only eleven books have appeared on this subject; this is the
best. Another reviewer says that the CIA tried to suppress it. This volume is
meticulously researched; it has 79p. of reference notes arranged by chapters. Its
approach is serious, rather than sensational. The main theme is the Vietnam
war connection. The author traces the history of heroin, via the Mafia, Iran and
China (whose cessation as a source of supply by 1955 was an important factor
cf. appendix by Adams), up to the present major world source, the 'Golden
Triangle' represented by Burma, Thailand and Laos. Thai government policies
encouraging the trade to supply addicts within the country, in 1947, and to stop
the trade, in 1959, are noted in the context of the still continuing KMT (Chinese
Nationalist Kuomintang Army) presence established in the triangle in the after
math of the Second World War and of Thai, Lao, Vietnamese and US government
post-war policies. Material cited includes the Meo involvement in opium production
centred on Ban Wat village and the trading role of Haw tribes from Yunnan in the
Fang area of northern Thailand near the Burma border.

493   **On the trail of the ancient opium poppy.**
       Mark David Merlin.   London: Associated University Presses,
       1985. 320p. bibliog.

This is a biogeographical account of *Papaver somniferum* dealing with its botanical
archaeology and dispersal, both by natural and human means, to its present range
of ominous economic and social importance.

494   **Freed for life.**
       Rita Nightingale.   London: Marshall, Morgan & Scott, 1982.
       192p.

The author, a nurse, spent some time in prison in Thailand following a drugs
offence; she was set free by an act of royal discretion. Her personal observations
of British prisoners' conditions in the late 1970s form the subject of these
reminiscences.

Politics

General

495 **The Sarit régime, 1957-63: the formative years of modern Thai politics.**
Thak Chaloemtiarana. Ann Arbor, Michigan: University Microfilms International, 1974. 566p. bibliog. (PhD thesis for Cornell University).

The subject matter of this thesis is the personality and politics of F. M. Sarit. An introductory section covers the coup to 1947, the involvement of Pridi Phanomyong, and the triumvirate of 1948-57. Factionalism in politics, the bureaucracy and the monarchy, and fears of an independent Isan (northeast Thailand) are aspects of internal affairs during Sarit's régime; the flare-up in Laos is an external factor which brought America closer to Thailand. Sarit himself, despite his massive misappropriations of public funds and excesses in the realm of sexual affairs, emerges as a figure Thai people could nevertheless admire: a headstrong risk-taker (*nakleng*).

496 **Thai politics, 1932-57.**
Edited by Thak Chaloemtiarana. Bankok: Thammasat University, 1978. 884p. (Social Science Association of Thailand).

This compilation will be of use to research students. It comprises texts from selected documents illustrating the development of Thai political life through most of the constitutional period dating from 1932. Aspects covered include the crisis of royal authority, the post-war rise of a national bureaucracy, and the alternation of military power and civilian politics in the post-war decades. Some of the documents quoted relate to foreign policy.

497 **The diplomacy of Southeast Asia, 1945-58.**
Russell H. Fifield. New York: Harper & Row, 1958. 584p. bibliog. Reprinted, Orinda, California: Shoestring, 1968.

The author gives a good outline of Southeast Asian regional rehabilitation problems confronting the outside great powers in the immediate post-war period. Chapter 7 concentrates on Thailand.

498 **Thailand: society and politics.**
John Lawrence Scott Girling. Ithaca, New York: Cornell
University Press, 1981. 306p. map. bibliog.

This recommended study describes the growth and present structure of Thai
politics in relation to its background in the country's social structure.

499 **Foreign policy of Thailand.**
Ganganath Jha. New Delhi: Radiant Publishers, 1979. 195p.
bibliog.

This summary of Thailand's foreign policy covers early Western contacts briefly,
and then concentrates mainly on the post-war period.

500 **The devil's discus.**
Rayne Kruger. London: Cassell, 1964. 260p. bibliog.

An analysis of the events surrounding the death of King Ananda (Rama VIII),
in 1946, who was still a minor. The book itself ends with a question-mark, and
it may prove to be the last word on this tragic episode – given the paucity and
reticence of official documentation on the subject. It includes material illustrative of the society of Bangkok at the time, and particularly leading personalities, such as the prime minister, Pridi Phanamyong, who became the focus of
certain official suspicions in this matter. Phanamyong sought exile in Peking
for a number of years, which were crucial in Thailand's post-war political development, and ultimately settled in Paris, where he had been educated.

501 **Modern Thai politics: from village to nation.**
Edited by Clark D. Neher. Cambridge, Massachusetts:
Schenkman, 1979. 483p.

The collection of materials in this substantial volume provides an excellent all
round background to modern Thailand's government, politics and administration.

502 **Elites, power structures and politics in Thai communities.**
Chakrit Noranitipadungkarn. Bangkok: National Institute of
Development Administration, 1981. 201p. bibliog. (Technical
Publication Promotion Project).

The pre-constitutional governments of Thailand were as much oligarchic as
monarchic; this short study looks at the evolution of the pattern of élites,
formerly the result of royal patronage, in modern Thai society, and considers the
effect on the individual in politics and management.

503 **Portraits of Thai politics.**
Jayanta Kumar Ray. New Delhi: Orient Longman, 1972. 225p.

This volume contains memoirs of civilian political activity in the period following
the coup of 1932 which abolished the absolute monarchy. Three notable personalities discussed are: M. R. Seni Pramoj; Thawee Bunyaketu; and Lady Lu-iad
Pibul Songkhram (widow of the Field Marshal).

504 **Some observations on the elections and coalition formation in Thailand 1976.**
Somporn Sangchai. Singapore: Institute of South East Asian Studies, 1976. 51p. (ISEAS Occasional Paper no. 43).

This paper was written immediately after the election of 1976 and reflects the cut-and-thrust of politics in action in Thailand at a time when an attempt was being made to reassert a democratic framework after the student rising of 1973 had caused the overthrow of the unpopular military triumvirate consisting of Marshal Thanom Kittikachorn, Praphas Charusathien (the 'strong man' in the background), and Colonel Narong Kittikachorn (who achieved notoriety for his conduct of bloody armed security operations against the students). Twenty-two parties contested the election. The book is of interest for its details of these and of the politicians involved, including the two alternating civilian prime ministers, the very different half-brothers M. R. Seni Pramoj and M. R. Kukrit Pramoj, who led the coalitions of the mid-'70s.

505 **The Thai bureaucracy: institutional change and development.**
William J. Siffin. Honolulu: East-West Center Press, 1966. 291p. bibliog.

This book analyses changes in Thailand's administrative system and institutions in the period 1950-65. The author shows how these changes came about against the background of the re-definition of the functions of the Ministry of the Interior, which, in the administrative model inherited from Ayudha, had represented a rigid oligarchic instrument of royal control.

506 **Elections and parties in Thailand.**
David A. Wilson, Herbert P. Phillips. *Far Eastern Survey*, vol. 27, no. 8 (Aug. 1958), p. 113-19. (American Institute of Pacific Relations).

Provides a preliminary overview of the context of personalities and political machinery in which some of the early attempts at democratic government took place in Thailand after the war, following the elections of 1952.

507 **Politics in Thailand.**
David A. Wilson. London: Oxford University Press; Ithaca, New York: Cornell University Press, 1966. 307p.

This perceptive sketch of the Thai political scene could provide a useful working basis towards the reading of fuller and more recent studies.

508 **Reflections on the collapse of democracy in Thailand.**
Robert F. Zimmerman. Singapore; Institute of Southeast Asian Studies, 1978. 117p. (Occasional Paper, no. 50).

This paper examines the aftermath of the student uprising of 1973. By way of background, the author postulates an analytical model of Thailand's political structure.

Radicalism: the student uprising, 1973

09 **Asie du Sud-est: l'enjeu thaïlandais.** (Southeast Asia: the Thai domino.)
Sylvia Cattori, Jean Cattori, preface by Jean Ziegler. Paris: Editions l'Harmattan, 1979. 253p. bibliog.

he subject-matter of this political polemic in French is the period immediately ollowing the student uprising of 1973. The Swiss co-authors, resident in Bangkok uring 1975-77 as a journalist and a UN official respectively, describe visits to ungle hideouts used by student members of the Communist Party of Thailand; hey extend the argument to illustrate the social conditions prerequisite to evolution. Readers may find the book useful as an example of international ommunist propaganda using Thailand as a peg.

10 **Thailand: origins of military rule.**
David Elliott, foreword by Malcolm Caldwell. London: Zed Press, 1978. 190p. map. bibliog.

This is an example of the Marxist analysis of the historical-political situation of Thailand. The author places an appreciation of the economic, banking and financial *status quo*, with a section on the controversial rice export premium, in the context of American imperialism.

11 **The Thailand Communist Movement and China-Vietnam competition in Asia.**
Kay Möller. Cologne, GFR: Federal Institute for Asian and International Studies, 1981. 32p.

The author considers the conflicting outside power interests involved on the Thai-ndochina border in relation to the Thai Communist Movement.

12 **Political conflict in Thailand: reform, reaction, revolution.**
David L. Morell, Chai-anan Samudivanija. Cambridge, Massachusetts: Delgeschlager, Gunn & Hain, 1981. Paperback edition, 1982. 362p. bibliog.

This is the fullest available account of the political upheavals in Thailand during the 1970s. The two authors combine the research resources of Princeton and Chulalongkorn universities for documentary source materials, and the work also includes interviews with Prime Minister M. R. Kukrit Pramoj and other contemporary politicians. The main thesis concerns the interplay of the forces of reaction and revolution in post-war Thai politics, especially as exemplified in the student uprising of 1973 and its aftermath. The authors trace the growth of political structures from 1932 (the coup abolishing absolute monarchy), and measure the extent of military intervention in the ensuing series of administrations, particularly the post-war Thanom-Phrapas clique; the last government mentioned is that of General Kris.

131

Politics. Radicalism: the student uprising, 1973

513 **Thailand's student activism and political change.**
Ross Prizzia, Narong Sinsawasdi. Bangkok: D. K. Book House, 1974. 221p. bibliog. photos.
This is a close-up account of the student uprising of 1973, with photographs of the events of that time, together with an impression of the political context from which they sprang.

514 **The Thai Young Turks.**
Chai-anan Samudavanija. Singapore: Institute of Southeast Asian Studies, 1982. 101p. bibliog.
The author analyses the role of the Thai Young Military Officers Group in the unsuccessful coup of 1 April 1981. The author traces the background of the military element in Thai politics from 1932-76, noting the attitudes of the middle officers, some of whose views are quoted, as expressing impatience with the politicians' use of the army to assert their own control.

515 **Buddhism and politics in Thailand: a study of socio-political change and political activism of the sangha.**
Somboon Suksamran. Singapore: Institute of Southeast Asian Studies, 1982. 179p. bibliog.
The main theme of this study is the emergence of radicalism among the monkhood in the 1970s, with a Young Monks Front coinciding with the eruption of student revolt in 1973. Political reformism was nothing new to the monkhood, and it was heightened by perception of the dangers of communism; from this background arose a new class of radical monks.

516 **Thailand: roots of conflict.**
Edited by Andrew Turton, Jonathan Fast, Malcolm Caldwell. Nottingham, England: Spokesman Books, 1978. 196p. map.
This is a study of radicalism and social conditions in Thailand. Malcolm Caldwell one of the editors, was murdered when, as a sympathizer with, and one of the first Westerners to do so, he re-entered Kampuchea, in 1978, after the Khmer Rouge takeover. For a further contribution by Caldwell cf. 'Thailand: toward the revolution', *Race and Class*, vol. 18, no. 24 (1976), which includes a good bibliography on this subject.

517 **Communism in Southeast Asia.**
Justus M. van der Kroef. London: Macmillan, 1981. 342p. bibliog. (Macmillan International College Editions).
This is an outline study of communist policy and party organization in Southeast Asia following the victory in Indochina. The author deals with ASEAN and Indochina; rifts between Peking and Moscow in the region; and the region's contemporary political environment, including that in Thailand, in relation to communist pressures. Thai politics are mentioned *passim*; Thai organizations referred to include the Federation of Patriotic Workers, the Independence Movement, the Patriotic Front, and the Muslim People's Liberation Armed Forces.

518   **The Thai radicals and the Communist Party: interaction of ideology and nationalism in the forest, 1975-80.**
Yuangrat Wedel.   Singapore: Maruzen Asia, 1983. 87p. bibliog.
(Institute of Southeast Asian Studies Occasional Papers, no. 72).

The author presents from personal experience a detailed day-by-day account of the student uprising of 1973, and the subsequent movements of radical student groups into the jungle, where intensive exchanges of Marxist and nationalist ideological views took place.

Insurgency and refugees

519   **Political change and modernization: northeast Thailand's quest for identity and its political threat to national security.**
Kanala Sukhabanij Eksaengsri.   Ann Arbor. Michigan: University Microfilms International, 1977. 590p. bibliog. (PhD thesis for the New York State University, 1977).

This thesis considers insurgency problems in the northeast against a pattern of village discontents. The incompatibility of ethnic élites within the country's central political structure is advanced as a factor in local instability. The bibliography contains useful material on defence and insurgency questions.

520   **Fighters, refugees and immigrants: a story of the Hmong.**
Mace Goldfarb.   Minneapolis, Minnesota: Carolrhoda Books, 1982. 48p. map. col. photos.

The author, an American pediatrician, portrays the life of Meo refugees from Laos. The text, liberally illustrated with colour photographs, shows life at the Ban Vinai refugee camp (founded in 1975 near the Mekong River), in a lively and positive light. Its Meo inhabitants, many of whom fought on the American side in Laos, tend to be accepted as immigrants in the United States.

521   **Thai government programs in refugee relocation and settlement in northern Thailand.**
Robert M. Hearn.   Auburn, New York: Thailand Books, 1974. 273p. foldout maps. bibliog. photos.

Hearn worked among the refugee areas of northern Thailand in a Peace Corps capacity and reports on local administrative conditions, welfare and insurgency problems. His report includes family budget expenditures of Meo refugees.

522 **Wider war.**
Donald D. Kirk. London: Pall Mall, 1972. 305p.

Kirk, a war correspondent, gives his impressions of the impact of the war in Vietnam on Thailand.

523 **China and 'people's war' in Thailand 1964-69.**
Daniel D. Lovelace. Berkeley, California: University of California Center for Chinese Studies, 1972. 99p. bibliographic notes.

This study assembles the evidence for Chinese Maoist influence in the phase of insurgency in Thailand in the 1960s.

524 **Promise of dawn: pages from a Thailand diary.**
Ruth Nickerson. Tring, England: Lyon, 1982. 56p.

The author describes her own observation of refugees in Thailand from across the Lao border.

525 **Thai insurgency: contemporary developments.**
R. Sean Randolph, W. Scott Thompson. Beverly Hills, California: London: Sage, for the Center of Strategic and International Studies, 1981. 88p. maps. bibliog. (Washington Papers, no. 81. Sage Policy Papers).

The subject matter of this US study is the impact of externally-influenced rebellious trends in Thailand between 1965 and 1980, with special reference to the student uprising of 1973.

526 **The quality of mercy: Cambodia, holocaust and modern conscience.**
William Shawcross. London: André Deutsch; New York: Simon Schuster, 1984. 464p.

An account, by a distinguished British journalist, of the plight of Cambodia (Kampuchea), touching on the effect of the refugee problem on Thailand.

527 **L'indochine vue de Pékin: entretiens avec Jean Lacouture.**
(Indochina seen from Peking: discussion with Jean Lacouture.) Prince Norodom Sihanouk. Paris: Centre d'Etudes Asiatiques et Africaines, 1955. 634p.

The author renounced his title to the Cambodian throne and became a key figure in the politics of Indochina throughout the turbulent period following the Second World War. He discusses the time when he had taken refuge in Peking, the involvement of Cambodia in the final stages, and the sequel of the war in Vietnam which resulted in border threats and refugee problems for Thailand. These memoirs are an important contribution to the documentation of the period.

Government and Administration

528 **Thailand's government (including all Ministries, Agencies, and dictionary locator).**
Gordon H. Allison, Auratai Smarnond. Bangkok: Siam Security Brokers, 1972. 155p.

This is a useful list of governmental and quasi-governmental institutions of the whole country, arranged in English alphabetical order, with their locations. Entries include 'The Queen', 'Radio engineers', and 'SEATO Graduate School of Engineering' (now the Institute of Asian Technology).

529 **Marketing in north-central Thailand: a study of socio-economic organisation in a Thai market town.**
Preecha Kuwinpant. Bangkok: Chulalongkorn University Social Research Institute, 1980. 234p. maps. bibliog.

This book, revised from the author's thesis for the University of Kent (1979), describes the administrative structure of one of the market towns which acts as a centralizing link for a network of villages.

530 **Covering a metropolitan area in Thailand: a study of public policies in Bangkok metropolis.**
Patom Manirujana. Ann Arbor, Michigan: University Microfilms International, 1978. 311p. bibliog. (PhD thesis for Syracuse University, New York).

The Bangkok Metropolitan Administration (BMA) is the only major city government in Thailand. This dissertation examines its policies, finances and membership, with particular reference to the internal (city) and external (national government, political) forces acting upon it. The author measures the effects of the coups of 1958 (Sarit) and 1971 (Thanom) and of the constitution of 1968 and the student uprising of 1973. In addition to providing a demographic, statistical and political portrait of the capital, the dissertaton throws some sidelights on the impact of these national events.

Government and Administration

531 **The ecology of public administration.**
Frederick Warren Riggs. London: Asia Publishing House, for the
Indian Institute of Public Administration, 1975. 144p.

Compares public administration structure in Thailand with those of the Philippines
and the United States.

532 **Problems of politics and administration in Thailand.**
Edited by Joseph L. Sutton. Bloomington, Indiana: Institute
of Training for Public Service (Department of Government,
Indiana University), 1962. 205p.

This volume comprises short analytical outline papers by Edgar L. Shor (on public
services); Frederick J. Horrigan (on provincial government and administration);
John W. Ryan (on municipal government); William J. Siffin (on economic
development); Fred W. Riggs (on clientèle groups); and Joseph B. Kingsbury
(on public administration, the monkhood and taxation).

533 **The civil service of Thailand.**
Kasem Suwanagul. Ann Arbor, Michigan: University Microfilms
International, 1962. 274p. bibliog. (PhD thesis for New York
State University).

This dissertation looks at the history and present situation of the civil service in
terms of organization, recruitment and pay. It concludes that improvements in
pay and conditions are needed to make it more effective. A useful picture of the
country's civil service emerges.

534 **Local authority administration in Thailand.**
Edited by Fred R. von der Mehden, David A. Wilson. Los
Angeles: University of California, 1970. 250p. bibliog. (Academic
Advisory Council for Thailand Paper, no. 1).

This report contains material arising from a three-day conference on rural administration and management problems and publications, attended by specialiists of
the University of California (UCLA), Royal Thai Government (RTG) and United
States Operations Mission Thailand (USOM). The report contains a bibliography
by W. J. Siffin and Charles F. Keyes.

The Law and the Police

The legal system

535 **Family law in Asia and Africa.**
Edited by J. N. D. Anderson. London: Allen & Unwin, 1968.
300p. (School of Oriental and African Studies. Studies on
Modern Asia and Africa, no. 6).

Thailand, with no colonial history, stands out as an exceptional case in relation to
regional studies of family law, as shown in this collected edition.

536 **The constitution of the kingdom of Thailand: official translation.**
Bangkok: Juridical Council of Thailand, 1968. lxxxiv, 50p.

This is the official translation of the 1968 constitution into English, by the
Juridical Council of Thailand. The text is given in Thai and English.

537 **Representative government in Southeast Asia.**
Rupert Emerson. Cambridge, Massachusetts: Harvard University
Press, 1955. 197p.

Outlines the early post-war processes of legislation in Thailand which were the
prelude to intermittent attempts to establish a durable civilian government.

538 **Gerichtsverfassung und Zivilprozess in Thailand: ein Überblick
mit einem Anhang: Verzeichnis der wichtigsten Gesetze Thailands.**
(Law and litigation in Thailand: with an appendix: index of the
principal laws of Thailand.)
Frankfurt-am-Main, GFR: Alfred Metzner, 1960. 76p. (Asian
Institute, University of Hamburg, vol. 6).

This analysis in German explains the principles of law and litigation in Thailand,
with a list of the principal laws.

The Law and the Police. The legal system

539 **Trial by ordeal in Siam and the Siamese law of ordeals.**
G. E. Gerini. *Asian Quarterly Review*, vol. 9, nos. 17 & 18
(Jan.-April 1895), p. 415-24, and vol. 10, nos. 19 & 20 (July-
Oct. 1895), p. 156-75.

This article, continued from one volume to the next of the *Asiatic Quarterly
Review*, later called the *Asian Review* (q.v.), describes administration of justice
in Siam by Hindu *dharmaśastra* laws involving subjection of the accused or
litigants to ordeals of purification by fire or water. A common ordeal consisted
of staying under water for prescribed lengths of time (a case so tried by King
Taksin on rebel monks in 1770); those who were unsuccessful were executed and
burnt, their ashes being mingled with temple putty. Another ordeal involved
retrieval of gold objects from boiling oil. A Lolo (northern tribal) practice
required chewing of raw white rice in which any pink traces of bleeding gums
betrayed guilt.

540 **A concise legal history of Southeast Asia.**
Michael Barry Hooker.   Oxford, England: Oxford University
Press, 1978. 306p. bibliog.

Provides an overview of modern legal practice in Southeast Asia and its antecedents in India and elsewhere. The author deals *passim* with modern Thai law
(*thammasat*) and extraterritoriality, with a background in Indian and French law,
and antecedents in Champa and Cambodia.

541 **An index of officials in traditional Thai governments: the law of
civil hierarchy and the law of military and provincial hierarchies.**
Yoneo Ishii, Osamu Akagi, Shigeharu Tanabe.   Kyoto, Japan:
Kyoto University Press, 1974. 179p. (Center for Southeast Asian
Studies. Discussion Paper, no. 76).

This paper contributes a listing which illuminates the intricate pattern of royal-
conferred titles and administrative functions in the pre-Bangkok period. Cf. also
a review of this paper by M. Vickery in JSS vol. 63, no. 2 (1965), p. 275-84.

542 **L'esclavage privé dans le vieux droit siamois.** (Private slavery
in old Siamese law.)
Robert Lingat.   Paris: Domat-Montshrestien, 1931. 395p. bibliog.

This volume contains translations and discussions of former laws on private
slavery in Siam, with comparisons to foreign traders' laws, laws regulating military
service, and laws inherited from Khmer sources. The author refers to the revisions
of 1805 and 1860, and the abolition of the slavery laws in 1905.

543 **Evolution of the conception of law in Burma and Siam.**
Robert Lingat. *Journal of the Siam Society*, vol. 38, part 1
(Jan. 1950), p. 9-31.

Traces the origin of the canon law, as re-codified in the case of Thailand by
Rama I at the outset of the Bangkok dynastic period (1782). The legal basis at
that time stemmed from Indian *dharmasastra* laws, an equivalent of the Roman
lex naturale. The king, though absolute, would refer to laws documented in
this way. It was not until Rama IV (King Mongkut 1851-68) that Thai law was
liberated from such a rigid system; modernization was completed by Rama V
(King Chulalongkorn 1868-1910). Cf. also the article by M. R. Seni Pramoj, 'King
Mongkut as a legislator' (JSS vol. 38, no. 1, p. 32-66).

544 **Introduction bibliographique à l'histoire du droit et à l'ethnologie
juridique.** (Bibliographic introduction to the history of law and
juridical ethnology.)
Robert Lingat. Paris: R. Lingat, 1965. 17p.

This legal bibliography includes material in all relevant languages, arranged under
the subjects of ancient and modern law, treaties (extraterritoriality), and
Buddhism.

545 **Vinaya et droit laïque: études sur les conflits de la loi religieuse
et la loi laïque dans l'Indochine hinayiste.** (Canonical precepts
and lay law: conflicts in religious and lay law in Hinayanist
Indochina.)
Robert Lingat. *Bulletin de l'Ecole Française d'Extrême-Orient*,
vol. 37, no. 2 (July 1937), p. 415-77.

This article deals with conflicts between canonical and secular law in relation to
the legal position of Thai monks on entering the *sangha* (monkhood). Marriage
and property laws are examined in this context as presenting particular problems,
since a married man would expect simply to abandon both wife and possessions
on entering the monastery and joining the *sangha*.

546 **Credit and security in Thailand.**
Chitti Tingsabadh, David E. Allan, Mary E. Hiscock, Derek
Roebuck. St. Lucia, Australia: University of Queensland Press,
1974. 154p. (Legal Problems of Development Finance Series).

This study is the result of a research project carried out for the Asian Development Bank and the Law Association for Asia and the Western Pacific, and refers
to the Industrial Finance Corporation of Thailand. The conclusions concern the
legal, constitutional and economic infrastructure to provide security relative to
development finance.

The police

547　**United States national security policy and aid to the Thailand police.**
Thomas Lobe. Denver, Colorado: University of Denver, 1977.
161p. map. bibliog. notes. (Graduate School of International
Studies Monograph Series on World Affairs, no. 14, book 2).

The author is professor of political science at the University of South Dakota.
Most of the material in the study was gathered in Washington or in Thailand
during a field research project in 1972-73 for the Michigan University research
operation on United States police assistance for the Third World. It deals with the
search for social controls in areas like Thailand during the Kennedy administration. The result is a down-to-earth analysis of CIA central and village security
operations, offshoots of the Vietnam war, and forebodings of the making of a
police state. In a postscript on the student rising of 1973, the author shows a
picture of a burning police station and wonders to what extent the involvement
of the United States was responsible for it.

Defence and the Armed Forces

548 Alternative in Southeast Asia.
Eugene R. Black. New York: Praeger, 1969. 192p.

Though the strategic situation on which it was based is now superseded, this argument in favour of support for state regionalism among the countries bordering the Mekong River remains of interest to students interested in the evolution of the United States defence policy with relation to Thailand and Southeast Asia generally.

549 Village security: pilot study.
D. J. Blakeslee. Bangkok: Thai-U.S. Military Security and Development Center, 1964. 387p.

The considerations underlying local security requirements remain relevant in the new circumstances which have arisen on Thailand's borders since this study was carried out.

550 Southeast Asia in turmoil
Brian Crozier. London: Penguin, 1968. rev. ed. 224p.

A discussion of the strategic problems, which were confronted by SEATO (the Southeast Asia Treaty Organization), which was formed as part of the defensive aftermath of the Geneva settlements following the French defeat in Vietnam.

551 Conflict in Laos.
Arthur J. Dommen. New York: Praeger, 1972. rev. ed. 454p.

The author, an American war correspondent, views the looming problems for Thailand of the conflict along the borders with Laos and Cambodia.

552 Southeast Asia in U.S. policy.
Russell H. Fifield. New York: Praeger, 1963. 488p.

This is a contemporary study of problems raised for the United States and SEATO (the Southeast Asia Treaty Organization) by military-political pressures in Laos in the early 1960s. They are seen in the context of regional superpower interests with ramifications including Japan and India.

Defence and the Armed Forces

553 **A short history of the Royal Thai Air Force.**
William M. Leary. *Aerospace History*, vol. 29, no. 2 (1982),
p. 93-97. 8 photos. 22 notes.

The Thai defence forces are a significant factor in the military potential of mainland Southeast Asia, and also influences the non-military Association of Southeast Asian Nations (ASEAN), comprised of Thailand, the Philippines, Indonesia, Singapore and Malaysia. The structure of the armed forces is described in the official and non-official yearbooks and handbooks; for a full description cf. the *American Army Department HQ Country Study*, by Harold D. Nelson, edited by F. M. Bunge (1981, q.v.). The Royal Thai Air Force is perhaps the most modern element in the country's and the region's defences. This article outlines its growth from small beginnings in the First World War and through the Second World War to become a strong and well-equipped arm in the strategic balance of Southeast Asia today. The author traces French and American influence in the history of the RTAF, and notes its expansion after 1961 and during the Vietnamese war, during which it operated alongside the USAF.

554 **Thailand and SEATO.**
Corinne Phuangkasem. Bangkok: Thai Watana Phanich, 1973.
106p. bibliog.

Thailand joined the Southeast Asia Treaty Organization (SEATO) in 1956. This book outlines the advantages of membership for Thailand in the fields of counter-subversion, mutual economic, social and cultural assistance, especially in the shape of the Graduate School of Engineering in Bangkok, and which was later called the Asian Institute of Technology (AIT).

555 **Thailand's relations with the United States: a study in foreign involvement.**
Irvine M. Rice. Ann Arbor, Michigan: University Microfilms International, 1970. 365p. bibliog. (PhD thesis for the American University, Washington DC).

This thesis documents the growing involvement of the United States in Thailand as a result of economic and strategic problems of the post-war resettlement of Southeast Asia.

556 **Trial in Thailand.**
George K. Tanham. New York: Crane-Russak, 1974. 175p.
map.

The author argues from first-hand experience in this critique of American policy towards Thailand's defence; he states that over-dependence on US material supplies impaired the effectiveness of Thailand's response to insurgency.

Foreign Relations

General

557 Articles on Siam's foreign relations from the *Siam Society Journal.*
Bangkok: Siam Society, 1954-59.
This compilation includes volumes 7 and 8 of the *Selected articles from the Siam Society Journal* (q.v.). Volume 7 deals with relations with Portugal, Holland and the Vatican; volume 8 deals with relations with France, England and Denmark.

558 Relations between Burma and Thailand.
Papers collected by King Bagyidaw of Burma. Bangkok: Siam Society, 1959. 2 vols.
A collection of documents on relations between Burma and Thailand, seen from the Burmese side, is of interest; it requires considerable interpretative re-assessment in the light of the romantic character of the Burmese chronicles on which it is based.

559 Sir John Bowring and the Chinese and Siamese commercial treaties.
G. P. Bartle. *Bulletin of the John Rylands Library*, vol. 44, no. 2 (March 1962), p. 286-308.
This article, compiled from papers in the John Rylands Library, and from letters sent to the Earl of Clarendon located at the Bodleian Library in Oxford, sheds sidelights on the multifarious personality of Sir John Bowring. He was the architect of the Anglo-Siamese treaty of 1855 and author of *The land and people of Siam* (q.v.). The author discusses the scope of his activities, and especially his zeal for free trade.

560 **The Burney papers.**
Henry Burney. Bangkok: Vajiranana National Library, 1910-14.
Reprinted, Farnborough, England: Gregg, 1971. 5 vols.

The papers published in these volumes constitute a major source for research into the diplomatic history of Anglo-Siamese relations in the early 19th century. They comprise the collected letters and reports of Henry Burney, military secretary at Penang (up to 1842) and of his co-negotiator, Major James Low, concerning their missions on behalf of the East India Company and the British government following the Siamese occupation of Kedah in 1821, and the Malay-Siamese war of 1838. A substantial part of the collection deals with Burney's subsequent posting to Ava, the vicissitudes of Anglo-Burmese relations leading towards the Anglo-Burmese war of 1852, and the ultimate administrative settlement of the territory formerly contested at length between Siam and Burma.

561 **The 1940 Franco-Thai border dispute and Phibun Songkhram's commitment to Japan.**
E. Thadeus Flood. *Journal of Southeast Asian History*, vol. 10, no. 2 (Sept. 1969), p. 304-25.

This article provides a useful summary of research by the author into documentation of the period in Thai and Japanese sources. For a British official account of the Japanese landing at Singora and Patani cf. *The war against Japan*, vol. 1, by Major-General S. Woodburn Kirby (London: HM Stationery Office, 1957 [History of the Second World War, U.K. Military Series], chapter 11: 'The Japanese invasion of Malaya').

562 **Siam in British foreign policy 1855-1939: the acquisition and the relinquishment of British extraterritorial rights.**
Vikrom Koompirochana. Ann Arbor, Michigan: University Microfilms International, 1982. 284p. map. bibliographic essay. (PhD thesis for Michigan University).

The treaty negotiated by Sir John Bowring in 1855 regulated trade between Britain and Siam in a new and equal manner, and formed a model for similar treaties concluded by other Western nations in Asia. At the same time it conferred certain extraterritorial legal rights on British traders, which were modified and finally abrogated by a series of subsequent agreements, culminating in those of 1925 and 1935, which were made with the assistance of American advisers to the Siamese government, especially Francis B. Sayre (q.v.). This dissertation traces the course of these negotiations in detail, mainly from contemporary British diplomatic records.

563 **Buddhism, imperialism and war: Burma and Thailand in modern history.**
Trevor Ling. London: Allen & Unwin, 1979. 163p. map. bibliog.

The theme of this book is the political role of Buddhism in Burma and Thailand and its influence on the historical relations and conflicts of the two neighbour countries up to the present day.

64 **Foreign trade, foreign finance and the economic development of Thailand, 1956-65.**
Chatthip Nartsupha. Bangkok: Prae Pittaya, [n.d.] . 186p. bibliog.

A general overview of factors involved in Thailand's foreign trade. Subjects considered include export structures and the balance of payments, rice production and export trends, rubber, tin and maize, allocation of foreign aid, and budgetary and government accounts.

65 **France and Siam.**
Sir H. N. D. Prendergast. *Imperial and Asiatic Quarterly Review*, vol. 1, 3rd series, (April 1890), p. 225-31.

This is the first of a sequence of contemporary articles on the Mekong incidents involving France, Siam and British interests in the Far East in the late 1880s. The sequence includes: 'The Mekong-Menam arrangement', by General A. R. McMahon (p. 232); 'The Mekong treaty', by W. A. Pickering (p. 241); 'The future of Siam from a Siamese standpoint', by Muang-Thai [pseudonym] (p. 248); 'A French view of the question', by Baron Textor de Ravisi (p. 255); and 'The Siam government and the Indian government', by the editor (p. 258-60).

66 **A short survey of Luso-Siamese relations 1511-1900.**
A. da Silva Rego. Macau: Imprensa Nacional, 1979. 28p.

Macau's dependence on Siam, and on other alternative trade contacts opened up by Albuquerque's landing at Malacca in 1511, was heightened by the banning of Christians from Japan, the previous main outlet, in 1614. This useful short outline of trade contacts with Siam and those principally engaged in developing them is taken from the Arquivos de Macau. For a full account of Portugal's overseas trade history cf. Charles R. Boxer, *The Portuguese seaborne empire 1415-1825* London: Hutchinson, 1969).

67 **A history of Malaysia and Singapore.**
N. J. Ryan. Kuala Lumpur: Oxford University Press, 1976. 322p. maps. bibliog.

This definitive history of Malaysia and Singapore describes Thailand's foreign contacts from the 15th to the 19th centuries, concerning trade routes and territorial disputes at issue with the Malay sultanates and British India. The book outlines the growth of Malacca and Penang in this context, and includes a discussion of the circumstances of the Anglo-Siamese treaty of 1826 regulating the then-contested states of northern Malaya. It may also be consulted for a useful summary of the Japanese invasion of 1941-42 (map, p. 247) and of the Malayan Emergency, culminating in the retreat of Chin Peng, the Chinese Communist leader, with his jungle force into southern Thailand in 1960.

568 **U.S.-Thai diplomatic relations during World War II.**
Vivat Sethachuay. Ann Arbor, Michigan: University Microfilms
International, 1977. 371p. bibliog. (PhD thesis for Brigham
Young University).

After a brief summary of Thai-American relations from the 1830s, this study
examines the positions of both sides in the two war-time phases before and after
Pearl Harbour. It covers the Thai leaders' postures during the phase of American
neutrality in the Second World War and the American response to the Thai
declaration of war against the Allies in 1942 – and the consequent formation of
the Free Thai Movement under Ambassador Seni Pramoj. The effect of the eve-of-
war negotiations with France is also taken into account.

569 **Off-shore petroleum resources of Southeast Asia: potential
conflict situations, and economic considerations.**
Corazon Morales Siddayao. Kuala Lumpur: Oxford University
Press, 1980; Singapore: Institute of Southeast Asian Studies,
1978. 205p. maps. bibliog.

A study of the implications of oil reserves in the Gulf of Thailand and other
Southeast Asian waters considers legal definitions proposed at the third Law of
the Sea Conference in relation to jurisdictional issues. The author looks at
Thailand's dispute with Cambodia over oil resources in the Gulf of Thailand
and general questions of demand, supply and development.

570 **Thai-American relations in the Laotian crisis of 1960-62.**
Surachai Sirikrai. Ann Arbor, Michigan: University Microfilms
International, 1980. 384p. bibliog. (PhD thesis for the New
York State University).

This thesis considers an interesting phase of the US policy of containment at the
height of the cold war, when a neutralist coup in Laos brought Prince Souvanna
Phouma to power; Marshal Sarit and the Americans supported the royal Rightists
in Laos in the hope of keeping the communist Pathet Lao from gaining the
upper hand in a supposedly neutral coalition.

571 **Unequal partners: Philippine and Thai relations with the
United States (1965-75).**
W. Scott Thompson. Lexington, Massachusetts: Lexington
Books, 1975. 183p. bibliog.

This two-country study considers the effects on the Philippines and Thailand of
the American involvement in the Vietnam war: in the first phase, Thailand experienced the effects of a much closer relationship with the United States, both
military and economic; the second phase, one of a general reduction of American
commitments in the region after the war ended, presented Thailand with fresh
problems of adjustment and adaptation cf. 'Thailand' (p. 117-36).

ASEAN

572 **Revenue system of ASEAN countries: an overview.**
Mukul G. Asher.   Singapore: Singapore University Press, 1980.
66p. bibliog.
This financial overview of ASEAN (Association of Southeast Asian Nations) outlines government sector revenue and tax structures, with tabulated aggregate revenue statistics. It has a useful bibliography of Thailand and general material on the subject.

573 **The dimensions of conflict in Southeast Asia.**
Bernard K. Gordon.   Englewood Cliffs, New Jersey:
Prentice-Hall, 1966. 201p.
The author reviews American strategic concern with the post-war development of Southeast Asia, and traces the beginnings of post-war regional economic co-operation which led eventually to the formation of ASEAN (Assocition of Southeast Asian Nations).

574 **Thai-American relations in contemporary affairs.**
Edited by Hans H. Indorf.   Singapore: Executive Publications,
for Chulalongkorn University, 1982. 234p. map.
This compilation of reports on Thai-American relations was published to make the bicentenary of the Chakri dynasty. The earliest American diplomatic relations with Siam were undertaken by the American consul in Batavia in 1830; a trade treaty followed in 1856, modelled on the one negotiated by Sir John Bowring. The volume covers the post-war concerns of Thai-American relations in the cultural, strategic and economic fields. The most recent phase expresses American interest in regional self-help patterns, from the American interest in the ASEAN Joint Conference on Management at Manila in 1967, and up to President Reagan's policies in the 1980s.

575 **United States economic policy for ASEAN: meeting the Japanese challenge.**
L. B. Krause.   Washington, DC: Brookings Institute, 1982. 98p.
This is a US policy document outlining the history and economic benefits of ASEAN and its relations with the outside world including Japan, and making recommendations for improved facilities for US trade with it.

576 **ASEAN bibliography.**
Project co-ordinator Patricia Lim.   Singapore: Institute for
Southeast Asian Studies, 1984. 487p.
An exhaustive compilation of ASEAN research materials.

577 **The invisible nexus: energy and ASEAN security.**
Edited by Kusuma Sukhumband Paribatra. Singapore: Executive
Publications, 1984. 238p.

This is an edited report of an international seminar held in 1981 at the Chulalong-korn University in Bangkok, under the auspices of the Institute of Security and International Studies. The seminar considered offshore energy resources, sea-lanes, potential conflict centres of the South China Sea, and opportunities for regional co-operation. The point was made that, whereas such energy and security questions were a matter of prominent governmental concern in the West, they had so far remained 'invisible' in the ASEAN region.

578 **Aspects of ASEAN.**
Edited by Werner Pfennig, Mark M. B. Suh. Munich, GFR:
Weltforum Verlag, 1984. 395p. (Schittenreihe Internationales
Asienforum, no. 2).

A useful handbook which discusses aspects of ASEAN, and how it has so far handled matters like regional politics, security, its own internal contradictions, economic cooperation, relations with the EEC in technology, and relations with Japan.

579 **ASEAN: eine Dokumentation zur Gipfelkonferenz.** (ASEAN:
documentation for the summit conference.)
Edited by Klaus-Albrecht Pretzell. Hamburg, GFR: Institute for
Asian Affairs, Asia Documentation Center, 1976. 2 vols. bibliog.

These two preparatory volumes have text in German providing general documentary information on ASEAN matters in advance of the two summit meetings; one at Bali, 23-24 February 1976 (vol. 1); the other at Kuala Lumpur, 4-5 August 1977 (vol. 2). The compilations are useful for extensive reproductions of press articles in English on various ASEAN topics taken from the presses of countries of the region.

580 **ASEAN financial cooperation in banking, finance and insurance.**
Michael T. Skully. London: Macmillan, 1985; Singapore:
Institute for Southeast Asian Studies, 1979. 269p. bibliog.

This is an overview of inter-governmental and private financial institutions of ASEAN countries, with a comparison of their domestic development and financial arrangements. The author covers the ASEAN Bankers' Association and the ASEAN Swap Agreement in appendixes. Cf. also Michael T. Skully, *Merchant banking in ASEAN: a regional examination of its development and operation*, (Kuala Lumpur: Oxford University Press, 1983. 200p. bibliog.); and *Financial institutions and markets in Southeast Asia* (London: Macmillan, 1984. 411p. bibliog.)

581 **ASEAN: regional cooperation in the ascendant?**
Edited by Mark B. M. Suh. Berlin: FU Occasional Papers, 1982.
243p. maps. bibliog. (FGS AP – Area Research Papers).

This is a general critique in English of ASEAN problems during the period 1967-80 (with a chronology of events) dealing *inter alia* with Japanese export-import in Thailand; intra-ASEAN trade: ASEAN and Vietnam; and resettlement of refugees. The latter problem is viewed in the context of the Geneva conference of 1979, at which the extra-ASEAN powers showed a willingness to accept refugees, while the intra-ASEAN participants feared the possible use of refugees to infiltrate a communist 5th column.

582 **Directions in Thai foreign policy.**
Sarasin Viraphol. Singapore: Institute for Southeast Asian Studies, 1976. 69p. (ISEAS Occasional Paper, no. 40).

Discusses the balance of interests for the Thai government's foreign policy between regional partnerships inside ASEAN, and the strategic involvement in Southeast Asia of the superpowers from outside it: China, Russia, Japan and the United States.

Economy

583 **The political economy of productivity: Thai agricultural development 1880-1975.**
David H. Feeny. Vancouver, British Columbia: University of British Columbia Press, 1982. 238p. bibliog. (Asian Studies Monographs, no. 3).

Provides an in-depth study from an economic standpoint of the evolution of rural society throughout the period of modernization in Thailand. Topics include the technology of rice production (1880-1940); the shifting of property rights; and Thailand's response to the expansion of world trade in a colonial environment. Appendices contain economic data on primary products (rice, tin, teak, rubber), and trends in manufacturing and oil requirements.

584 **The fifth national economic and social development plan, 1982-86.**
Bangkok: National Economic and Social Development Board, 1982. 351p. map.

The plan (in English) gives an excellent general profile of the Thai economy and of the government's social goals. Among those mentioned are: alleviation of poverty in backward rural areas; development of border provinces; spreading knowledge of the Thai language in Muslim areas; and decentralization of social welfare organizations in defined areas with social problems.

585 **Economic change in Thailand 1850-1970.**
James C. Ingram. Stanford, California: Stanford University Press, 1971. 352p. map. bibliog.

This is a revision of the author's original work, published in 1954, following a further research visit to the country. The book reviews export and import patterns in the light of the effects of Thailand's exposure to modern Western trade. Tin and rice are major elements of trade exchange; the author considers other types of produce, and the revenue accruing from governmental control of external trade, as against the promotion of private investment policies. The material analysed poses the question whether gradual but uninterrupted growth has impeded some aspects of manufacturing and development.

150

586 **Rural society and the rice economy of Thailand 1880-1930.**
David Bruce Johnston. Ann Arbor, Michigan: University
Microfilms International, 1975. 443p. map. bibliog. (PhD thesis
for Yale University).

The author examines the growth of Thailand's rice economy against the back-
round of social conditions and change. Factors such as crime, labour, the Chinese
immigration, and land tenure are considered in relation to changes in the produc-
ion and management of rice, with the conclusion that patterns of expansion,
on the whole, still follow along the lines of traditional methods.

587 **Marriage, fertility and labour force participation of Thai women:
an economic study.**
Kenneth Maura, Rosalinda Ratajcak, T. Paul Schultz. Santa
Monica, California: Rand, for the Agency for International
Development and Rockefeller Foundation, 1973. 54p. bibliog.

This study in family economics highlights the role of women in market and non-
market production. The report collates economic constraints with migration and
fertility of women.

588 **The rice industry of mainland Southeast Asia 1850-1914.**
N. G. Owen. *Journal of the Siam Society*, vol. 59, part 2 (1971),
p. 75-143.

This article includes an account of the steady growth of the rice industry of the
central Chao Phraya basin of Thailand, under the influence of irrigation, marsh
and jungle clearance and expanding rail, river and road communications. The
industry dominates the country's export trade.

Industry, Development and Planning

589 **Industrial development in Thailand.**
Narongchai Akrasanee, for the World Bank. Washington, DC:
World Bank (IBRD), 1977. 87p. appendices.

This World Bank report outlines growth patterns in Thai industry in relation to
export-import and foreign investment. Appendix 3 (18p.) discusses the fourth
National Plan project (1977-81), noting measures designed to counteract
problems met with in the first and second plans. The report appends numerous
tables on individual products, employment and industrial location.

590 **The manufacturing sector in Thailand: a study of growth, export
substitution; and effective protectionism 1960-69.**
Narongchai Akrasanee. Ann Arbor, Michigan: University Microfilms International, 1973. 295p. bibliog. (PhD thesis for Johns
Hopkins University).

The purpose of this thesis was to measure indicators of manufacturing conditions, such as consumer demand and promotion of export substitution, against
changes in production and tariffs, in order to estimate the effectiveness of protec-
tionist policies during the decade under review. The research calculations (set
forth in appendices), and an extensive bibliography are very useful guidelines to
the manufacturing sector of the country's post-war economy.

591 **Macroeconomic and distributional implications of sectoral
policy interventions: an application to Thailand.**
Piyasvastri Amranana, Wafik Grais. Washington, DC: World
Bank, 1984. 179p. bibliog. (World Bank Staff Working Papers,
no. 627).

The effects of a drop in world oil prices on Thai economic policy are assessed in
this paper. The authors compare fiscal rice policy and energy price policy, and
conclude that farmers' incomes would benefit more from a reduction in the rice
export tax rate than from a reduction in energy prices. The frame of reference for
this study is model 'Siam 2', a multi-sectoral, multi-household general equilibrium
model of the Thai economy; 'Siam 1' was used for an earlier World Bank study
*Aggregate demand and macroeconomic imbalances in Thailand; simulations with
the Siam 1 model* (WBSWP, no. 448 [World Bank, 1981]).

152

592 **Marketing and development: the Thailand experience.**
Dole A. Anderson. East Lancing, Michigan: Michigan State
University, 1970. 214p. bibliog. (MSU International and Business
Studies).

This business study examines the economic and social environment of retail trade
in Thailand, and contrasts the market conditions of town and country, especially
specific products such as kenaf and maize versus rice. Part one deals with economic
history, the family and the role of women in marketing; part two deals with
retail conditions and consumers, road and rail infrastructure, and governmental
controls. The author considers the significance of Bangkok as a market in comparison with other Asian cities.

593 **Industrial development strategy in Thailand.**
Bela Belassa. Washington, DC: World Bank, 1980. 59p. (East
Asian and Pacific Regional Office, World Bank Country Study).

The report of a country study mission, by the chief of the mission, sent to
Thailand by the World Bank in 1979.

594 **Aggregate structures of production and domestic demand for rice
in Thailand: a time series analysis, 1951-73.**
Olarn Chaipravat. Bangkok: Bank of Thailand, 1975. 36p.
bibliog. (Economic Research Department Paper, no. 4).

This paper – one of a series on trends in national economic demand, production,
banking and finance – estimates changes in rice farmers' requirements of fertilisers,
credit and general crop and output decisions over a period of 24 post-war years.
The report contains numerous pullout tabular charts. Earlier papers in the series
deal with: 'Thai commercial banks' revenue and cost structures' (no. 1, 1974
[q.v.]); 'The demand for currency notes' (no. 2, 1974); and 'Thai commercial
banks' (no. 3, 1974).

595 **An economic model of world rice markets.**
Olarn Chaipravat, Sayan Pariwat. Bangkok: Department of
Economic Research, Bank of Thailand, 1976. 34p. (Discussion
Paper DP/76/14).

A paper which was prepared for the 1976 Pacific Basin Central Bank Conference
on Econometric Models at the Bank of Korea in Seoul.

596 **Thailand: an analysis of structural and non-structural adjustments.**
Arne Drud, Wafik Grais, Dusan Vujovic. Washington, DC: World
Bank, 1982. 93p. (World Bank Staff Working Papers, no. 513).

This a publication of the World Bank's 'Thailand Country Programs', by the
Development Research Department of the East Asia and Pacific Region. It
discusses changes in Thailand's economic environment with, and without, policy
interventions, in terms of investment, agricultural growth and incomes. Trends in
the 1980s could involve changes in energy utilization for higher efficiency, and
changes in fiscal policy to bring about a transformation in agriculture.

153

Industry, Development and Planning

597 **Asia in the 1980s: interdependence, peace and development.**
Edited by Yoshiyuke Hagiwara. Tokyo: Institute of Developing
Economies, 1982. 207p.

This compilation is the result of a symposium held in Tokyo in 1981 on the
politico-economic prospects for Asia. ASEAN (the Association of Southeast
Asian Nations) is dealt with in several papers. Another topic of Thai concern is
the Cambodia problem. The volume gives an overview of Japan's relations with
Southeast Asia, which will be of interest in view of the growth of Japanese
investment in Thailand.

598 **The economic development of Southeast Asia.**
Edited by Shinichi Ichimura. Kyoto, Japan: Kyoto University,
1975. 393p. (Kyoto University Center for Southeast Asian
Studies Monographs, and University of Hawaii East-West Center).

A country-by-country survey showing Japanese interests in this region. The
chapter on 'Thailand' (p. 129-78), deals with structural changes of the previous
decade and provides a bibliography.

599 **Major causes and effects of Thailand's export instability 1961-75.**
Piboon Limprapet. Ann Arbor, Michigan: University Micro-
films International, 1979. 132p. bibliog. (PhD thesis for the
University of Illinois).

This thesis reviews the relevant literature, and goes on to analyse export concen-
trations by market and product, relating these to economic growth. The conclusion is that short-term fluctuations are a deterrent to growth.

600 **Background information relating to environmental guidelines for
zones in the Gulf of Thailand.**
H. F. Ludwig, and the Southeast Asia Technology Company.
Bangkok: National Environment Board and the US Agency for
International Development (Thailand), 1976. 66p. maps. bibliog.

This report considers products of the region adjoining the Gulf of Thailand (tin,
rubber, rice, coconut, palm oil, and tourism), in relation to environmental risks
and the need for regulatory measures. Maps and tables are included, dealing with
salinity and currents in the Gulf, the coral industry, and port construction.

601 **The development of labor institutions in Thailand.**
Bevars D. Mabry. Ithaca, New York: Cornell University Press,
1979. 144p. (Southeast Asia Program Data Paper, no. 112).

Mabry covers the history of labour in Thailand, including the Chinese element,
and then describes the process of union formation and of labour and union legislation, and traces the practical effects of these in several case studies.

02   Economic development and policies: a case study of Thailand.
     G. A. Marzouk, foreword by Jan Tinbergen (professor of
     development and planning, The Netherlands School of Econ-
     omics).   Rotterdam, The Netherlands: Rotterdam University
     Press, 1972. 472p. bibliog. notes by chapters.

his study presents a full and thoroughly researched background to the availability
nd utilization of Thailand's economic resources. Its main purpose is to assess
1e effects of incentives towards productivity and development. The author's
nalysis contrasts the workings of profit motivation in the promotion of sectional
ersus national interests in the application of land, labour and capital resources.
he principal subject matter of the book consists of Thailand's experience during
1e 1960s in demography and population policies; the rice economy and agricul-
ural diversification; growth in the manufacturing sector; foreign exchange and
xternal trade; and public finance, credit and tax policies. The material would
ake a useful base for any further study of development potential.

03   The economic role of Thai women.
     Kanitta M. Meesook.   Bangkok: Department of Economic
     Research, Bank of Thailand, 1980. 21p. (Discussion Paper
     DP/80/34).

utlines the implications of the high participation of women in the Thai
conomy.

04   Income distribution in Thailand.
     Oey Astra Meesook.   Bangkok: Thammasat University, 1975.
     183p. (Faculty of Economics Discussion Paper Series).

he materials in this paper were presented at two conferences, one in Bangkok
1962) and the other on Tokyo (1974), in conjunction with the Japan Economic
esearch Centre. Questions of rent, home ownership and welfare, and the
roblem of defining poverty are discussed. The key question is whether income
rowth will raise rural poverty levels without specific policies to iron out inequality
n national income levels.

05   The economic development of Thailand, 1956-65.
     Chatthip Nartsupha.   Bangkok: Prae Pittaya, [n.d.] . 186p.
     bibliog.

Provides a concise overview of the main elements in the country's assumption of
1ew economic directions in the decade after the post-war resettlement: foreign
rade and finance; infrastructural development; private and foreign investment;
1nd industrial development.

155

606   **South Thailand regional planning study.**
       National Economic and Social Development Board, Ministry of
       Overseas Development. Bangkok: Hunting Technical Services,
       1974. 220p. (Draft final report, no. 2).

This paper by the British Ministry of Overseas Development, presents a complete
tabulated, demographic and physical profile of the southern development area of
Thailand, with reference to British aid and co-operation projects specializing in
this area.

607   **Census of Business, Trade and Services: Annual Report.**
       National Statistical Office. Bangkok: Office of the Prime
       Minister, ca 1965- . annually.

This comprehensive series of interim reports is published in the intervals between
national census publications, covering specific aspects of the census concerning
business, trade and services; various sections cover the kingdom as a whole, the
metropolis, and each region and province.

608   **Asian economic development.**
       Edited by Cranley Onslow, foreword by Sir Sydney Caine.
       London: Weidenfeld & Nicolson, 1965. 243p.

A relatively early compilation of studies on development needs in Asia and
foreign investment. The politico-economic situation of Thailand is dealt with
(p. 151-74) by Puey Ungphakorn (a member of the war-time Free Thai movement
in London), who came into renewed prominence at the time of the 1973 student
uprising, as a politician in whom the students had confidence, and in whom the
then military rulers accordingly did not.

609   **Thailand's interzonal input-output tables in reference to east
       Thailand.**
       Borawornsri Somboonpanya. UN Asian and Pacific Develop-
       ment Institute, 1980. 3 vols. (2p. of tables).

This is an American-style regional input-output study. The first descriptive
volume, appendix A1 (p. 33-69), gives a full, detailed inventory of natural and
manufactured products of east Thailand which could be of general interest or
useful for research purposes.

610   **The co-operative movement in Thailand.**
       Thailand Co-operative Promotion Department, Technical Division.
       Bangkok: The Department, 1974. 55p.

Describes the co-operative movement in Thailand. An English translation of the
Co-operative Societies Act of 1968 is also available (1973).

11 **Thailand: prospects and policies.**
London: Economist Intelligence Unit, 1984. 198p. map. bibliog.
(Available from the unit, 40 Duke Street, London W1).

This large-format paper is a complete economic profile of Thailand in the 1980s.
It gives the political background, with a section on the military tradition and
the (current) government of General Prem, followed by an overview of the
economic record to date and the direction of domestic economic policy. The
third section looks at the prospects up to 1987 of energy, forestry, agriculture,
fisheries, mining, industry, tourism and seaboard development.

12 **Consumer emancipation and economic development: the case of
Thailand.**
Hans B. Thorelli, Gerald D. Sentell. Greenwich, Connecticut:
London: JAI, 1982. 376p. map. bibliog. (Contemporary Studies
in Economic Analysis, no. 37).

This study uses Thailand as a typical, less developed country to examine consumer
reaction to modern product retailing. The authors have compiled the most
thorough, available profile of the Thai consumer in town and country, and of the
market structures serving him. The book deals with shopping habits, market
research techniques, and product awareness against a background of demographic,
geographic and cultural features of the communities of Bangkok, on the one
hand, and rural settlements on the other. The bibliography consists mainly of
material on general marketing theory.

13 **Thailand: towards a development strategy of full participation.**
World Bank. New York: World Bank East Asia & Pacific
Regional Office, 1978. 232p. maps. (A Basic Economic Report).

The report advocates planned assistance to the depressed sector of the farming
community in Thailand in order to enable it to participate more fully in the
country's rising standard of living. The conclusions are supported by thorough
statistical analysis of agricultural sectors concerned, and by a demographic break-
down from 1976.

14 **A public development program for Thailand.**
World Bank Mission, chaired by Paul T. Ellsworth. Baltimore,
Maryland: Johns Hopkins University Press, for the International
Bank for Reconstruction and Development, 1959. 301p. pullout
maps.

A report of the World Bank Mission requested by the Thai government on how
funds should be allocated for social and economic planning. Sections analysed
in the report include: requirements for the rubber industry, irrigation and
fertilizers in farming, forestry and fisheries, diversification, and trade education.

157

Finance and Banking

615 **Impacts of monetary, fiscal, debt management and exchange rate policy changes in the Thai economy; a macronometric simulation.**
Olarn Chaipravat, Kanitta M. Meesook, Siri Ganjarerndee.
Bangkok: Department of Economic Research, Bank of Thailand, 1977. 93p. bibliog. (Discussion Paper DP/77/22).
A paper prepared for the third Pacific Basin Central Bank Conference on economic modelling, in Wellington, New Zealand (1977).

616 **Model of the Thai monetary sector: a progress report of the Bank of Thailand's financial research program.**
Olarn Chaipravat, Siri Ganjarerndee. Bangkok: Economic Research Department, Bank of Thailand, 1977. 33p. (Discussion Paper DP/77/21).
This paper on the monetary sector in Thailand was presented to the first ASEAN central bank workshop on economic modelling hosted by the Bank of Indonesia at Bandung, in 1977.

617 **Revenue and cost structures of Thai commercial banks: a cross-section time series analysis, 1963-70.**
Olarn Chaipravat. Bangkok: Department of Economic Research, Bank of Thailand, 1974. 18p. (Bank of Thailand Papers, no. 1).
Analyses and tabulates commercial banking experience in Thailand through most of the 1960s.

618 **Revenue stamps of Thailand: a provisional listing.**
Compiled by Peter Collins. Wimbourne, England: Thailand Philatelic Society, 1979. 20p. illus.
This is the first listing for over sixty years of the fiscal stamps of Thailand.

619   The financial institutions of Southeast Asia: a country-by-country
      study.
      Robert F. Emery.   New York: Praeger, 1970. 748p. bibliog.
      (p. 735-48). (Praeger Special Studies in International Economics
      and Development).

The Thailand section (p. 558-637) of this very thorough financial handbook
covers public and private institutions, including pawnbroking, the Bangkok Stock
Exchange, non-agricultural credit cooperatives, development finance corporations,
and the organization of the Bank of Thailand.

620   Income and price policy.
      Kanitta M. Meesook.   Bangkok: Department of Economic
      Research, Bank of Thailand, 1980. 34p. bibliog. refs. (Discussion
      Paper DS/80/30/(S)).

This paper analyses indexation of price and purchasing power as a basis for
income and price policy in Thailand. It is one of a valuable series by the Bank of
Thailand's Economic Research Department on specific aspects of the economy;
among other papers in the series the following may prove useful adjuncts to
further research: 'Econometric modelling experience in the Bank of Thailand'
(DP/79/20, 17p.); 'Bank of Thailand model of the Thai economy' (DP/79/25,
95p.); 'Commercial banks of Thailand, a regional analysis' (DP/76/16, 53p.);
'The economic role of Thai women' (DP/80/34, 21p.); 'The relationship between
money and credit and economic activity' (DP/81/36, 51p. q.v.).

621   International aid to Thailand: the new colonialism.
      Ronald C. Nairn.   New Haven, Connecticut: Yale University
      Press, 1966. 228p. bibliog.

The author's study of the effectiveness of UN aid agencies in establishing useful
contact with their opposite numbers in Thailand is based on fieldwork which he
carried out for Unesco in several villages in the central region. His conclusions are
that, on the whole communications between UN aid agencies and their Thai
counterparts proved defective, especially at the individual level. The book
examines the Thai social and institutional background which made interlinking
difficult, and also provides a list of foreign personnel working on UN aid projects
of the period.

622   Balance of payments and monetary developments: Thailand
      1947-73.
      Chanpen Puckartikom.   Ann Arbor, Michigan: University Micro-
      films International, 1977. 140p. bibliog. (PhD thesis for the
      University of Rochester, New York).

This analysis of Thailand's payment structure adopts the monetarist approach.
It considers merchandise trade accounts, exports and imports, domestic credit
creation and the balance of payments in the light of restrictive domestic policies
operated by the Bank of Thailand. Another factor taken into account is the effect
of US military expenditure connected wth the Vietnam war.

Finance and Banking

623 **Finance and banking in Thailand: a study of the commercial system, 1888-1963.**
Paul Sithi-Amnuai. Bangkok: Thai Watana Panich, 1964. 224p. bibliog. statistical tables. pullout leaf.

This is an exhaustive account of the origins, growth and activities of the banking system in Thailand by the vice-president of the Bangkok Bank. The book contains a brief outline of the country's historical economic and export condition; a review of the generation and development of financial institutions at the end of the 19th century, and during the constitutional period, the Japanese occupation, and the post-war period. There is also a description of the legal and commercial operating system of the banks (including the central bank – the Bank of Thailand). The bibliography covers Thai and world banking practice and theory, and lists thirty-nine publications which give economic information, by sixteen Thai government departments; a pullout leaf summarizes the capital positions of twenty-nine Thai and foreign banks operating in Thailand. The book makes an invaluable conspectus to the country's financial and banking arrangements for its home and foreign trade and industry.

624 **Thailand: income growth and poverty alleviation.**
Washington, DC: World Bank, 1980. 56p. map.

One of the World Bank's special-subject studies.

625 **Tax and investment profile: Thailand.**
Touche Ross International. Bangkok: Jaiyos, 1982. 20p.

Gives prospective businessmen visiting Thailand a profile of the tax structure they are likely to encounter.

626 **Thailand's monetary experience: the economics of stability.**
Paul B. Trescott. New York: Praeger, 1971. 342p. (Praeger Special Studies in International Economics and Development).

This study outlines the structure of Thailand's monetary and banking system and considers factors which have preserved the stability of the financial system during times of relative disturbance.

Trade and Investment

627 **Hints to Exporters: Thailand.**
British Overseas Trade Board.   London: HM Stationery Office,
1980- . bibliog. 18-monthly.
This annually revised booklet provides a useful summary of information for
visitors, primarily on business, and lists export intelligence services available.
Previously published as *Hints to businessmen: Thailand.*

628 **Thai exports.**
Thai Export Directory.   Bangkok: The Directory, 1974. 163p.
An official guide to some 500 products of Thailand available for export, with
details of export-oriented manufacturers.

629 **Thailand welcomes foreign investment.**
Thailand Board of Investment.   Bangkok: Thailand Board of
Investment, 1976. 30p.
This publication contains descriptive sections on the food industry, mining
machinery, electrical goods, and machine tools, in which foreign investment is
invited.

Agriculture, Forestry and Fisheries

630 **Keys for the identification of aphids (Homoptera): winged aphids of species economically important in Thailand.**
Hans Bänziger. Bangkok: Ministry of Agriculture and Co-operatives, 1976. 41p. bibliog. (Plant Protection Service Technical Bulletin, no. 36).
This pamphlet is a useful pest control tool, indicating sources for further similar material; it includes a glossary in English and Thai.

631 **Supply response in underdeveloped agriculture: a case study of four major annual crops in Thailand 1937-63.**
Jere R. Behrman. Amsterdam: North Holland, 1968. 446p. maps. bibliog.
A thorough empirical study of the four crops rice, cassava, corn and kenaf in Thailand. The author employs an outline model technique, showing conclusions in tabular form. The study includes a physiographic profile of the demographic, health, educational and social background against which agricultural decisions are made.

632 **Preliminary list of insect pests and their host plants in Siam.**
Samual Beller, Prasert Bhenchitr. Bangkok: Department of Agriculture and Fisheries, 1936. 68p. (Technical Bulletin, no. 1).
This pre-war pest report, in English and Thai, could still be of value as a basis for estimating the consequences of later changes in cultivation, pest control, especially by chemicals, and cropping. The booklet also includes a useful relevant vocabulary in Thai.

633 **Thailand: rural growth and employment.**
Hans Binswanger (leader of the World Bank Team), Ruchaniwan
Uthaisri, (co-ordinator of the Thai team). Washington, DC:
World Bank, 1983. 194p. bibliog. (World Bank Country Study).

This study which is a report of the joint Thai-World Bank team is the application
of rural and national resources to education, planning, farming and non-farming
employment, with an overview of provincial manufacturing and pricing policies.

634 **The origin of Thai silk.**
Stephen Browne. *Arts of Asia*, vol. 9, no. 5 (Sept. 1979),
p. 91-100.

The author, an industrialist in Bangkok, mentions earlier articles on the subject
in the same journal. He gives his opinion that the first Thai immigrants brought
the art of sericulture with them from China, though it survived only as a domestic
producer in northeast Thailand until Jim Thompson developed its potential as a
nationwide and international source of trade silk in 1945. The industry still
uses imported production equipment. The article includes illustrations of this, and
of some of the *ikat* (*madmi*) traditional Thai designs. Cf. also Mary Cable, 'The
silk of Thailand' in *Atlantic*, vol. 217 (Jan. 1966), p. 107-11, which includes an
interview with Jim Thompson at his house in Bangkok.

635 **Hill farms and paddy fields: life in mainland Southeast Asia.**
Robbins Burling. Englewood Cliffs, New Jersey: Prentice-Hall,
1965. 180p.

A useful introduction to traditional agricultural systems from an anthropological
standpoint.

636 **Contributions to the development of integrated rice pest control.**
Tokyo, Bangkok: Japan International Cooperation Agency
(JICA), 1981. 204p. bibliog.

This report, in English, of a research project carried out at the request of the Thai
government by a JICA team on the role of pest predators in relation to cultivation
systems, chemical intervention and resilience breeding in protecting and improving
rice yields in Thailand.

637 **An interdisciplinary perspective of cropping systems in the
Chiang Mai valley: key questions for research.**
Gordon Conway, with the Multiple Cropping Project Research
Team (Chiang Mai University). Chiang Mai: Chiang Mai Univer-
sity, 1980. 238p. maps. bibliog.

This research report, issued by Chiang Mai University's faculty of agriculture,
tabulates the general crop and infrastructural resources of the low-lying irrigated
and river-valley agricultural production zone of northeast Thailand.

163

Agriculture, Forestry and Fisheries

638   Rice field ecology in northeast Thailand: the effect of wet and
       dry seasons on a cultivated ecosystem.
       Charles W. Heckman. The Hague: W. Junk, 1979. 228p. bibliog.
The wet-rice culture of the Thai-Indochinese region has been extant with relatively
slight alteration for at least two millennia, and presents a social, agricultural,
economic and biological phenomenon of the greatest significance. This study does
it justice in all aspects, and therefore has a 'spin-off' value well beyond its main
purpose, which was to examine the ecosystem of a man-made aquatic subzone
(a wet ricefield in Udorn Dhani) for the year 1975; it observes changes in the wet
and dry seasons in its entire complement of flora and fauna, pests, and cultivated
fish. Apart from the rice itself, the author demonstrates the subspeciation of plant
and animal life, making the paddy field an important source of aquatic food,
filling the village market with delectations like the walking catfish. The bibliography (p. 207-16 in large-format close type) covers a wide variety of works in
Western languages dealing, in part, specifically with Thailand, and more generally
with the whole range of subject matter raised by the study on a regional or world
basis.

639   An illustrated guide to some natural enemies of rice insect pests
       in Thailand.
       Tokyo, Bangkok: Japan International Cooperation Agency
       (JICA), 1982. part 1. 71 plates.
The plates contain drawings and descriptions of 71 common predators and
parasites of rice pests.

640   Thailand: a rice-growing society.
       Edited by Yoneo Ishii, translated from the Japanese by Peter
       Hawkes, Stephanie Hawkes. Kyoto, Japan: Kyoto University,
       1978. 340p. maps. bibliographic refs. figs. (Monographs of the
       Center for Southeast Asian Studies, English Language Series,
       no. 8).
This monograph is a good introduction to Thailand's main economic focus: by
means of a sequence of contributions by Japanese specialists on selected themes,
the book gives a complete picture of the country as a rice-growing society, from
its earliest conjectural beginnings five or more millennia ago, through its historical
evolution under a series of Thai dynasties, and up to the stage of modern technology and planning. The book covers each phase of production, according to
location, terrain, type of rice and method, with its corresponding evolution of
infrastructural water systems, transport, labour, productivity, yields, export
potential and future prospects. The treatment provides an easily intelligible con-
tinuity, with liberal use of diagrams, sketch-figures and maps.

641   **Dry rice agriculture in northern Thailand.**
       Laurence C. Judd.   Ithaca, New York: Cornell University Press,
       1964. 82p. maps. bibliog. (Southeast Asia Program Data Paper,
       no. 52).
This paper deals with climate, soil, vegetation, dry rice and other crop cultivation
methods, fishing and general agricultural subsistence farming in north Thailand.

642   **Farming in the forest: economic development and marginal
       agriculture in north Thailand.**
       Edited by Peter Kunstadter, E. C. Chapman, Sanga Subhasri.
       Honolulu: Honolulu University Press, 1978. 402p. bibliog.
       photos. (East-West Center, East-West Population Institute).
The principal subjects of this agricultural review of northern Thailand are the
Lua', Skaw Karen and the Meo, who constitute the main tribes inhabiting the area
under examination. The contributors establish the cultural, demographic and geographical setting, and then analyse the system of *swidden* (slash-and-burn)
cultivation and recommend future policies to limit its deleterious effects on the
living standards of these upland tribes in comparison with the lowlanders. Topics
covered include marketing and the dilemma posed by opium controls (with some
observations of Sir Stamford Raffles on cropping and coercion in relation to
pepper procurement in 19th-century Sumatra), and problems of forestry. The
book makes an excellent compendium, liberally illustrated with charts, tables and
photographs, of the northern upland agriculture and possible courses for its
amelioration.

643   **Review of the economic insect pests of cotton in Thailand:
       description, infestation and control.**
       Terence H. Mabbett.   Bangkok: Ministry of Agriculture (Cotton
       Pests Research Branch). 1979. 80p.
This is a report by an adviser attached to the Cotton Pests Research Branch of the
Thailand Ministry of Agriculture, on cotton pest control in Thailand, especially
methods of dealing with recent serious attacks of boll-worm.

644   **Forestry economic models for Thailand (1977).**
       Sompetch Mungkorndin.   Ann Arbor, Michigan: University
       Microfilms International, 1979. 209p. bibliog. (PhD thesis for the
       New York State University).
Working on the economic model method, this study brings out all the factors
involved in forestry management in Thailand. Satellite photography shows the
progressive depletion of the country's forestlands for reasons of probably mis-
placed economic incentives; the question posed by the author is whether what
remains will be enough, without intensive conservation measures, to satisfy future
demands for housing a growing population.

Agriculture, Forestry and Fisheries

645 Agricultural census report, 1978.
National Statistical Office. Bangkok: Office of the Prime Minister, 1978.

This census is the counterpart of the national census (q.v.) and is also published in Thai and English, in separate parts dealing with the whole country, with main regional subdivisions, and with each province. It shows crop and fruit-tree areas, forestlands, sizes of holdings, and represents an important agricultural, statistical source.

646 Agricultural development planning in Thailand.
Edited by Kenneth J. Nicol, Somnut Striplung, Earl O. Heady. Ames, Iowa: Iowa State University Press, 1982. 326p. map.

Analyses zonal crop potentials on the basis of national models, rice storage capacities, demography and general economic requirements.

647 Thailand: agriculture.
P. D. O'Reilly, P. I. McDonald. Budapest: Akademiai Kiado, 1983. 98p. bibliographic refs. (Hungarian Academy of Science, Geography of World Agriculture, no. 12).

This concise geographical report on Thailand describes the country's physical and social characteristics as a setting for its rice-export dominated economic needs. The authors stress the paramount importance of water supplies. Topics include upland and tribal agriculture, rubber and fruit cultivation, and general prospects and potentials.

648 A host list of the insects of Thailand.
Compiler Thol Pholboon (for the Ministry of Agriculture), with the United States Operations Mission in Thailand. Bangkok: Ministry of Agriculture, 1965. 3rd ed. 149p.

A useful compilation of plants and their insect pests, including a large selection of caterpillars, grubs, beetles, aphids, plant louse, bolls, seed-bugs and grasshoppers. The plants and insects are listed under English, Thai and scientific names.

649 Locusts and grasshoppers of economic importance in Thailand.
Jeremy Roffey. London: Centre for Overseas Pest Research, 1979. 200p. maps. bibliog. (Anti-Locust Memoir, no. 14).

This pest control study contains data on 55 locust and allied species dangerous to various crops in Thailand. The author lists about 300 types of food plants attacked (p. 192-200). The book contains an extensive bibliography (p. 139-50). For a full study on rice cf. D. H. Grist and H. J. A. W. Lever, *Pests of rice* (Longman, 1969. 520p).

650 **Morphology and genesis of gray podzolic soils in Thailand.**
Santhad Rojanasoonthon. Ann Arbor, Michigan: University
Microfilms International, 1972. 226p. bibliog. (PhD thesis for
Oregon State University).

Gray podzolic soils are prevalent throughout Southeast Asia, and present in
several tracts in Thailand, especially the northeastern plateau and the western
strip and river and marine coastal terraces of the central rice-growing area. Their
infertile character gives low agricultural yields. This thesis suggests studies which
could lead to improved soil management and use in the affected areas. The author
describes the climatological and cultural background (mentioning the problem of
termite mounds), provides a general soil map of Thailand, and extensive tables
of X-ray results. The bibliography contains further useful material on soils.

651 **Some aspects of rice farming in Siam.**
M. C. Sithiporn Kridakara. Bangkok: Suksit Siam, 1970. 187p.

The author, Prince Sithiporn, a distinguished authority on national agricultural
policies and popular welfare, puts in a plea in this book for relieving the rice
farmers of the onerous effects of the rice export premium tax system. The book
cites the views of numerous specialists on this subject.

652 **The spices and essential oil crops of Thailand.**
Tem Smitinand, T. Santiruk. *Natural History Bulletin of the
Siam Society*, vol. 29 (Sept. 1981), p. 85-128.

Discusses the cultivation, management, marketing and export of Thailand's
economic aromatic plants, among which are mint, basil, and cardamom.

653 **Forests of Southeast Asia.**
Russell C. Stadelmen. Princeton, New Jersey: R. C. Stadelmen,
1966. 245p. bibliog.

Thailand is dealt with separately (p. 174-200) in this study of the forests and
forestry of this region; it also includes a useful bibliography. Common and scientific names of trees are indexed.

654 **Fishery development in Thailand.**
K. Tiews. *Archiv für Fischwissenschaft*, vol. 24 (1973),
p. 271-91. bibliog.

This article, in English, provides a good background to Thailand's fishery industry,
and has a useful bibliography for further reading on the subject. An earlier official
publication, *Fisheries in Thailand* (Bangkok: Ministry of Agriculture, 1961, 50p.
illus.) outlined the position at that date. Cf. also 'First guide to the literature of
the aquatic sciences and fisheries in Bangkok', *Kasetsart University Fishery
Research Bulletin*, no. 2 (1965).

655 **The accounting price of rice in Thailand: calculation of
a conversion factor.**
Mike Veitch. Bradford, England: University of Bradford, 1979.
33p. bibliog. (Project Planning Centre for Developing Countries.
Occasional Paper, no. 4).

Considers Thailand's rice industry as a special case in price accountancy. The author discusses existing literature on the subject, and offers a calculation taking into account tax policies, handling charges, and export-import rates, as well as other economic factors.

656 **Co-operation for survival: an analysis of an experiment in
participating research and planning with small farmers in Sri
Lanka and Thailand.**
Kuenrad Verhagen. Amsterdam: Royal Tropical Institute, 1984.
253p. bibliog.

This paper sets forth in technical and tabular form a comparative field study of unnamed poor villages in Sri Lanka and Thailand, showing patterns and possibilities of self-help through co-operatives.

Transport and Communications

657 **The impact of road development in the central plain of Thailand.**
Janes Allen Hafner. Ann Arbor, Michigan: University Microfilms
International, 1977. 309p. maps. bibliog. (PhD thesis for
Michigan University).

This thesis, presented in 1970, considers the effects of road development in
central Thailand on rural economies, marketing networks and traditional transport
systems. The author considers questions of delay in the lower central plain due to
capital shortages, and notes the effect of road development on types of water
transportation, increasing specialization and raising the size of cargo boats.

658 **The role of the state railways in Thailand 1892-1932.**
David Frederick Holm. Ann Arbor, Michigan: University Micro-
films International, 1977. 300p. maps. bibliog. (PhD thesis for
Yale University).

This detailed historical review covers a period when there was growing Western-
power economic interest in Thailand. One general conclusion from it is that the
ensuing development gave the railway network an over-riding role in relation to
other infrastructural requirements, such as roads and irrigation. The need for
railway development was a consequence of Bowring's treaty of 1855; competing
French interests in Indochina hastened the scramble to complete the rail contracts.
The import of foreign labour was essential for their fulfilment. Internal and
external dissensions set in, resulting in procrastination. It was not until after the
First World War that the Thai national interest began to supervene; by then, an
important and efficient, but unduly predominant railway network was well under
way.

659 **Reappraisal of a rail project in Thailand; an application of the Harvard transport models.**
Arturo Israel.   Washington, DC: World Bank, 1972. 116p. 54p. of annexes. (International Development Association, Economic Staff Working Paper, no. 132).

This paper from the Transportation and Public Utilities Division reviews the somewhat delayed implementation of a rail development project in Thailand arising from a World Bank loan in 1961. The conclusions refer to the desirability of competitive transport systems, including highway development.

660 **Transport in Thailand; the railway decision.**
P. J. Rimmer.   Canberra: Australian National University Press, 1971. 203p. bibliog. (Department of Human Geography Publication, no. HG 6).

This is a report of the joint research project of the Research School of Pacific Studies (Australian National University), the Applied Scientific Research Corporation of Thailand, and the University of Michigan. The report analyses freight densities in road, rail, and inland waterway systems, considers problems of integration, and reviews the decision to develop the railways in the early 1960s in the light of the need for balanced highway facilities and local provincial road development.

Philately and Numismatics

661 **The Thai Times. Journal of the Thailand Philatelic Society.**
Edited by Peter Collins. Wimbourne, England: Thailand
Philatelic Society, 1958- . irregular.

The society's occasional publications (twenty-seven in all, 1958-85 and continuing)
deal with all aspects of the philatelic history and current postal developments of
Thailand.

662 **Thailand: mail to and from prisoners-of-war and internees
1942-45.**
Compiled by Peter Collins. Wimbourne, England: Thailand
Philatelic Society [n.d.]. 24p. illus.

This is a handbook of covers (illustrated by plates) of correspondence received or
sent by prisoners-of-war and internees during the war in Thailand. The book is
prefaced by a brief historical summary of the circumstances in which the letters
were written, or received, supported by a short list of non-philatelic books.

663 **Royal Siamese Postal Service (the early years).**
Bonnie Davis. Bangkok: Siam Stamp Trading Company, 1983.
168p.

A wittily presented anthology of excerpts from newspaper files in Bangkok
containing otherwise little-known information on postal matters 1869-1908.

664 **Air post in Thailand.**
C. W. Fawdry. Batley, England: Harry Hayes, 1972. 18p.

This booklet, first published in 1935, gives a full account of the early internal and
external mail-carrying flights of Thailand.

Philately and Numismatics

665 The postage stamps of Siam.
Alex Holland. Boston, Massachusetts: Boston Philatelic Society, 1904. 28p.

This is of interest, as the first privately produced handbook on Thai philately. It contains comprehensive, not always completely accurate, information on the stamps, and a geographical background.

666 Siamese coins and tokens: an anthology.
Reginald Le May (vol. 1), Harding W. Kneedler, Ulrich Guehler (vol. 2), H. A. Ramsden (vol. 3). London: Andrew Publishing, 1977. Re-edited. 3 vols. in one. 389p. bibliog. plates.

This volume is, in effect, a single compilation in three parts on the coinage and tokens of Thailand, having been re-edited from several publications of the Siam Society from 1932 onwards. It begins with an account of the 'bullet' (*pot duang*, or twisted snake) coins of the Mon period, and goes on to deal with Ayudhyan coinage and finally with the Bangkok period. The third part deals with porcelain tokens. The work is liberally illustrated with black-and-white plates.

667 Siam: its posts and postage stamps.
Fred Melville. London: Stamp Collectors Fortnightly, 1906. 53p.

This issue covered Siam's postal regulations and stamps 1881-1905.

668 Postal progress in Siam 1885-1925.
Ministry of Communications. Bangkok: Ministry of Communications, 1925. 36p.

This official publication reports internal and international postal service routes in operation and outlines the history and organization of the Post Office. It also gives a tabulated listing of stamps with colour illustrations.

669 The date of the early Funanese, Mon, Pyu and Arakanese coinages (symbolic coins).
Michael Mitchener. *Journal of the Siam Society*, vol. 70, nos. 1 & 2 (Jan. & July 1982). p. 5-12. bibliog. 2p. of plates.

The text, photographs of coins and bibliography of this article will all be of interest both to numismatologists and historians, as illustrating early migrations and contacts in the pre-Thai period in the region stretching from Burma to South Vietnam.

670 Postage stamps & post & letter cards of Siam 1920.
Bangkok: Siam Philatelic Society, 1920. 129p.

Presents a comprehensive description of posts and postal services up to 1920, with details of technical processes used and the variant calendric and dating systems involved.

671 **Postal organisation of the kingdom of Siam.**
Paris: Siamese Legation, 1885. 42p.
This publication carried excerpts from the postal regulations and reproductions of stamps.

672 **Adhesive postage stamps of Siam.**
R. W. H. Row.   London: Junior Philatelic Society, 1913. 75p.
This detailed study of the technical aspects of stamp production in Thailand up to 1913 is of particular value to students of philately.

673 **Siam 1939-1948.**
Bangkok: Siam Philatelic Society, 1949. 60p. plates.
A definitive account of the postage stamps, postal rates and postmarks of the war years, with a list of the stamps produced in the country.

Statistics

674 **The markets of Asia-Pacific: Thailand.**
Asia-Pacific Centre. Aldershot, England: Gower, 1981. 141p.
This is a useful compilation from official statistical sources showing Thailand's potential as a consumer market, with population distribution charts, wage and employment patterns and market structures.

675 **Foreign Trade Statistics of Thailand.**
Department of Customs. Bangkok: The Department, 1954- .
monthly.
The monthly figures for all imports and exports are published cumulatively, presenting an annual statement up to December, which is isued in the following June.

676 **Thailand trade nomenclatures.**
Department of Customs. Bangkok: The Department, 1974.
350p. In English and Thai.
A trade nomenclature of all categories in Thai with a conversion to the standard international trade classification.

677 **Thailand: Facts and Figures.**
Department of Technical and Economic Cooperation. Bangkok: The Department, 1965- . annually.
This is a useful source of general and statistical information on a wide variety of public, social, business and technical departments of Thailand. It includes topographical and historical background summaries and foreign trade statistics.

678   **Thailand: prospects and policies.**
      Economist Intelligence Unit.   London: Economist Intelligence
      Unit, 1984. 198p. map. bibliog. (Available from the unit,
      40 Duke Street, London W1).

This large-format paper is a complete economic profile of Thailand in the 1980s.
It gives the political background, with a section on the military tradition and the
(current) government of General Prem, followed by an overview of the economic
record to date and the direction of domestic economic policy. The third section
looks at the prospects up to 1987 of energy, forestry, agriculture, fisheries,
mining, industry, tourism and seaboard development.

679   **Statistics Asia and Australasia: sources for social, economic and
      market research.**
      Compiled by Joan M. Harvey.   Beckenham, England: C. B. D.
      Research Limited, 1983. 2nd ed. 440p. (Obtainable from the
      publishers, 154 High Road, Beckenham, Kent, BR3 1EA).

A valuable publication, providing descriptive text and listings of statistical
materials for social, economic and market research: (Thailand, p. 368-79).

680   **Thailand.**
      Hong Kong and Shanghai Banking Corporation.   Hong Kong:
      The Bank, 1981. 2nd ed. 27p. (Business Profile Series).

Presents a good statistical profile of Thailand and its economic potential.

681   **Review of demographic sample surveys for Asia and the Pacific,
      1970-79.**
      Richard Leete.   UN Economic & Social Commission for Asia
      and the Pacific (Statistical Division), 1980. 109p. bibliog.

The Thailand census system is described on p. 98-103, in relation to the 1970
census and the 1975 fertility census.

682   **Agricultural Statistics of Thailand.**
      Ministry of Agriculture.   Bangkok: The Ministry, 1954- .
      annually. In English and Thai.

This is an important source of statistical information on the whole range of
Thailand's agricultural production.

683   **Census 1970.**
      National Statistical Office.   Bangkok: Office of the Prime
      Minister, 1977.

The 1970 census was published (in Thai and English) in parts, covering the whole
nation; the main regions; and each province (*changwat*) in separate volumes. The
census contains a mass of general social information and statistics, including
housing.

Statistics

684 Census of Business, Trade and Services: Annual Report.
National Statistical Office. Bangkok: Office of the Prime Minister, ca 1965- . annually.

This comprehensive series of interim reports is published in the intervals between national census publications, covering specific aspects of the census concerning business, trade and services; various sections cover the kingdom as a whole, the metropolis, and each region and province.

685 Statistical Summary of Thailand.
National Statistical Office. Bangkok: Office of the Prime Minister, 1974- . annual. In English.

This annual summary is a good source of official statistical information on public health and social services; it also includes statistics on prices, production and employment.

686 Statistical Yearbook.
National Statistical Office. Bangkok: National Statistical Office, 1909- . annually.

Collates records available to the National Statistical Office to provide a complete national profile. It is arranged under nineteen main headings ranging from area, population and climate to production and business activity; a final miscellaneous section deals with electricity, water resources, religion, and cinemas. The material is up to one or two years prior to publication. The office also issues a quarterly bulletin of statistics, comprising similar information over several years up to three months prior to its publication; it has a library which is open to visitors who wish to consult its wide range of subject publications.

687 Census subject reports.
Chintana Pejaranonda, Fred Arnold, for the National Statistical Office. Bangkok: Office of the Prime Minister, 1981. 2 vols. In Thai and English.

These reports form parts of a decennial project, and are based on the 1970 census population and housing figures. The reports cover economic characteristics (vol. 1); and migration (vol. 2). A valuable feature of these reports consists of excellently-presented whole-page graphic charts in colour, illustrating the statistical trends under analysis.

688 The Siam Directory: the Book of Facts and Figures.
Bangkok: Tawanna Publishing, 1947- . annually.

Supplies an annual economic, export-import and general statistical summary.

689   **The Statesman's Year-book; Statistical and Historical Annual of the States of the World.**
London: Macmillan, 1864- . annually.

This admirable and reliable annual summarizes statistical and official information on all countries. The section on Thailand will be found to be a concise and useful profile of the country's area, population, government and governmental services, economy, communications, and education.

690   **The Thai Chamber of Commerce Business Directory.**
Bangkok: Marketry Media LP, ca 1965- . annually.

A complete telephone-book type of directory, divided into sections dealing with financial and banking, industrial and business activities in Thailand.

691   **Thailand Official Yearbook.**
Bangkok: Office of the Prime Minister, 1965- . annually.

This is an all round handbook of official information and statistics. Subject headings include defence and armed forces, social welfare, tourism and sport.

Education

692 **Education in Thailand: a century of experience.**
Bangkok: Ministry of Education, Department of Elementary
and Adult Education, 1970. 142p. rev. ed. bibliog.

This book consists of a translation into English of ten papers presented by Thai
educationists at a seminar held in Bangkok in 1961. The seminar was designed to
elicit their conclusions, both positive and negative ones, from the educational
experience in the country over the past decades.

693 **Compulsory education in Thailand.**
M. L. Manich Jumsai. Paris: UNESCO, 1951. 98p. (Studies in
Contemporary Education, no. 8).

A good, simple account by a leading Thai educationist. It covers the palace
education system (1871-88); state education (1887-1921); compulsory education
(1921-32); and developments up to 1950.

694 **Buddhism and education in Burma and Thailand.**
Trevor Ling. *Religion*, vol. 14, no. 1 (Jan. 1984), p. 53-65.
bibliog.

This article contrasts the effects of 19th-century colonialism in South East Asia
on Buddhist educational practice in Burma and Thailand.

695 **Autobiography: the life of Prince Patriarch Vajiranana of Siam 1860-1921.**
Translated from the Thai, edited and introduced by Craig James Reynolds. Athens, Ohio: Ohio University Press, 1979. 88p. bibliog. (Southeast Asia Translations Series).

Prince Patriarch Vajiranana was King Chulalongkorn's younger brother, a monk and one of the leading intellectuals of the reign. He undertook a major reform of Buddhist teaching and organization throughout the country and was one of those at the heart of the integration of monastic and state education. His memoirs, even though they cease at the early age of twenty-one, accordingly shed valuable light on the religious and educational structure of his day, and on the changes brought about in it by King Chulalongkorn in the early 1900s. For further background reading cf. review articles by Manas Chitakasem, BSOAS, vol. 44, no. 3 (Dec. 1981, p. 623-25), and Sulak Sivaraksa, JSS, vol. 69 pt. 2 (July 1981) p. 174-76.

696 **The humanities and education for development in Thailand.**
Mattani Mojdara Rutnin. Bangkok: Thai Khadi Research Institute, Thammasat University, 1980. 48p. bibliog.

Deals with the direction of higher education in the humanities in Thailand. The author has specialized in drama and modern literature.

697 **The impact of Buddhism on higher education in Thailand.**
Prachaksha Saisang. Ann Arbor, Michigan: University Microfilms International, 1981. 123p. bibliog. (PhD thesis for Indiana University).

Reviews the inscriptions at Buddhist monasteries dating from 1292-1361, and introduces the educational records of Sukhothai and Ayudhya, followed by the Thonburi-Bangkok era when education was entirely in monastic hands until 1868. King Chulalongkorn's modernization programme, the foundation of the university bearing his name in 1916, and all developments up to 1970 are considered.

698 **The development of the modern library and library education in Thailand.**
Uthai Sangpichitara. Ann Arbor, Michigan: University Microfilms International, 1981. 215p. bibliog. (PhD thesis for Michigan University).

This thesis reviews the educational system of Thailand and relates it to the libraries at various levels: the National Library, public and university libraries, and school libraries. The study discusses policy options in relation to conditions and educational facilities available for librarians, including salaries, establishments and the Library Association.

Education

699 **The Thai professorial role: an assessment of role expectations.**
Rapée Suvanajata. Bangkok: Research Center, 1977. 199p.
bibliog. tables.

This is a study of motivations and expectations in the higher educational system
of Thailand. The author examines conflicts of conception and administration,
both intra- and extra-positional, and also assesses the expectations of professorial
staffs of faculties.

700 **Historical analysis of the department of teacher training in the
Ministry of Education in Thailand, 1954-76.**
Aravan Chamnankit Tulayasook. Ann Arbor, Michigan:
University Microfilms International, 1981. 315p. bibliog. (PhD
thesis for Chicago University).

The author of this thesis on teacher training experience in post-war Thailand
considers economic, political and religious influences which have affected it, and
deals with its administrative, curriculum, research and rural aspects.

701 **Educational development in Thailand.**
Keith Watson. Hong Kong: Heinemann Asia, 1980. 295p.
bibliog. (Asian Studies Series).

This is a comprehensive textbook dealing in three main sections with: a. the geographical, historical and social background which gave rise to Thailand's modern
educational needs; b. foreign involvement in education (including Western, Protestant and the progression of Chinese education from assimilation and cooperation
to conflict); c. nationalist and post-war trends, teacher training, higher education,
agricultural, trade and adult education. The author offers some conclusions on
problems presented by rigidity of class structure and central control to the
achievement of equality in education on the lines set up by King Chulalongkorn.

702 **The beginnings of modern education in Thailand, 1868-1910.**
David K. Wyatt. Ann Arbor, Michigan: University Microfilms
International, 1967. 698p. bibliog. (PhD thesis for Cornell
University).

Presents a full and thorough survey of the evolution of Thailand's educational
system. It begins with Sukhothai and Ayudhya, and goes on to deal with Bangkok
and the politics of reform, 1868-80. The vital role of King Chulalongkorn himself,
with the strong support of Prince Damrong, is a feature of the further development
and modernization of the system from 1892. The king's tour abroad (the first by
a Thai monarch) marks the transition to ministerial educational policy from 1902;
also compulsory education followed soon afterwards. The entire evolutionary
process in education is viewed by the author against the background of contemporary politics.

703   **The politics of reform in Thailand: education in the reign of
      King Chulalongkorn.**
      David K. Wyatt. New Haven, Connecticut: Yale University Press,
      1969. 425p. bibliog. (Yale Southeast Asia Studies, no. 4).

The author traces in detail changes set in motion by King Chulalongkorn in
Thailand's educational system. These amounted to a creative, rather than, as
formerly, a defensive response to challenges arising from Western contacts to
outmoded social conditions bequeathed by the traditional absolute monarchy.
Key elements in Chulalongkorn's programme – one of transition from slavery to
reform – involved the collaboration of a generation of outstanding Thai educationists and historians like Prince Damrong, and the participation of the
monastery schools in an overall process of educational rationalization. The book
contains a useful glossary of administrative institutional and personal terms.

Libraries, Museums and Archives

704 **Guide to the exhibits in the National Museum.**
Luang Boribal Boribhand, A. B. Griswold. Bangkok: Fine Arts
Department, 1962. lxiii, 54p. 16 plates.

The National Museum in Bangkok is housed in several fine buildings of the forme
'front' palace of the second king (*uparat*). Each major art period is allocated t
one of the buildings or halls. This valuable catalogue (in English and Thai
contains extensive illustrations and explanations of the exhibits. Most of th
regional or provincial museums of Thailand, including those under the directio
of the Fine Arts Department (for instance, at Sukhothai, Chiang Mai an
Ayudhya) have a bookstall; at least some of the informational materials availabl
in these is likely to be in English.

705 **The Vajiranana National Library of Siam.**
George Cœdès. Bangkok: National Library, 1924. 39p.
30 plates.

This attractive and liberally-illustrated handbook of the National Library i
Bangkok is by the distinguished French scholar George Cœdès, who was at th
time its chief librarian. The booklet describes the organization of the library'
holdings of Pali and Siamese manuscripts on palm leaves, Siamese manuscripts o
paper, and foreign printed books.

706 **Directory of libraries and special collections on Asia and
North Africa.**
Robert Lewis Collison. London: Lockwood, 1970. 123p.

A list of 158 libraries in Britain and Northern Ireland describing their facilities
Asian resources, and access rules. Libraries are listed geographically. There ar
two useful indexes: one contains the names of special collections and all librarie
referred to in the text, the other is a subject index. The South Asia library grou
is the dominant regional one in the collection.

707 **An account of a field trip, 1958-9.**
Cecil Hobbs. Ithaca, New York: Cornell University Press. 1960.
(Southeast Asia Program Data Paper, no. 40).

An account of a journey to elucidate library and publication sources in Thailand
and other Southeast Asian countries. Though dated, it could form a useful basis
for further research.

708 **Library resources on Thailand in Singapore.**
Compiled by Saengthong M. Ismail. Singapore: Institute for
Southeast Asian Studies, 1974. 130p. (Library Bulletin, no. 9).

The Singapore library holdings are listed by type, alphabetically by author, and
are unannotated.

709 **Library Catalogue, School of Oriental and African Studies,**
University of London. Vol. 20 Subject Catalogue: Southeast Asia
and Pacific Islands: Thailand. Boston, Massachusetts: G. K. Hall,
1963. p. 305-16.

This catalogue is in 28 volumes and occasional supplements (1947-), reproducing
over 540,000 cards from the SOAS card indexes, arranged by author, main geographical areas (African and Asian), and countries, and 14 subject parts dealing
with archaeology, art, and politics. The pages cited here contain the entries listed
under Thailand in the Southeast Asia volume. Cf. also the comparable library
catalogue of the substantial holdings on Thailand in the library catalogue of
Cornell University, Ithaca, New York.

710 **Materials on Siam in the India Office Library.**
Bangkok: National Library, 1915-22. 5 vols.

This compilation of records relates to Siam in the 17th century, and contains in a
convenient form a variety of material made available for the publication in
Bangkok.

711 **Materials on Thailand in the library of the Royal Institute of
Linguistics and Anthropology, Leyden.**
Compiled by G. A. Nadelkerke. Leyden: The Institute, 1975.
63p.

The materials in this compilation include the library's holdings on Thailand, and
articles from the *Journal of the Siam Society* (q.v.).

712 **Some information about Thai manuscripts.**
Kwandee Rakpongse. London: K. Rakpongse, for the School
of Oriental and African Studies, University of London, 1967.
16 leaves (32p. of typescript).

This is a valuable survey of historical Thai manuscripts, including a description of
methods, sources, languages, bibliographic references and locations inside and
outside Thailand.

713 **A guide to the India Office Library with a note on the India Office records.**
Stanley C. Sutton. London: HMSO, 1971. 122p.

Manuscripts in the India Office Library, London, constitute the largest collection of documents pertaining to South and Southeast Asia in the world outside South Asia. This volume, written by a former India Office librarian, lists the major collections and also includes a brief history of the library and information on its book and pamphlet collection.

714 **A guide to western manuscripts and documents in the British Isles relating to South and South East Asia.**
Mary Doreen Wainwright, Noel Matthews. London: Oxford University Press, 1965. 532p.

This comprehensive guide covers both official archives and private papers in all the main British and Irish centres, including record offices, libraries, and learned institutions. India Office Library manuscripts are excluded. Entries are arranged chronologically under individual depositories. While holdings of the Public Records Office are covered in a general way, Cabinet Office records are excluded.

715 **The house on the klong: the Bangkok home and Asian art collection of James Thompson.**
William Warren, photographs by Brian Brake. Washington: Walker, 1968. 87p. 63 plates (32 col.).

The Thompson House is one of Bangkok's most important museums, both as a typical teak house and as a collection of Thai and Asian classical art objects. This book catalogues the collection with illustrations, some of which may have the additional value of recording items lost through thefts.

716 **The World of Learning.**
London: Europa Publications, 1950- . annually.

The World of Learning carries a comprehensive and valuable list of Thailand's learned societies, research institutions, libraries and archives, museums, and universities and technical institutions (p. 119-26 in the 1983-84 edition).

The Arts

General

717 **The art of Srivijaya.**
M. C. Subhandradis Diskul. Kuala Lumpur: Oxford University Press, 1980. 68p. bibliog. 66 plates.

Srivijayan art is derived from the seaborne Indianized empire, during the second half of the 1st millennium AD. Its precise extent and definition have become controversial, but it seems to have had an important, if not its principal, centre at Chaiya on the eastern coast of peninsular Thailand. The temples, sculpture and other art objects are mainly Hindu or Mahayanist. Some magnificent examples found in Thailand are reproduced in this large-format volume (many of them are now in the National Museum in Bangkok), along with others from the Indonesian part of the empire. They are of particular interest for the pre- or early Buddhist images, including the multi-armed Indic types, which disappear from the Thai Theravadist art of Sukhothai onwards.

718 **Towards a history of Sukhodaya art.**
A. B. Griswold. Bangkok: Fine Arts Department, 1967. 68p. 40 plates. 3 maps (one folded).

This is a reconsideration of the documentation on the origins of the 'golden age' of Thai art, especially that of Sukhothai around the 14th century and continuing in subsequent centres for several centuries. The plates are of particular value.

719 **Art on peninsular Thailand prior to the 14th century.**
Piriya Krairiksh. Bangkok: Fine Arts Department, 1980. 264p. maps. bibliog. plates.

This book of fine black-and-white plates introducing and recording an exhibition in Bangkok shows examples of the Indian-influenced art forms of the Mon sea trading kingdoms in southern Thailand during the 5th-8th centuries. The late 8th-century types are controversially characterized as 'Srivijayan', and the 11th-13th century types as Khmer. The illustrations are valuable for their depiction of the rarer historical Hindu and Mahayanist sculptural forms.

720 **A concise history of Buddhist art in Siam.**
Reginald Le May. Cambridge, England: Cambridge University
Press, 1938; Reprinted, Rutland, Vermont: Tuttle, 1962. 165p.
bibliog. 205 b/w plates.

This is an excellently illustrated description of the temple and sculptural art of
Thailand in a historical context from the early centuries of the 1st millennium AD
to the 16th century. Mon, Dvaravati, Funan and Khmer objects are displayed in
their unchanging splendour, though some of the art periods to which they are
assigned have been revised in the light of later researches since the first publication
of this book.

721 **Hindu gods of peninsular Siam.**
Stanley J. O'Connor. *Artibus Asiae*, 1972. 76p. 8 b/w plates.
cover maps. bibliog. (Supplement no. 28).

The principal conclusion of this interesting and important study of the early
Indian cultural impact on peninsular Thailand is that this distinctive crescent of
territory evolved a Hindu civilization in its own right. The author traces successive
influxes of Indic influence via India and Burma, which were a consequence
of the India-China trade link by portage across the Kra Isthmus until the 5th
century AD. Pictures showing archaeological evidence for the author's conclusions
include some fine, large-format plates of statues of Śiva and Viṣṇu found in
peninsular Thailand, which are compared to prototypes found in India in Pallava,
Mathura and Gujarati styles.

722 **The art of Sukhothai: Thailand's golden age.**
Carol Stratton, Miriam McNair Scott, drawings by Turachai
Kamphu na Ayudhya. Kuala Lumpur: Oxford University Press,
1981. 163p. maps. bibliog. illus.

Sukhothai saw the first, and in many ways the greatest efflorescence of truly Thai
art forms. They were evolved from Indian examples and inspiration; but especially
in the distinctive Buddha images, it established a refined style of its own during
the period 1250-1450 AD approximately. These styles continued to be transmitted
to later kingdoms for several centuries.

Architecture

723 **The sights of Rattanakosin.**
Bangkok Bicentennial Committee. Bangkok: Bangkok Bicentennial Committee, 1982. 332p. illus.

Prompted by the 1982 bicentenary of the Chakri dynasty (Rattanakosin), this
superbly illustrated volume (captioned in English) places on record the best of the
historic architecture of the capital, from the Grand Palace to the outer temples
and monuments.

724 **Der Bot in den siamesischen Tempelanlagen.** (The *bot* in Siamese
temple designs.)
Karl Döhring. Berlin: Gustav Ascher, 1914. 65p. plates. plans.
(PhD thesis for Friedrich-Alexander University, Erlangen).

The *bot* or *ubosoth* is the main building of a monastery complex (*wat*). This thesis
gives an excellent all round view (with pictures) of the structure and decorations
of representative types of *bot* and provides numerous ground-plans of their layouts.

725 **Wat pra yün reconsidered.**
A. B. Griswold. Bangkok: Siam Society, 1975. 87p. map. illus.
(Siam Society Monograph, no. 4).

A good example of an illustrated study of one of the historic temples of Thailand.

726 **Pimay: étude architecturelle du temple.** (Phimai: an architectural
study of the temple.)
Pierre Pichard. Paris: Ecole Française d'Extrême-Orient, 1976.
53p. 6 b/w photos. 9 foldout plans.

The temple complex at Phimai (assumed to have been Mahidharapura of the
Khmer empire) in northeast Thailand, constructed from the 11th century as a
provincial centre by representatives of the dynasty of Angkor, is one of the
country's more interesting and important archaeological and architectural sites.
Part of the decoration is Mahayanist. The author's research analysis of the temple,
carried out after a highly successful reconstruction of it by the Fine Arts Department, is excellently presented and illustrated in this large-format boxed cahier.

Sculpture

727 **The heritage of Thai sculpture.**
Jean Boisselier, Michel Beurdeley, translated from the French by
J. Emmons. New York: Weatherhill, 1975. 269p. bibliog.
chronology.

Sculpture of the classical period in Thailand refers essentially to the Buddha
image; and its several distinct schools comprise an entire branch of religious art.
This finely illustrated volume deals with the antecedents of this art form and its
iconography, concerning which the same general considerations apply as in the
author's companion work, *Thai painting* (q.v.).

728 **Dated Buddha images of northern Siam.**
A. B. Griswold. *Artibus Asiae*, 1957. 97p. 57p. of b/w plates.
map. (Supplement 16).

This fine, large-format volume is lavishly illustrated with plates of the Buddha
images under discussion. The point of the text is that the dating of Buddha image
is difficult and tends to be dubious. Copying of propitious and venerated image
over several centuries is not uncommon. The statues (constructed in section
which can be dismantled and carried by elephants) are frequently moved and
re-housed in temples at some distance from the original sites, and inscriptions are
relatively rare. The author draws his conclusions on the dating of important
genres of northern Thai Buddha images from those with inscriptions which offer
sufficient clues. The text of the book provides a historical sketch of Lan Na
including the religious work of King Tiloka of Chiang Mai. Among northern
genres of the Buddha image discussed is Phra Singh, the narrow-waisted 'lion
Buddha', which was originally at Wat Phra Singh in Chiang Mai, and is now in
Bangkok.

729 **Life of Buddha in Indian sculpture: an iconological analysis.**
Ratan Parimoo. New Delhi: Kanak Publications, 1982. 142p.
128 plates.

An account of the early history of Buddhist sculpture in India recommended
as a basis of comparison, showing the iconographic parentage of parallel forms of
Thai sculpture representing the Buddha and episodes from the life of Buddha. The
earliest such sculpture found in Thailand is either of Indian origin, or (Dvaravati)
pure Indian style; subsequent genres establish distinctively Thai interpretation
from the same iconographic bases.

Ceramics

730 **The ceramics of Southeast Asia: their dating and identification.**
Roxanna Brown. Kuala Lumpur: Oxford University Press, 1977.
82p. 43p. of plates. bibliog. large-format.

This excellent and well-illustrated study shows the separate national genres of
ceramics in Southeast Asia and traces the cross-fertilization of some styles with
neighbouring styles — e.g. Thai and Khmer. In addition to colour plates, the book
provides drawings of the main design themes of the various schools of pottery.

731 **Thai ceramics.**
Introduction and descriptive notes by Dick Richards, photographed by J. Turner. Adelaide, Australia: Art Gallery of South Australia, 1977. 208p. 311 plates (some col.). bibliog.

This is the catalogue of an important collection of ceramics from Ban Chiang and the northern Thai kilns at Sawankalok, including some Khmer-style wares, assembled by the Art Gallery of South Australia in Adelaide from 1969 onwards. Cf. also *A ceramic legacy of Asia's maritime trade*, from the Southeast Asian Ceramic Society, West Malaysia Chapter (Kuala Lumpur: Oxford University Press, 1985, 160p., 213 colour plates, 40 black-and-white illustrations, 3 maps.). This is the catalogue of the exhibition held at Kuala Lumpur in 1985, based on 1,600 ceramic finds found on the island of Tioman, illustrative of maritime trade between China, Southeast Asia and the Middle East over eight centuries.

732 **Northern Thai ceramics.**
John C. Shaw. Kuala Lumpur: Oxford University Press, 1981. 270p. maps. bibliog. illus.

This beautifully illustrated handbook of the northern schools of pottery in Thailand covers the Kalong, Haripunchay and Samkampaeng kiln periods, producing rain-cloud and black-and-white celadons, between 1000-1620 AD. The author includes a discussion of the various schools of thought on the origins of these kilns, and suggests that their provenance lay in general displacement of Chinese and other expert potters rather than in direct appeals for them to the Yüan court.

Painting

733 **Thai painting.**
Jean Boisselier, captions by Jean Michel Beurdeley, translated from the French by Janet Seligman. Tokyo: Kodansha, 1976. 270p. maps. bibliog. glossary. chronology. plates. (col.)

It is impossible to discuss the mural temple and other classical visual art forms of Thailand without also describing the country's religious scriptures and folk stories. The author does both with the clarity and thoroughness of a leading master, making this finely illustrated book a major source of information not only on Thailand's art, but also on its religious and spiritual history. Specific aspects of analysis and explanation include: the techniques and natural substances used in mural and lacquer work; the *jatakas* (stories of previous incarnations of the Buddha) and episodes from the life of the Buddha; the Sanskrit and Pali terminology involved in these; the iconography of the depictions of Buddha and of the gods, semi-gods and goddesses, and *bodhisattvas* (Buddhas-in-waiting) who comprise the inhabitants of Indra's heaven and of the Himalayan uplands leading to it; and the rich records of contemporary Thai village life which Thai artists, especially of the period ca 1790-1868, tended to intersperse among the backgrounds of scenes from the classical religious imagery. The volume contains an exhaustive bibliography on Thai and related art and religious themes in Western languages, and a full glossary.

734 **Sawasdi Jantisuk 1925- : Thai artist.**
Karawok Chakrabandhu. *Artasia*, vol. 1, no. 1 (winter 1965), p. 44-48. plate.

This article from the first issue of *Artasia*, describes the work of a modern Thai artist of international repute with illustrations of his work.

735 **Wat Chong Nonsi.**
Photographs by Chamnong Sinuan. Bangkok: Muang Boran, 1982. 87p. (Mural Paintings of Thailand Series).

This is one of the illustrated monographs with explanations in Thai and English, published by the archaeological journal publishers in Bangkok, showing mural paintings from individual temples.

736 **Wat Yai Intharam.**
Photography by Chamnong Sinuan. Bangkok: Muang Boran, 1982. 88p. illus.

This example of the monograph pictorial records of specific historic art sites in Thailand shows the murals of a famous provincial temple in Chonburi, with historical explanations in English and Thai.

737 **The lacquer pavilion at Suan Pakkad Palace.**
Princess Chumbhot na Nagara Svarga. Bangkok: The Author,
1960. 24p. 20 plates. (5 col.).

The Lacquer Pavilion further described and briefly illustrated in J. Boisselier,
Thai painting (q.v.) was brought to the Suan Pakkad Palace in Bangkok from the
vicinity of ruined Ayudhya by Prince Chumbhot na Nagara Svarga as a present to
the author, his wife, who later published this beautifully illustrated volume about
it in his memory. The pavilion, presented by the king to the patriarch as a library
and scriptorium, contains some of the late Ayudhya-early Bangkok period's finest
gold-leaf-on-black-lacquer work on its inner teak walls, depicting *jatakas* and
scenes from the life of Buddha and from the *Ramakien.*

738 **Mural paintings in Thailand.**
Klaus Wenk. Zürich, Switzerland: Inigo von Oppersdorff, 1975.
3 vols.

These three massive volumes constitute an art in themselves, and are of world
importance for art history. Prepared in collaboration with the Thailand Fine
Arts Department, they place on record all the temple murals of the country.
Among their particular merits is that they provide permanent examples of an art
form which is suffering serious deterioration for climatic reasons, so that many
of the originals are being either lost or restored, with variable chances of success.
This publication, therefore, is rapidly becoming the only complete extant
repository of the murals, which are the most characteristically Thai of the
country's art forms. It is a product of the religious traditions inherited from Sri
Lanka and Burma and developed, mainly during the late Ayudhya and early
Thonburi and Bangkok periods, with the aid of Moghul miniaturists, and of
Chinese as well as Thai master painters. Volume one consists of introductory and
explanatory material; volumes two and three consist of very fine, extra-large
format colour reproductions of the murals.

739 **Thailändische Miniaturmalereien.** (Thai miniature paintings.)
Klaus Wenk. Wiesbaden, GFR: Franz Steiner, 1965. 116p.
20 double-sided, 6 single-sided col. plates.

This large-format volume contains superb reproductions, with the essential gold
ingredients fully displayed, of illustrations from a Thonburi manuscript of 1774
in the Berlin Museum (Indian Art Department), forming part of the extant
re-publication of the *Traibhum* by King Taksin. The manuscript is the fullest
contemporary re-working of painting instructions for illustrating the *Traibhum*,
the life of Buddha and the *jatakas* in the Thai Buddhist canon, and concurrent
geographical material. The author adds a history of Thai painting from Dvaravati
onwards and sets the Berlin manuscript in the context of the few extant parallel
manuscripts in Thailand.

740 **Ten lives of the Buddha: Siamese temple paintings and Jataka tales.**
Elizabeth Wray, Clare Rosenfield, Dorothy Bailey, photographs by Joe D. Wray. New York: Weatherhill, 1973. 154p.

This pleasant pictorial record gives a concise representation of the temple mural paintings depicting the Great *Jatakas*, or ten final pre-incarnations of the Buddha. The pictures in the book are accompanied by short, simple accounts of the temple locations photographed and the individual *jatakas* illustrated in them.

Music

741 **Kaen playing and mawlum singing in northeast Thailand.**
Henry Ellis Miller. Ann Arbor, Michigan: University Microfilms International, 1977. 676p. bibliog. (PhD thesis for Indiana University).

This thesis by a musicologist consists of an examination of the musical culture of the Lao-speaking area of northeast Thailand. A *kaen* is a reed organ peculiar to this region; *mawlum* is a mode of popular singing there, embodying animist, Buddhist, and courtship and other folk rituals and practices. The study is of value both for its musical interpretation and also for its illumination of the regional culture. It has a glossary of local dialect terminology.

742 **The traditional music of Thailand.**
David Morton. Los Angeles: University of California Press, 1976. 258p. bibliog. discography. illus.

This is the later and much fuller version of the author's work on the traditional music of Thailand, and provides a complete account of the subject for the specialist. An earlier and shorter edition under the same title was published in 1968. It covers general and particular musical forms, and deals in particular with various local types of songs and instruments. The argument is liberally supported with illustrations of musical ensembles of various regions, translations into English, and transcriptions in Western musical notation. The book appends a discography of relevent extant recordings.

743 **Die Mundorgel bei den Lahu in Nord Thailand.** (North Thailand: the Lahu mouth-organ.)
Gretel Schwörer. Hamburg, GFR: Karl Dieter Wagner Verlag, 1982. ca 50 leaves of music. (Beiträge zur Ethnomusikologie, no. 10, part 2).

A transcription of the words (with annotations in German) and music (in Western notation) of Lahu songs and mouth-organ music from northern Thailand.

Dance drama and crafts

744 **Nang: Siamesische Schattenfiguren im KGL Museum für**
Völkerkunde zu Berlin. (Nang: Siamese shadow-play puppets
in the Berlin Ethnographic Museum.)
F. W. K. Müller. Leiden, The Netherlands: Brill, 1894. 26p.
11 col. plates. (Supplement to Internationales Archiv für Ethno-
graphie, no. 7).

This large-format brochure contains 11 fine, colour plates, reminiscent of Japanese
prints, showing leather puppets from Ligor and Phuket, presented to the Berlin
Ethnographic Museum in the 1880s. The text (in German) describes the provenance
of the exhibits depicted in the plates and gives transliterated and translated
excerpts, with a plate of reproductions, of passages from shadow-play episodes
from the *Ramakien* in which they were used.

745 **Contemporary Southeast Asian arts and crafts.**
Thelma R. Newman. New York: Crown Publishers, 1977. 306p.
illus.

Thailand's handicrafts are to some extent common to other Southeast Asian
countries, with important variations in originality. This compendium of regional
arts and crafts includes a sketchy historical retrospect; the book is useful as a
reference source on present-day activities, of which it offers numerous photographs.

746 **The Siamese theatre: a collection of reprints from the** *Journal of*
the Siam Society.
Edited by Mattani Rutnin. Bangkok: Siam Society, 1975. 291p.
bibliog. illus.

The articles in this volume, mainly in English, with some in French, include a
number from the collection published by the Siam Society in honour of their
author, Prince Dhani (q.v.). They present an excellent all round view of the types
of performance which have grown up in the Thai theatre, from classical (*khon*) to
popular (*lakhon*), and the now dying shadow-puppet form (*nang*). The book
contains a useful general introduction, a discussion of the provenance of the
Ramakien, a good set of photographs of historical hide puppets and a full
bibliography of works in Western languages and Thai.

747 **Malay shadow puppets: the wayang siam of Kelantan.**
Amin Sweeney. London: British Museum, 1972. 83p. 36 plates.

This finely-illustrated volume uses examples of puppets from the British Museum
which were used in the shadow plays of northern Malaya and southern Thailand.
The author discusses the social setting in which they were used, and the evidence
for their origins in Javanese puppetry.

193

748 **The art of mother-of-pearl in Thailand.**
Klaus Wenk, translated from the German by Sean O'Loughlin,
Elizabeth O'Loughlin. Zürich, Switzerland: Inigo von
Oppersdorff, 1980. 140p. illus.

This book describes Thailand's mother-of-pearl industry. The craft represents
one of the most original of the country's localized minor arts, rising to considerable heights of imaginative working in colour in vivid, free-flowing depictions
of natural scenery by the post-war era.

Cuisine

749 Thai cooking.
Jennifer Brennan.   London: Jill Norman & Hobhouse, 1981.
232p. glossary.

This excellent cookery book makes available, to those who use it, the full range and delicacy of Thai food, which, like Thai painting, has absorbed influences from China, India and elsewhere to develop into an art form which is quite distinctively Thai in character. The book has a useful vocabulary indexed in both Thai and English.

750 Seafood of Southeast Asia.
Alan Davidson.   London: Macmillan, 1978. 366p. map. bibliog.
illus. (some col.).

An admirable, large-format volume which consists of an illustrated catalogue of the edible fish, crustaceans, molluscs and other sea creatures of Southeast Asia, illustrated by drawings and some fine, full-page colour-plates, followed by a collection of recipes from each of the countries of the region ('Thailand' p. 233). The book also has an interesting and useful section on ingredients in common use in the region, including herbs and spices. Nomenclature is provided throughout in English and vernacular languages.

751 Herbs: how to grow, treat and use them.
Ethelind Fearon.   London: Barrie & Jenkins, 1977. 96p.

The author's account of the cultivation and culinary uses of herbs includes Thai and Filipino recipes.

752 The complete Asian cookbook.
Charmaine Solomon, photographs by Reg Morrison, edited by
Peter Hutton, Wendy Hutton.   Dee Why West, Australia:
Windward, 1976. 511p. glossary.

This coffee-table-style book relies as much on its full-page, colour plates of traditional dishes of Southeast Asia as on the simplified instructions for their preparation. Exceptionally, not only Thailand's recipes are covered, but also dishes of the closely-related but subtly different neighbour cuisines of Burma, Laos and Cambodia.

Cuisine

753 **Everyday Siamese dishes.**
   Sibpan Sonakul. Bangkok: Prachand Press, 1969. 5th imprint.
   81p.

This excellent little cookbook contains an introduction, 160 Thai recipes, an appendix (Tips from R. L. and A. M. Pendleton, consisting of appreciations of Thai cooking traditions), and an illustrated glossary of plants, implements and ingredients, with equivalents in Thai script.

Periodicals

754 **Arts of Asia.**
Editor Tuyet Nguyet. Hong Kong: Tuyet Nguyet, Arts of Asia
Publications, 1970- . bi-monthly.
This is a photogravure-set illustrated magazine of the arts, crafts and art history of
Asia, carrying occasional articles on Thailand and Southeast Asia. The magazine
also carries advertisements by art dealers of Asia, Europe and of London.

755 **ASEAN Business Quarterly.**
Singapore: Asia Research, 1977-81. quarterly.
This periodical gave trends, facts and comment for ASEAN financiers, investors,
shippers and traders, surveying both the region as a whole and individual members,
and dealing with production, tourism, and finance.

756 **Asian Review.**
London: Oriental University Institute, Woking. 1866- .
During its rather chameleon-like existence, this journal carried a long series of
authoritative articles on current themes of imperial or colonial importance, a
number of which remain of interest in relation to events affecting Thailand. It was
formerly published as the *Asiatic Quarterly Review*, vols. 1-10 (1886-90),
continued as *Imperial and Asiatic Quarterly Review*, 2nd series, vols. 1-10
(1891-1912), and as *Asiatic Quarterly Review*, new series, vol. 1, no. 1-vol. 48,
no. 176 (Jan. 1913-Oct. 1952), and later as *Asian Review Quarterly*, 4th series,
up to vol. 60 (1964), after which it was finally absorbed into the *Journal of the
East India Association.*

757 **Asian Survey.**
Berkeley, California: University of California, 1960- . monthly.
This small-format monthly journal maintains a steady flow of contributions on
general Asian affairs, dealing occasionally with Thai matters.

Periodicals

758 **Asian Thought and Society: an International Review.**
New York: New York State University, 1976- . 3 times a year.

ATS publishes in substantial volumes international specialist contributions in English on a whole range of Asian subject matter including book reviews. Materials on Thai or related affairs appear irregularly.

759 **Bank of Thailand Annual Economic Report.**
Department of Economic Research, Bank of Thailand. Bangkok: The Bank, 1943- . annually. statistical addenda.

The Bank of Thailand's annual report, published in English, comprises overall surveys of economic, financial and production conditions in the country and reports on Southeast Asian, Australian and New Zealand and other banking corporations. Each issue contains a substantial addendum consisting of statistical summaries of economic and production indicators. The Bank of Thailand also publishes annual retrospect and prospect reports, in the form of discursive pamphlets, in which annual trends are discussed and evaluated. Bank of Thailand monthly bulletins were discontinued in 1975.

760 **Bank of Thailand Quarterly Bulletin.**
Department of Economic Research, Bank of Thailand. Bangkok: The Bank, 1961- . quarterly.

The Bank of Thailand's quarterly bulletin, published in English, is a valuable source of general reports and statistics on economic conditions, commodity production, and banking and finance in Thailand.

761 **Bulletin de l'Ecole Française d'Extrême-Orient.**
Paris: The School, 1901- . annually.

This substantial journal, of over 400p. per issue, published in French, includes contributions by French and other specialists, mainly in the fields of Indo-Chinese and related materials. Numerous articles on Khmer history, architecture and inscriptions, and occasional articles on Tai, Shan and other tribal cultures have appeared. The BEFEO was first published in Hanoi in 1901, and remains one of the major research outlets and sources for current Asian studies. This school is also an important publisher of monographs; an up-to-date list of which can be found on the back pages and cover of each issue.

762 **Bulletin of the School of Oriental and African Studies, University of London.**
London: The University, 1917- . 3 times per year.

This wide-range collection of specialist papers, covering both Asian and African (including Middle Eastern) affairs, provides a vehicle for research contributions by faculty members and associates of SOAS. Each issue contains a substantial book-review section, cumulatively indexed by book-author. The material includes occasional contributions or reviews of Thai interest.

198

763 **Contemporary Southeast Asia.**
Singapore: Institute for Southeast Asian Studies, 1968- .
quarterly.

This regional affairs journal of the National University of Singapore contains book reviews and articles on economic and social issues, human rights, banking and rural and economic development, and similar material from individual countries of the region.

764 **Contributions from the Biological Laboratory, Kyoto University.**
Kyoto, Japan: The Laboratory, 1955- . irregular.

The content of this well-presented and illustrated thick, scientific journal consists of substantial articles and research papers in English on Japanese and Southeast Asian biology, including themes related to Thailand.

765 **Far Eastern Economic Review.**
Hong Kong: South China Morning Post, 1946- . weekly.

A valuable source for material on political and economic affairs of the Far East, including articles, statistical surveys and special numbers. Thai and related affairs form part of its regular coverage. The publishers also publish annually the *Asia Yearbook* (q.v.), which contains a section reviewing Thailand's economic and trade performance with a factual introduction to the country, its people, trade, industry and agriculture.

766 **Foreign Affairs Bulletin.**
Bangkok: Ministry of Foreign Affairs, Information Department, 1962- . monthly.

Contains announcements and reports of Thai diplomatic interests.

767 **The Gardens' Bulletin.**
Singapore: Botanic Gardens, Parks & Recreations Department, Ministry of National Development, 1912- . irregular.

This bulletin reports on plant collecting and on tropical flora, especially of peninsular Malaysia and Thailand. Cf. *The Zingiberaceae of the Malay Peninsula*, vol.13, no. 1 (June 1950), by R. E. Holttum, who was the then curator of the gardens.

768 **Journal of Asian Studies.**
Ann Arbor, Michigan: Association for Asian Studies, 1956- .
quarterly.

This is a substantial publication sponsored by the universities of California and Michigan. It carries wide-ranging material reviewing east and south Asia, with occasional articles on Thai affairs, and the adjacent Pacific Islands, and includes book review sections.

Periodicals

769   **Journal of the Royal Asiatic Society.**
London: The Society, 1834-63 (vols. 1-20); 1865- . new series.
2 or 3 times per year.

The full title (not normally used in citation) is the *Journal of the Royal Asiatic Society of Great Britain and Ireland.* The present journal was preceded by one published in Calcutta and London, entitled *Asiatic Researches: or transactions of the society instituted in Bengal for inquiring into the history and antiquities, the arts, sciences, and literature, of Asia.* That subtitle remains a good description of the editors' aims. The JRAS has been a major source of reports and articles on Asian affairs generally, with occasional material on Thai matters and especially on relevant Hindu-Buddhist religious foundations, beliefs and literature. The journal contains a valuable section of book reviews. The Malaysian Branch is also a significant occasional source of materials on matters affecting Thailand, as is also the China Branch.

770   **Journal of the Siam Society.**
Bangkok: The Society, 1904- . twice yearly (Jan. & July), or occasional.

Throughout its publication history this journal has been the principal source of specialist research papers, historical surveys, archaeological reports, and articles on all aspects of national culture of Thailand. Authors include both Thai and Western specialists; and articles appear mainly in English or occasionally in French, either originally or as translations from the Thai. The journal also contains book reviews and review articles. In addition to the journal and the *Bulletin of Natural History* (q.v.) the society publishes monographs and *Felicitation volumes* (q.v.) and occasional *Collected articles* (q.v.) from past volumes. Volumes 33-35 were published during the Japanese occupation of Thailand under the title *Journal of the Research Society of Siam.*

771   **Journal of Southeast Asian History.**
Singapore: University of Malaya, 1960-69. biannually.

This journal was continued from 1970 as *Journal of Southeast Asian Studies* (q.v.).

772   **Journal of Southeast Asian Studies.**
Singapore: McGraw-Hill, 1970- . biannually.

This journal of the Department of History of the University of Singapore, appeared as the *Journal of Southeast Asian History* (q.v.) until 1969. Both journals have provided a forum for international specialists in various aspects of Southeast Asian studies, with occasional special numbers e.g. N. Tarling, *Australia, New Zealand and Southeast Asia*, vol. 2, no. 1 (March 1971).

773   **Kew Bulletin.**
London: HM Stationery Office, 1887- . quarterly.

The *Kew Bulletin* is a major source of world botanic reports and articles, carrying occasional contributions on findings in Thailand, and in neighbouring areas having flora in common with Thailand.

774 **Kontyu.**
Tokyo: Entomological Society of Japan, 1950- . quarterly.
An excellently presented technical journal on entomology. Contributors are both Japanese and international; the articles are written mainly in English (a few in Japanese), and deal with Japanese and general tropical, Far Eastern and Southeast Asian entomological topics, including some which are of direct or indirect Thai interest.

775 **Malayan Nature Journal.**
Kuala Lumpur: Malayan Nature Society, 1947- . annually.
Articles deal with birds, insects, mammals, reptiles and general aspects of the flora and fauna of the Malay peninsula, some dealing directly with Thailand.

776 **Muang Boran.** (Archaeology.)
Bangkok: Muang Boran Publishing House, 1974- . approx. quarterly. illus.
This is a well-produced magazine of the ancient sites, arts and antiquities of Thailand, liberally illustrated with high-standard colour plates. General presentation and most articles are in Thai, with translations in English. The publishers also produce illustrated booklets on selected sites. The magazine is recommended not only for tourists and anyone interested in the subject range (which extends well beyond archaeology as such and into the fine arts), but also for advanced students of Thai.

777 **Natural History Bulletin of the Siam Society.**
Bangkok: The Society, 1904- . annually, or less often.
This journal, like the *Journal of the Siam Society* (q.v.), is a substantial collection of articles, mainly in English, by Thai and Western authors. The line of separation is broadly between humanities and literary subjects and topics on flora and fauna.

778 **Nature and Life in Southeast Asia.**
Edited by Tatuo Kira, Tadeo Umesao. Kyoto, Japan: Fauna & Flora Research Society, 1961-76. irregular.
The editors, respectively Professor of Botany at Kyoto University and Professor of Animal and Human Ecology at Osaka University, used this journal title for a series of special reports on research projects in Southeast Asia, amounting to seven volumes in all. The initial volumes, running to some 450p. each, dealt principally with the results of a joint research expedition to Southeast Asia, one of whose main target areas was Thailand. The project was concluded with a final publication in 1976.

779 **Notes from the Royal Botanic Gardens.**
Edinburgh: HM Stationery Office, 1900- . irregular.
The Edinburgh notes carry announcements and reports of general botanical interest, especially concerning Zingiberaceae, an interesting species, several families of which are found in Thailand's forests, village cultivations, and markets.

Periodicals

780 **Orientations.**

Edited by Elizabeth Knight. Hong Kong: Pacific Magazines, 1969- . monthly.

A large-format magazine in photogravure, for connoisseurs and collectors. It carries saleroom information from various parts of the world, and carries articles on Chinese and general Asian archaeology and art history, some numbers consisting of illustrated monographs. Topics include occasional material on Thai subjects.

781 **Oryx.**

Oxford, England: Blackwell, 1950- . quarterly.

This journal, formerly published by the Society for the Preservation of the Wildlife Fauna of the Empire, carries descriptive and informational articles on wildlife, and especially endangered species, including occasional items from Thailand.

782 **Phuket Marine Biological Centre Bulletin.**

Phuket, Thailand: The Centre, 1971- . irregular.

Phuket Island is ideally situated for marine research. It is part of a chain of islands off the western shore of peninsular Thailand; the group leads southwards via the Langkawi Islands to Penang. Phuket is also mentioned in 19th-century literature as a domicile of Captain Light, the founder of British Penang, and remains an attractive tourist resort, especially for gourmets of seafoods. Since Thai-Danish collaboration was established at the centre in 1971 (a few years after its original foundation), the station has published a series of research papers on various specific aspects of marine biology.

783 **Social Science Review.**

Social Science Association of Thailand, 1976- . irregular.

This journal, together with the association's occasional papers, provide a well-presented and useful source of information in English on current research in a variety of social science fields.

784 **South East Asia: an International Quarterly.**

De Kalb, Illinois: University of Southern Illinois, Center for Vietnamese Studies, 1971- . quarterly.

A multi-disciplinary journal covering a wide spectrum of Southeast Asian topics. The first issue contained an article entitled 'A view of Southeast Asia', by Charles A. Fisher.

785 **Southeast Asian Journal of Tropical Medicine and Public Health.**
Bangkok: SEAMED Regional Tropical Medicine and Public
Health Project (TROPMED), 1970- . quarterly.

The member countries of TROPMED consist of the 5 members of ASEAN
(Thailand, Singapore, Indonesia, Malaysia and the Philippines) with the addition
of Cambodia, Laos and Vietnam — 8 in all. The type of material parallels that of
the *Journal of Tropical Medicine and Hygiene* (London), but relates exclusively to
Southeast Asian medical and public health topics, which the London journal, with
a more general coverage including Africa, carries only rarely. The TROPMED
journal carries regular research reports from Thailand.

786 **The Southeast Asian Review.**
Edited by Sachchidanand Sahai. Gaya, India: The Asian Trust,
1976- . biannually.

This journal of the Gaya Centre for Southeast Asian Studies carries material on all
aspects of Southeast Asian culture, humanities and social sciences, and has included
major items on Thai anthropological subjects.

787 **Thailand Yearbook.**
Editor-in-chief Ivan Mudannayake. Bangkok: Temple
Publication Services, 1965- . annually.

This massive volume is admirably arranged under subject headings, flagged by
projecting alphabetic keys. Its data sections include various historical summaries:
the 1985 edition, for instance, carries a history of printing and type fonts in the
country, the first of which, designed by the missionary Dan Beach Bradley in
1837, is still the prototype model. Data sections also include the various branches
of the economy, social services departments, media and trade, and diplomatic and
personal directories.

788 **University of Kansas Science Bulletin.**
Lawrence, Kansas: University of Kansas, 1902- . annually.

This well-presented and illustrated thick bulletin contains extended scientific
announcements and articles at irregular intervals by members of the science
faculties of the University of Kansas. Several of them specialize in Thai and
Southeast Asian fauna.

Newspapers and Broadcasting

789 Bangkok Post.
Bangkok: Allied Newspapers, 1946- . daily.

This is the best established daily paper in English. It has the type of coverage one might expect to see in the *New York Times* or the London *Daily Telegraph* or *Express*, dealing with national and international news. It publishes occasional supplements on matters of major national interest and, in general, provides a valuable record of events and personalities in Thailand. The paper also lists home and foreign broadcasts.

790 Bangkok World.
Bangkok: Allied Newspapers, 1957- . daily.

A later-established companion (originally a competitor) of the *Bangkok Post*, carrying general news features on home and international affairs.

791 Daily News.
Bangkok: Borisat Siphaya Kanphim, 1953- . daily.

Despite its English title, this paper is published in Thai. It is a popular illustrated Bangkok daily, covering social affairs and tending towards home affairs to a rather greater degree than the other main dailies. The paper has a sensationalist slant, carrying material on sex and crime reminiscent of London's *News of the World*.

792 The Nation.
Bangkok: Suthichai Yoon for the Business Review Company, 1975- . daily.

The paper is the latest-established of Bangkok's three dailies in English. The outlook tends towards the radical viewpoint in presenting the same general area of coverage as the *Bangkok World* (q.v.) and the *Bangkok Post* (q.v.).

793 **Burmese and Thai newspapers: an international union list.**
Compiled by G. Raymond Nunn. Taipeh: Ch'eng-wen, 1972.
43p. bibliog. (Chinese Materials and Research Aids Service
Center).

Thai newspapers are listed under each language (English, Chinese, Thai), and
location (Bangkok and provincial towns). Papers are indexed in English transliteration and in Thai. The locations of files maintained abroad are also listed,
together with the extent of the files by dates. For a listing of holdings of some
twenty Thai-language serials in the Oriental Manuscripts and Printed Book department of the British Libarry, cf. *Catalogue of the OMPB* at the British Library
(OPL) on microfiche. A separate catalogue lists manuscript and printed book
holdings in Thai at the OMPB department. The holdings are located at Stone
Street, London.

794 **Sayam Rat. (Siam.)**
Bangkok: Sombat Pookarn, 1950- . daily.

This is the nearest vernacular approach to a paper of the type and standing of the
London or New York *Times*, having a broad coverage of political and general
home and international affairs. Its distinguished founder and original editor, M. R.
Kukrit Pramoj, later became an accomplished contributor over a number of years,
often gently chiding the lack of lasting constitutional and democratic progress in
the country. He was himself a successful civilian prime minister of the 1970s, and
author of the historical novel *Si phaen din* (q.v.).

795 **Summary of World Broadcasts, parts I and III.**
Caversham Park, England: Monitoring Service of the British
Broadcasting Corporation, 16 Aug. 1939- . daily.

These are two parts of a daily digest (known as the SWB) of world broadcasts.
Part 1: USSR; part 2: Eastern Europe; part 3: Far East; part 4: Middle East and
Africa. The four parts are produced jointly by the BBC Monitoring Service and
the United States Information Service (USIS). The SWB comprises a selection
of monitored and edited extracts from the home and foreign broadcasting output
of virtually all countries, including official announcements, news and comment,
information and propaganda; it also includes press reviews and articles and reports
of national assembly or parliamentary and conference proceedings. It constitutes
an unmatchable source of contemporary records on home and foreign affairs of
the countries whose broadcasts are monitored, or to which broadcasts are directed.
In the case of Thailand, this involved matters like the Thai home service's output
during the 1973 student rising, and Soviet and other propaganda intended for
Thai audience on Thai-Southeast Asian affairs, insurgency problems, and world
affairs generally.

796 **Thai Rat. (Thailand.)**
Bangkok: Borisat Chaloemkiat, 1955- . daily.

This is a rather more popular-style national daily than *Sayam Rat*, with a similar
general news coverage.

Bibliographies

797 **The study of Thailand: analysis of knowledge, approaches, and prospects in art history, economics, history and politics.**
Edited by Eliezer B. Ayal. Athens, Ohio: Ohio University Press, 1978. 257p. (Center for International Studies, Southeast Asia Program Series, no. 54).

This bibliography amounts to a general critique of historiographic and related writings on Thailand. Each subject category of listings is introduced by a critical essay. On the editorial conclusions, cf. review by Peter J. Bee, BSOAS, vol. 44 (p. 415).

798 **Bibliography of materials about Thailand in Western languages.**
Bangkok: Chulalongkorn University, 1960. 326p.

The volume contains references to works principally in English, French and German, and includes a large number of contributions to specialist periodicals, mainly the *Journal of the Siam Society*, by foreign and Thai authors. Sections are divided under subject headings and unannotated. The wide variety of entries on medicine in the science section should be of particular value, especially in respect of a country with an exceptional range of rare diseases, and where medical research and health care provided one of the early areas of effective collaboration with the West.

799 **Thailand: a selected collection of doctoral dissertations 1861-1984.**
Edited by Sarah Marianne Bonnycastle. Ann Arbor, Michigan: University Microfilms International, 1985. 19p.

This is a selected compilation consisting of 1,028 doctoral theses on Thai subjects submitted to American universities. It is arranged under subject headings, and annual updatings are available from the publishers.

Bibliographies

800 The economic conditions of Southeast Asia: a bibliography of English-language materials 1965-77.
Compiled by Vieginai Chen. Westport, Connecticut: Greenwood Press, 1978. 788p. ('Thailand' p. 743-88).
Contains some information on economic periodicals and general works, but is mainly divided into country sections.

801 Research on Thailand in the Philippines: an annotated bibliography of theses, dissertations and investigations.
Compiled by Sia Chety. Ithaca, New York: Cornell University Press, 1977. 90p. (Southeast Asia Program Data Paper, no. 107).
A review of studies in English on Thai themes, conducted in the Philippines.

802 Bibliography on demography of Thailand up to 1979.
Nopphawan Chongwatthana. Bangkok: Chulalongkorn University, 1981. 53p.
The materials cited in this compilation on demography are from sources in Thai and English.

803 The Zoological Record.
Compiled under the direction of Marcia A. Edwards (Zoological Society of London), by the staff of BIOSIS (Biological Sciences Information Services, United Kingdom and Philadelphia). London, Philadelphia: BIOSIS, 1965- . annually.
This is an annual analytical guide to zoological publications written mainly in English. Each annual volume is issued in twenty-seven separate sections dealing with animal groups, general publications and new announcements. One publication may occur in several different sections. The arrangement within sections is by author-index, geographical region, subject and various systematic references.

804 Population research in Thailand: a review and bibliography.
James Fawcett, Alan Howard, Kajorn Lekagul Howard, Peter Kunstadter, Robert Rutherford, Wisit Prachuabmoh, Anuri Chintakananda Wanglee. Honolulu: East-West Center, 1974. 123p. (East-West Population Institute, Chulalongkorn University Joint Project).
This joint research compilation contains 634 entries on population studies in Thailand.

207

Bibliographies

805 **A selected bibliography of mangrove literature.**
Compiled by Dawn W. Frith. *Phuket Marine Biological Centre, Research Bulletin*, vol. 19 (1977), 142p.

The compiler lists more than 2,600 references to works on mangrove coastal swamp biology and ecology, indexed according to subject, area and author. Over a hundred entries deal specifically with Thai mangroves; many more cover relevant regional materials, or general theoretical work based on various parts of the world.

806 **Bibliography of Thai botany.**
Bertel Hansen. *Natural History Bulletin of the Siam Society*, vol. 24, nos. 3 & 4 (Jan. 1973), p. 319-408.

The author of this botanical bibliography, from the Botanical Museum of Copenhagen University, has assembled a large collection of papers announcing new discoveries up to 1969, and refers to a previous collection by E. H. Walker, NHBSS, vol. 15 (1952), p. 27-88.

807 **Thailand: an annotated bibliography of bibliographies.**
Compiled by Donn Vorhis Hart. De Kalb, Illinois: Northern Illinois University, 1977. 96p. (Center for Southeast Asia Studies Occasional Paper, no. 5).

The material in this compilation is in several languages, with descriptive comments.

808 **Thai culture, values and religion: an annotated bibliography of English-language materials.**
Philip J. Hughes. Chiang Mai, Thailand: P. J. Hughes, 1982. 56p.

This annotated bibliography is arranged by subject. Religious entries include information on Christianity.

809 **Bibliography of Thai studies.**
Toshio Kawabe. Tokyo: University of Foreign Studies, 1957. 60p.

A useful short bibliography of books in English up to 1957, unannotated, author-indexed, categorized according to type of publication.

810 **Entomology in Thailand up to 1964.**
Banpot Napompeth. Bangkok: Kasetsart University, 1965. 109 ref.

This is a list of 109 papers and works on entomology in Thailand written in Western languages.

811 **Bibliography on water resources of Thailand.**
Compiled by the National Documentation Centre. Bangkok:
Applied Scientific Research Corporation of Thailand, 1971. 49p.

This annotated bibliography in English lists 229 documents on national planning and development with reference to water resources.

812 **Statistical bibliography.**
National Statistical Office. Bangkok: Office of the Prime
Minister, 1961- . irregular.

This occasional listing (separately published in English and Thai) sums up the statistical output of all Thai government departments (including sport).

813 **Thai government and its setting.**
Woodward G. Thrombley, William J. Siffin, Pensri Vayavananda.
Bangkok: National Institution of Development Administration,
1967. 514p. In English and Thai.

This NIDA publication covers official source material including chronicles, farming records and governmental institutions, substantially in Thai, but with a record in English sufficient to provide a useful checklist.

814 **Bibliography of bibliographic materials relating to Thailand.**
Compiled by Herbert Tillmann. Düsseldorf: H. Tillmann, 1978.
163p.

Prepared in English, this unannotated compilation contains 631 entries arranged by subject.

815 **Selected bibliography on manpower, education and employment with reference to Thailand.**
Rachaniwan Uthaisri. Bangkok: Thammasat University, 1978.
41p.

The sources cited in this specialized, unannotated bibliography are in Thai and in English, arranged according to subject. Materials cover Thailand and relevant general works.

816 **Thailand research bibliography: supplement II.**
Karl E. Weber, Sylvia Höfer. Heidelberg, GFR: University of
Heidelberg, 1974. 192p. (South Asia Institute, Thailand Research
Project Data Paper, no. 6).

The material in this bibliography written in English is arranged by type of publication, and includes books and articles.

209

Bibliographies

817 **Historical materials in Bangkok.**
David K. Wyatt, Constance M. Wilson. *Journal of Asian Studies* (Nov. 1965), p. 105-18.

A listing of a variety of historical and primary source materials available to scholars in Bangkok, compiled in the course of a research project in the early 1960s.

818 **Preliminary checklist of Thailand serials.**
David K. Wyatt. Ithaca, New York: D. K. Wyatt, 1973. 3rd rev. ed. 269p.

This is a valuable cumulative, unannotated compilation of 1,591 serials, from dailies to government department reports, from all sources (Thai and foreign) dealing with Thai affairs, and written in Thai, English, Japanese, and other languages. Entries are all romanized, and in roman alphabetical order throughout. Old and extinct serials are listed; locations of file holdings are given, and geographical and subject indexes are provided.

Index

The index is a single alphabetical sequence of authors (personal and corporate), titles of publications and subjects. Index entries refer both to the main items and to other works mentioned in the notes to each item. Title entries are in italics. Numeration refers to the items as numbered.

211

Agricultural census report, 1978 645
Agricultural development planning in Thailand 646
Agricultural products and household budgets in a Shan peasant village in northwest Thailand: a quantitative description 339
Agricultural statistics of Thailand 682
Agriculture 16, 26, 474, 630-633, 635-643, 645-647, 650-652, 656, 765
  annual cycle 459
  demographic analysis (1976) 613
  diversification 476, 602
  drift to towns 479-480
  education 701
  emergent 143
  environmental limits 18
  expansion 596
  farming records
    bibliography 813
  fiscal policy 596
  4th century 135
  Miao tribe 341
  modern 55
  prospects to 1987 611
  slash-and-burn 334, 359
  Southeast Asia 143
  statistics 613, 645, 682
  tribal 642, 647
  upland 642, 647
  vegetative propagation 135
Agronidae 145
Ahmad, M. 151
Aid, international 604
  from Britain 606
Air post in Thailand 664
AIT – Asian Institute of Technology 528, 554
Akagi, O. 541
Akha and Miao; problems of applied anthropology in Further India 332
Akrasanee, N. 589-590
Alabaster, A. 428
Albuquerque 89
  landing at Malacca (1511) 566
Allan, D. E. 546
Allbury, A. G. 320
Allen, B. M. 132
Allen, Sir Richard 207
Allison, G. H. 380, 528

Aloes 81
  wood bark as writing tablets 340
Alphabet; a key to the history of mankind 382
Alphabets 386
  history 37
  transitional 382
Alpheid shrimp of the Gulf of Thailand and adjacent waters 146
Alternative in Southeast Asia 548
Amathusiidae 152, 174
American Area Handbooks 26
American Army Department HQ Country Study 553
American Museum of Natural History 151
American Philosophical Society 231, 238
American theses
  bibliography 799
Ames 136
Amnuai, P. Sithi- 623
Amphoe [district]
  boundary maps (1959) 58
Amranana, P. 591
Amsterdam
  facsimile travel book 81
Amulets 449, 453
Ananda, King 301, 401
  death (1946) 500
Ancient cities in Thailand 193
Ancient Khmer empire 231
Ancient Siamese government and administration 248
Ancient Southeast Asian warfare 225
Andaya, L. 96
Anderson, D. A. 592
Anderson, J. 71
Anderson, J. N. D. 535
Angiosperms 120, 141
Angkor 63, 267
  'City of the Dead' 80
  Khmer inscriptions 238
  Wat 232
Angkor dynasty 726
Angkor: an introduction 232
Animism 36-37, 358, 428, 741
  see also Spirit beliefs; Spirit cults
Anna 83, 284, 460
Anna and the King of Siam 83
Annales du Siam, t. III: chronique de Xieng Mai 247

213

Arts and crafts *contd.*
  painting 37, 194, 391, 411, 733-740
    modern 734
  periodicals 754, 776
  puppets 744, 746-747
  religious art 194, 241-242, 443, 717,
    722, 727
    Buddhist 438
  see also Buddha images
  saleroom information 780
  sculpture 439, 727-729
  SOAS catalogue 709
  Srivijayan art 717, 719
  terms
    Greek 438
    Pali 438, 733
    Sanskrit 438, 733
    Theravadist art 717
    tribal 332
Arts of Asia 754
Arupa [perfection] 432, 440
Asahina, S. 145
Asceticism 433
ASEAN – Association of Southeast
    Asian Nations [Thailand,
    Singapore, Indonesia, Malaysia,
    Philippines] 475, 553, 572-582,
    755, 785
  central bank workshop (1977) 616
  financial overview 572, 580
  Islamic nations 374
  Joint Conference on Management,
    Manila (1967) 574
  periodicals
    financiers 755
    investors 755
    shippers 755
    traders 755
  politics 517
  problems (1967-80) 581
  prospects (1981 symposium) 597
  relations with EEC 578
    Japan 575, 578
    USA 575
  research materials 576
  seminar (1981) 577
  summit meetings (1976, 1977) 579
  TROPMED [ASEAN & Cambodia,
    Laos, Vietnam] 785
ASEAN Bankers' Association 580
ASEAN bibliography 576
ASEAN Business Quarterly 755

*ASEAN: eine Dokumentation zur
    Gipfelkonferenz* 579
*ASEAN financial cooperation in
    banking, finance and insurance*
    580
*ASEAN: regional cooperation in the
    ascendant?* 581
ASEAN Swap Agreement 580
Asher, M. G. 572
Asia 256
  antiquities 769, 780
  art dealers 754
  arts 769
  book reviews 758
  cultivated plants 136, 142
  current affairs 761
  east 220, 768
    history 238
  history 769
  literature 769
  modern
    problems and prospects 218
  sciences 769
  south 768
  Southeast *see* Southeast Asia
Asia in the making of Europe 256
*Asia in the 1980s: interdependence,
    peace and development* 597
Asia Yearbook 765
Asia-Pacific Centre 674
*Asia-Pacific Population Programme
    News* 329
Asian Development Bank 546
Asian economic development 608
Asian Institute of Technology – AIT
    528, 554
*Asian Perspectives: journal of archae-
    ology and prehistory of Asia and
    the Pacific* 195, 202
Asian Review 539, 756
Asian Survey 757
*Asian Thought and Society: an Inter-
    national Review* 758
Asiatic Quarterly Review
    1866-90 756
    1913-52 756
Asiatic Researches 769
Asie du Sud-est: l'enjeu thaïlandais
    509
Askins, K. 167
Askins, R. 168
Aspects of ASEAN 578

Chen, V. 800
Cheopsis aurifrons pridii 301
Chety, S. 801
Chi Han
    translation of *Flora of S.E. Asia* 135
Chia-sheng 238
Chiang Hung 294
Chiang Mai 42, 228, 252, 284, 356, 728
    chronicle 247
    dynasty 247
    growth 471
    guidebook 104, 704
    sacking 408
    snails 159
    University
        Faculty of Agriculture 637
Chiang Mai: the cultural center of the north 104
Chiang Mai University
    faculty of agriculture 637
Chiang Saen 79
Les chiens de Bangkok 491
Childbirth 342
    ceremonies 337
    in old Siam 29
Children of the Meo hilltribes 343
Chin Peng
    retreat (1960) 567
China 97, 135, 141, 230, 233, 333, 436, 567, 769
    archaeology 780
    art history 780
    ASEAN 582
    butterflies 152
    calendrical cycles 209
    cuisine 113, 135
    cultivation of rice 482
    Europe 220
    heroin 492
    influence on Thai food 749
    junk trade 212
    loess zone 136
    Maoism 523
    maritime trade 224
        ceramic finds 731
        4th century 135
    Sino-Indian trade 220, 721
    Sino-Siamese relations 219, 371, 392
    South 63
    soul-summoning 360
    trade 262, 634

Yüan (Mongol) court 244
China and 'people's war' in Thailand 1964-69 523
China seas
    South 321
        potential conflict 577
        trade 78
Chinese cooking 113
Chinese in Bangkok: a study in cultural persistence 367
Chinese medicine 118
Chinese minority 331, 367-373, 467
    Bangkok 367, 370
Chinese Nationalist Kuomintang Army (KMT) 492
Chinese pilgrims 208, 237
Chinese potters 732
Chinese society in Thailand: an analytical history 371
Chinese sources 238, 240, 244
Chinese-English dictionary 237
Chinese-Thai differential assimilation in Bangkok: an exploratory study 370
Ch'ing dynasty 219
Chitakasem, M. 382, 394-395, 695
Choisy, F. T. de, abbé 77, 253
Cholera
    isolation camp 322
Chomchai, P. 50
Chongwatthana, N. 802
Christianity
    banned from Japan (1614) 566
    bibliography 808
    conversion 77, 85
Chronica botanica 136
Chronicles
    Abdullah 290
    Ayudhya 250, 267, 269
    Bangkok 297
    bibliography 813
    Burmese 558
    Chiang Mai 247
    Chinese 244
    Haripunjaya 247
    Jengtung 258
    Khmer 260
    Lan Na 258
    Mon 242
    Padaeng 258
    Rama I 282
    Tamnan 258, 266

222

G

Gabaude, L. 445
Gait, Sir Edward 340
Galsworthy, J. 401
Games
  village 481
Ganjarerndee, S. 615-616
Garden, D. 410
Gardens' Bulletin 767
Garson, M. G. 49, 52, 141
Gastropods 184
Gatty, J. C. 73
Gaya Centre for Southeast Asian
  Studies 786
Gazetteer of the maps of Thailand 62
Geddes, W. R. 341
Gedney, W. J. 29, 379, 415-417, 474
Geldern, R. Heine- 458
General survey of crabs in Thailand
  181
Geneva conference on refugees (1979)
  581
Geneva settlements
  after French defeat in Vietnam 550
Geographic map of Thailand 62
Geography 16, 44-48, 50, 52-53,
  55-56
  biogeography 52
  economic 46-47, 55
  glossary of Malay terms 62
    Thai terms 62
  historical 66
  Thailand 235
  physical 47
  political 48
*Geography and the environment in
  Southeast Asia: proceedings of
  the Jubilee Symposium of the
  Department of Geography and
  Geology, University of Hong
  Kong, 21-25 June 1976* 50
*Geological environment of tin miner-
  alization in the Malay-Thai
  Peninsula* 49
Geological Society of America Bulletin
  56
Geology 45, 49, 51-52, 54-57
  economic 49
  regional 57
  stratigraphy 43

*Geology of Laos, Cambodia, southern
  Viet Nam and the eastern part of
  Thailand: a review* 57
*Geology of the tin belt in peninsular
  Thailand around Phukhet,
  Phangnga and Takua Pa* 49
Geophysics 52, 141
Geosyncline
  Burmese-Malayan 56
*Gerichtsverfassung und Zivilprozess
  in Thailand: ein Überblick mit
  einem Abhang: Verzeichnis der
  wichtigsten Gesetze Thailands*
  538
Gerini, G. E. 213, 236, 446-447, 539
German Foundation for International
  Development 484
German sources
  anthropology 356
  bibliography 798
  conferences on ASEAN 579
  fauna 144
  history 254
  law 538
  literature 396, 412-414
  religion 436
German-Thai relations 38
Gervaise, N. 251
Gesick, L. M. 271
Gething, T. G. 416
Gia Long, Emperor of Vietnam 274
*Gibbon and siamang I: evolution,
  ecology, behavior and captive
  maintenance* 178
  *III: natural history, social behavior,
  reproduction, vocalizations,
  prehension* 179
Gibbons 164, 171, 178-179
Gibson-Hill, C. A. 157
Gidal, S. 15
Gidal, T. 15
Gilchrist, Sir Andrew 311
Giles, F. H. 252
Giles, H. A. 237
Ginger 113, 119
Girling, J. L. S. 498
Gold 49
  artefacts 194
  leaf on black lacquer 737
Golden triangle 11
  heroin 492

H

Haas, M. R. 383, 388
Habe, T. 159
Hafner, J. A. 657
Hagensick, A. Clarke 471
Hagiography 453
Hagiwara, Y. 597
Hague, The 91
Hakluyt handbook 90
Hakluyt, R. 90
Hall, D. G. E. 214, 278
Hamada, General 311
Hamburg University 414
  Asian Institute Papers 38
Hamlyn historical atlas 66
Han times 360
  Chinese caravan route 235
Handbooks 1, 3, 6, 16, 26, 53, 211, 467
  financial 619
Hanks, J. R. 342
Hanks, L. M. 357
Hanoi 230, 761
Hansen, B. 806
Hardie, R. 326
Harem life 83
Haripunchay
  pottery kiln 732
Haripunjaya
  chronicle 247
  civilization 242
Harmony
  of self and universe 435
Harris, J. G. 415, 417
Harrison, B. A. 160
Hart, D. V. 807
Hartmann, J. F. 418
Harvard University 220
Harvey, J. M. 679
Haseman, J. B. 312
Hastings, W. 280
Hatting, T. 203
Haw tribes
  opium trade 492
Hawaii National Maritime Laboratory 146
Hawker, F. 343
Hawkes, P. 640
Hawkes, S. 640
Hayami, I. 175
Heady, E. O. 646

Health 479, 631
  services 488
  administration 488
  statistics 488-489
Health and welfare survey 489
Hearn, R. M. 521
Heaven 432
  Indra's 733
Heckman, C. W. 638
Heekeren, H. R. van 206
Heidelberg University
  South Asia Institute
    Institute of Tropical Hygiene and
    Public Health 484
Heine-Geldern, R. 458
Hell 432, 440
Henry Burney: a political biography 278
Herbert, J. 435
Herbert, Sir Thomas 81
Herbs and spices 115-116
  in cookery 750-751, 753
Herbs: how to grow, treat and use them 751
Heritage of Thai sculpture 727
Herklots, G. A. C. 113
Hernia 118
Heroin 491-492
Herpetology 186-187
Hideyoshi 268
Higashi, N. 486
Highlanders of Thailand 352
Hikayat [chronicle]
  Abdullah 290
Hikayat Patani: the story of Patani 290
Hildebrand's field guide 105
Hildebrand's travel map 64
Hill farms and paddy fields: life in mainland Southeast Asia 635
Hill, J. E. 161-162
Hill, R. D. 50
Hilltribes of northern Thailand: a socio-ethnological report 365
Himalayas 733
Hindu art 717, 721
Hindu canon 447
Hinduism 250, 434, 439, 441, 447
Hinduism and Buddhism 434
Hinton, P. 348
Hints to Exporters: Thailand 627
Hiouen Thsang 237

Leiden University
  see Leyden
Lekagul, B. 162, 166-168
Leonowens, A. H. 83, 84, 284, 292
Leonowens, L. 83, 284
Leprosy 486
Lerco, A. 491
Letters from John Chinaman 392
Letters from Thailand 392
Lewis, P. W. 351
Lewitz, S. 386
Leyden
  Royal Institute of Linguistics and
    Anthropology
    library holdings 711
  University 66
Li, H.-L. 135-136
Liangcharoen, M. 199
Librarians
  conditions 698
  education 698
Libraries 705-714, 716, 737
  Bodleian 559
  Cornell University 709
  directory to Asian resources 706,
    714
  foreign printed books 705
  India office 713
    17th-century records 710
  John Rylands 559
  Leyden 711
  Library Association 698
  manuscripts 705, 712
  National 705
    education system 698
  public
    education system 698
  Public Records Office 714
  school 698
  Singapore 708
  university 698
  SOAS 709
*Library Catalogue, School of Oriental
    and African Studies, University of
    London. Vol. 20 Subject Cat-
    alogue: Southeast Asia and Pacific
    Islands: Thailand* 709
*Library resources on Thailand in
    Singapore* 708
Life and customs 1-2, 15, 28, 53, 474
  Asian attitude 435
  contemporary 9

court 92
daily 2, 27, 39
  and Buddhism 464
domestic 98
family 2, 216
  northern Thailand 23
in Bangkok 2, 19
old Siam 29
19th century
  domestic 98
  religious 98
pre-war 13, 92
religious 98
seen by foreigners 13, 19
traditional 22
village 15
*Life and ritual in old Siam: three
    studies of Thai life and customs*
    29
*Life of Buddha in Indian sculpture: an
    iconological analysis* 729
Life of the farmer in Thailand 474
Life-cycle ceremonies 360
Light, Captain 213, 280, 782
Ligor 71
  leather puppets 744
Lim, P. 576
Limprapet, P. 599
Ling, T. 563, 694
Lingat, R. 291, 450, 542-545
Linguaphone Thai course 382
Linguistics 202
  Ahom dialects 417
  N. Thailand 235
  Shan 418
  Tai 416-417
  dialects 393, 418
  tonal structures 379
Linschoten, J. H. van 74
Lipsey, R. 438
List of the odonata from Thailand 145
*List of reference collection of algae,
    sea grasses, marine invertebrates
    and vertebrates* 169
Literature 7, 384-385
  Asia 769
  bibliographies 268, 404
  classical 394, 396
    translated 407
  essays 403
  family saga 392
  folklore 356, 392, 397, 405

247

Pallegoix, J.-B., Bishop 5, 88
  on tattooing 36
Palm
  oil 600
  manuscripts on palm leaves 12
  Siamese 705
*Panorama of Thailand: a guide to the
  wonderful highlights of Thailand*
  108
Papaver somniferum 493
Papilionidae 152, 174
Paribatra, K. S. 577
Paribatra, M. D. 400
Parimoo, R. 729
Paris 247
  Academy of Science 77
  bat collection 161
  Pridi 301, 500
  Sorbonne 287
Pariwat, S. 595
Pariwatworn, P. 175
Patani 252, 281, 290
  Japanese landing 561
Pathet Lao 570
Patriotic Front 517
Patronage 470
  royal 502
Pawnbroking 619
Paysans de la forêt 334
Peace Corps 521
Pearl Harbour 568
Pearn, B. R. 239
Pedicab drivers 479
Pegu 74
Pejaranonda, C. 687
Peking 224, 268, 527
  exile of Pridi 301, 500
  rift with Moscow 517
Peltier, A.-R. 449
Penang 71, 278, 280, 560, 782
  growth 567
Pendleton, R. L. 53
Peninsular Thailand
  art 717, 719, 721
  fauna and flora 141
  mammals 156
  Semang Negrito 344
  see also Population studies, tribes
Pennsylvania University 135, 197
People 3-5, 31
  see also Population studies
People of the sun 4
People's China 301

*Peoples of the earth, vol. 11: Southeast
  Asia* 361
*Peoples of the golden triangle: six
  tribes in Thailand* 351
Peoples of Southeast Asia 361
Peoples of Thailand 361
Pepper 119
Perak 278
Periodicals 754-788
  agriculture 765
  arts and crafts 754, 761, 769, 780
  Asian affairs 757, 762, 768, 784
  biology 764, 777
    marine 782
  botany 773, 778-779
  diplomacy 766
  ecology 778
  economics 763, 765
  entomology 774
  finance and banking 755, 759-760,
    763
  flora 767, 773
  history 761, 769, 771-772
  industry 765
  literature 769
  politics 765
  production 755, 759-760
  religion 769
  rural development 763
  social issues 763, 783
  stamp-collecting 661
  tourism 755
  trade 755, 765
  tropical medicine 785
  wildlife 781
Perry, L. M. 118
Persia 81
Persian sources 259
Persian traders 217
Pest control 630, 636, 649
  chemical 632, 636
  cotton pests 643
  cropping 632
  pre-war 632
  resilience breeding 636
  rice pests 636
  parasites and predators 639
Pests of rice 649
*Peter Floris: his voyage to the East
  Indies in the Globe 1611-1615*
  86
Peyton, E. L. 180
Pfennig, W. 578

253

Rego, A. da Silva 566
Rehabilitation
  post-war 497
Reincarnation 432, 440
Reischauer, E. O. 220, 238
Reitinger, F. F. 177
Relations between Burma and
  Thailand 558
Les relations entre la France et la
  Thaïlande (Siam) au XIXème
  siècle d'après les archives des
  affaires étrangères 287
Relationship between money and
  credit and economic activity 620
Religion 16, 26, 251, 411, 456, 466,
  479
  American Protestant missions
    460-464
  bibliography 808
  Buddhism 428-456
  history 258
  Indian 233
  minority 436
  Negrito 356
  19th century 98
  practices in old Siam 29
  procedures 225, 248
  statistics 686
  tribal 436
Die Religionen Südostasiens 436
Religious attitudes in Valmiki's
  Ramayana 411
Reluctant princess; a legend of love of
  Siam 400
Rent 603
Renunciation
  of material world 450
Representative government in
  Southeast Asia 537
Reptiles
  Malay pensinsula 775
Research institutions 716
Research material, bibliographies of
  in English 798, 801-802, 809, 815,
    818
    French 798
    German 798
    Japanese 818
    Thai 802, 815, 818
    Western languages 810
Research on Thailand in the Philip-
  pines: an annotated bibliography
  of theses, dissertations and
  investigations 801

Resources *see* Geology; Land
  resources; Minerals; Water
  resources
Restoration of Thailand under Rama I,
  1782-1809 282
Restricted faunas and ethnozoological
  inventories in Wallacea 138
Retail trade 592, 612
Retrospective view and account of the
  That Maha Ch'at ceremony 446
Return from the River Kwai 321
Revenue
  ASEAN
    government sector 572
    statistics 572
  government
    from trade 585
Revenue and cost structures of Thai
  commercial banks: a cross-section
  time series analysis, 1963-70 617
Revenue stamps of Thailand: a
  provisional listing 618
Revenue system of ASEAN countries:
  an overview 572
Review of demographic sample surveys
  for Asia and the Pacific, 1970-79
  681
Review of the economic insect pests of
  cotton in Thailand: description,
  infestation and control 643
Revision of the spider genus Liphistius
  Araneae mesothelae) 176
Revolution
  after World War II 229
  1688 95
Reynolds, C. J. 450, 695
Reynolds, F. E. 440
Reynolds, J. 426
Reynolds, M. B. 440
Rhizomes 116
Riau islands 78
Riboud, M. 40
Rice 18, 136, 354, 469, 481, 564,
  592, 594-595, 600, 602, 631,
  655
  cultivation 134, 137, 293, 360, 482
    4th century 135
    in dry conditions 338, 641
    tokens of account 195
  economic data 583
  export premium 476, 510, 591, 651
  fiscal policy 591
  industry 588
  prices 655

264

Map of Thailand

This map shows the more important towns and other features.

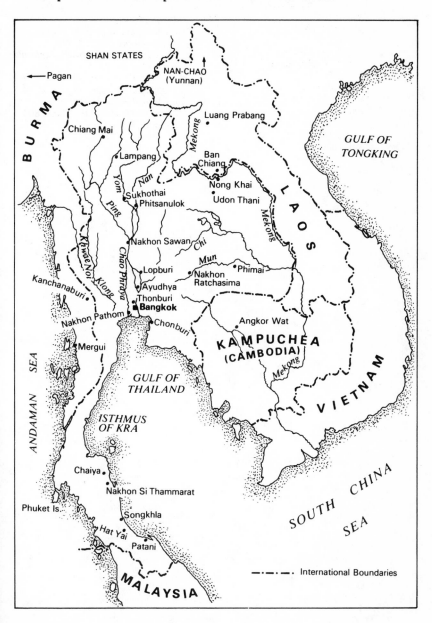

275